THE
EVERYTHING®
AFTER COLLEGE
BOOK

The Everything Series:

The Everything® Baby Names Book
The Everything® Bartender's Book
The Everything® Beer Book
The Everything® Bicycle Book
The Everything® Casino Gambling Book
The Everything® Cat Book
The Everything® Christmas Book
The Everything® College Survival Book
The Everything® Dreams Book
The Everything® Etiquette Book
The Everything® Family Tree Book
The Everything® Games Book
The Everything® Get Ready for Baby Book
The Everything® Golf Book
The Everything® Home Improvement Book
The Everything® Jewish Wedding Book
The Everything® Low-Fat High-Flavor Book
The Everything® Pasta Cookbook
The Everything® Study Book
The Everything® Wedding Book
The Everything® Wedding Checklist
The Everything® Wedding Etiquette Book
The Everything® Wedding Organizer
The Everything® Wedding Vows Book
The Everything® Wine Book
The Everything® After College Book

THE
EVERYTHING®
AFTER COLLEGE
BOOK

Real-World Advice for Surviving and Thriving on Your Own

Leah and Elina Furman

Adams Media Corporation
Holbrook, Massachusetts

aap-5934

TO OUR GRANDMOTHER, ETERI

Acknowledgments

We would like to thank our mother, Mira, for her support and creative assistance; John Nikkah for his extensive research and superior interviewing skills; and our editor, Pam Liflander, for her insightful suggestions and continuous enthusiasm.

An Everything® Series Book.
The Everything® Series is a registered trademark of Adams Media Corporation.

Published by Adams Media Corporation
260 Center Street, Holbrook, MA 02343

ISBN: 1-55850-847-3

Printed in the United States of America.

J I H G F E D C B A

Library of Congress Cataloging-in-Publication Data
Furman, Leah.
The everything after college book / by Leah and Elina Furman.
p.   cm.   —(Everything series)
ISBN 1-55850-847-3
1. College students—United States—Life skills guides. 2. College students—Employment—United States.
3. College students—United States—Conduct of life. 4. School-to-work transition—United States.
I. Furman, Elina. II. Title. IIII. Series.
HQ2039.U6F87   1998
646.7'0084'2—dc21   97-49329
CIP

This publication is designed to provide accurate and authoritative information with regard to the subject matter covered. It is sold with the understanding that the publisher is not engaged in rendering professional advice. If advice or other expert assistance is required, the services of a competent professional person should be sought.

Product or brand names used in this book may be trademarks or registered trademarks. For readability, they may appear in initial capitalization or have been capitalized in the style used by the name claimant. Any use of these names is editorial and does not convey endorsement of or other affiliation with the name claimant. The publisher does not intend to express any judgment as to the validity or legal status of any such proprietary claims.

ILLUSTRATIONS BY BARRY LITTMANN

This book is available at quantity discounts for bulk purchases.
For information, call 1-800-872-5627 (in Massachusetts, call 781-767-8100).

Visit our home page at http://www.adamsmedia.com

CONTENTS

CONTENTS

CONTENTS

PREFACE

Ahhh! At last, the long-awaited moment has arrived. As you proudly stride down the graduation aisle, you spot your excited and teary-eyed friends, that professor who introduced you to the genius of Dostoevski, and, of course, your supportive parents, who wouldn't be caught dead without their trusty camera at a moment like this.

What you do not yet know is that you are in for a rude awakening. The lovely graduation ceremony and the gifts lavished upon you are there for a very good reason. These are the last attempts to buffer your entrance into the real world, the proverbial spoonful of sugar to help the medicine go down.

Many questions like Where should I live? What should I be? and Who is going to take care of me? will begin merely as innocuous whispers, but will eventually snowball into the resounding, thunderous clamor of WHAT AM I GONNA DO?!

Take heart, you are not alone. There have been many others before you who have had to endure the degradation of being dragged, kicking and screaming, into what may seem to be the cold and unknown future. Most have survived.

College graduation is like getting on an elevator without any knowledge of which button does what. You aimlessly cruise up and down the various floors, using trial and error to find the right place. Now, on top of all this, imagine that you don't even know which room it is you are trying to find. You will have to become accustomed to getting off on the wrong floors, encountering rude occupants unwilling to give directions, or, worse yet, seasoned pranksters trying to steer you the wrong way. Sound confusing? Maybe even impossible? Well, take it from us, it's not.

To successfully navigate your course, you will need courage, perseverance, a sense of humor, and, most importantly, self-confidence. Cultivating the ability and desire to learn from your past mistakes will ensure future triumphs. Some problems you will be confronting include meeting new people, living in a new city, moving back home, and getting a fulfilling job. This book contains expert advice on how to overcome these and other obstacles blocking your entry into "the real world."

FRIENDS

Chapter One

BEGINNING A NEW LIFE, AGAIN

ROMANCE

We can assure you, this summer could turn out to be unlike any other you previously lounged through. First, many of your nearest and dearest summer-party-madness cohorts are not going to show up this time. And the friends who don't desert you will also change, often deciding to become responsible on the spur of the moment. To add insult to injury, the people who have actually enabled you to go out, get drunk, and have fun in days of old (your parents), may now look at you as if you're a parasitic worm for not making the expected returns on the money they poured into your education. Gasp! . . . some of them may even feel they have a right to charge you rent. Once you've accepted that nothing will be as it had been, you'll be ready to dance, paddle, and skip your way into a bright tomorrow of your own creation.

GREAT EXPECTATIONS

You're home from college. Your parents could not be happier to have you back. They are begging that you continue living at home, even though you have just picked a job (from a pile of offers) that will pay you enough to live in the style of British royalty. So you pack your bags and move into your new place. Your neighbors are also attractive people with successful and interesting careers. They all love you. They gather at your house for after-work cocktails, and you are the life of the party. You can still hear them laughing at all of your jokes. The most attractive one of them finds you unbelievably clever as well as physically alluring. You two become a hot item and the envy of everyone you meet. Your life is so great, you might as well . . . wake up, because this *dream* isn't getting any better.

Don't be let down if your life is not immediately exciting and joyful. Review your expectations and you will find that the dissatisfaction you feel toward your own life is simply a result of believing everything you hear about post-college life.

The Freedom Myth

So many fresh college graduates anticipate feeling something akin to a perpetual sigh of relief. Yes, exams *are* over and nothing is hanging over your head at the moment. You are free. But freedom is boring. If it weren't for the responsibilities we're all so busy trying to wiggle our way out of, life would be nothing but a mess of apathy and sloth.

G.P.A. ≠ IQ

A lot of you may have some trouble with this one. Being called smart by your college pals for acing exams without giving up your social life may convince you of your rightful superiority in life. But your good grades and the fact that they came easily for you are not sure signs that you are a genius life form. True intelligence will be measured by the school of life, and there is no grade curve in the real world. What you make of your opportunities, or your "luck," as some will have it, is how you'll arrive at a good estimation of your own brilliance.

The Swinging Pad

If you have fallen prey to the hackneyed misconceptions surrounding an aspect of life as ordinary as living space, take this as a good indication that you have built a castle in the air, one which you can't afford. The situation is as follows: After searching high and low for a reasonably priced apartment, you will invariably end up with a room the size of a sucking candy. While no one is there to keep track of your comings and goings (unless of course you are in the unenviable position of sharing your domicile with a bunch of nosy roommates), you are also apt to be lonely and to run up your phone bill out of desperation for human interaction. Doesn't sound like the idyll you thought it would be, does it? (And don't be surprised if all your other idealized notions about after-college life turn out to be mere clichés, not bearing the slightest resemblance to reality.)

Fast Friends

It is easy to get spoiled by the secure conditions of a college campus. Because a college town probably sees relatively few cases of serial killers and the like, people feel much more comfortable talking to strangers and thereby forming friendships. At this point, need we even tell you that your welcome in the real world will be

lukewarm at best? There are no brotherhoods/sisterhoods that you can join to make friends magically appear. It may seem like there will be no problems meeting new people when you're surrounded by them, but that is precisely when forming acquaintances becomes most difficult. It will take a serious effort on your part, an investment of your time, and many disappointments along the way before you can finally look at your social circle and see anything that comes close to suggesting the cast of *Friends*.

Because I had spent all of my time with my boyfriend, I never got the opportunity to form any close friendships. "Once we graduated, I felt that it was time to broaden my social sphere, as things between Brandon and me were getting pretty stale. I met one girl who I thought was pretty cool— a rare thing nowadays. Whenever I went out, she was invited; if she was sick, I brought her care packages. While I was being the selfless friend, she, I soon realized, was nothing but a selfish moocher. If it inconvenienced her in the slightest, she would begrudge me the most insignificant of favors. If I requested that she go five minutes out of her way to give me a ride home, she would quickly arrange to drop me off by cab. Well, I'm no masochist. And when she carried on in her unbeliev- ably egomaniacal habits, in spite of my positive example to the contrary, she soon found herself without my friendship, or anyone else's for that matter.

—CARA, UNIVERSITY OF CHICAGO, '93

While Cara went on to form many mature friendships, it was definitely not a smooth ride. She encountered a lot of people who tried to take advantage of her generosity or who simply did not measure up to her character standards. Overnight friendships are rarely long-lasting and usually prove to be a waste of time and emotional energy. People are not so many stamps to be collected (they are much more annoying than that!). So once you find some friends who don't make you want to cringe, give them your time and consideration; eventually you'll be happy with the bonds you've *chosen* to form.

The Career Mirage

Even if you are one of the select few who graduate with a job offer, you will soon learn that any entry-level job, no matter how full of opportunities for advancement, is still a job. What this means is that you will have to contend with a high stack of paperwork, get bossed around by higher-ups to their little hearts' content, and receive for all your efforts a meager bimonthly paycheck that will barely cover your cost of living. If you're lucky, the first several weeks may be exciting, but even with relatively enjoyable jobs, the initial thrill soon subsides. Just as nothing is as dismal as it appears, neither is anything quite as great.

Because I wanted to become a staff writer at my favorite music magazine, with carte blanche *to interview the rock stars of my choosing, I tried to show off my writing skills every chance I got. Each time I would add anything original, I was reminded that my place as an editorial assistant was not to alter the writers' style but to correct grammatical errors. It went on like this for over a year, during which time the only contact I had with the legends of rock was when I had to call them, only to transfer the call to that writer or editor who was actually working with them. Oh yeah, I also got to listen to them on the car radio. Basically, I was doing a lot of grunt work and not having any fun on the job. There were some perks, such as getting free tickets to concerts and movie premiers from time to time, but these hardly made up for the sad reality that eight hours of my day were spent proofreading and making photocopies.*

—BEN, NEW YORK UNIVERSITY, '92

STAYING IN TOUCH WITH FRIENDS

Now that you are a (wo)man about town, why would you take the time to address those "little people" who live beyond your city walls? Are you thinking that you've got bigger and more significant fish to fry—like that hot group of guys/gals next door, for instance? Well, we're glad to see you've got some serious aspirations, but what about those

Keeping Old Friends

PLUSES	MINUSES
There's always someone to listen to your problems.	You have to listen to someone else's problems.
You always have a place to crash.	Your place is a crash pad.
You always have someone from whom to borrow money.	You may find yourself in the uncomfortable position of having to lend money you can't really spare.
You always have a ride to the airport.	Volunteer chauffeuring may disrupt your social life.
You get more birthday gifts.	You have to give more birthday gifts.

promises to keep in touch, to write faithfully, to call often? Even though it may escape you now, you had good reason to make such vows. If you don't want to end up like Jan Brady after the junior high elections, you should keep the promises you made to the good friends you had.

The Treasure Amidst the Bills

No, we're not talking about the ten-million-dollar prize you may have already won compliments of Ed McMahon. We're talking letters here, real letters from real people. Neither Victoria's Secret catalogs nor supermarket coupons can compete with the mood-enhancing quality of a letter from a good friend. You think a postcard will suffice? Not a chance. The only purpose of postcards is to inspire your coworkers' envy of your European vacation. Your close personal friends do not merit such treatment. Letters to them should be well-thought-out impressions of and expressions on your life, considerate questions on the state of theirs, and any priceless bits of humor you may have picked up in their absence. Enclose nothing incriminating or easily misconstrued; remember, a letter is forever.

Reach Out and Touch Someone

Since the written word cannot be denied, you cannot impart anything in the least bit compromising by way of the United States Postal Service. The means by which you'll get to dish the serious dirt is that beautiful wire we owe to the genius of Alexander Graham Bell. The phone is not only the most convenient means of communication but also the most fun. A letter cannot provide you with a shared laugh, tap you into the sound of each others' voices, connect you in a simultaneous exchange of ideas, or in any way resemble a two-sided conversation. The phone, however, can. Nothing short of an actual physical encounter can remind you so well of why you became friends to begin with.

> *My best friend and I had a hard time taking leave of one another when it came to graduation. We were really so close; neither of us had ever met anyone with whom we could talk*

as freely. However, I was moving to Boston; she was going to Chicago. We'd both have time-consuming jobs, and visits would be infrequent. We promised each other that our calls would not be few and far between. It turned out really well; we spoke each week, knew all the events befalling one another, and had the best time over the phone. No one can make me laugh like Candice to this very day. I'm really glad that we made this commitment to our friendship, especially since I'm planning to move out to Chicago soon, and will have my best friend to show me around my new town.

—LISA, BOWLING GREEN UNIVERSITY, '93

While the price of calling may be exorbitant—many of us have spent more on the phone bill than on our food/clothing allowance—the pleasure derived might surpass the pain incurred by any cost. On the other hand, if your friend's phoneside manner is lacking, unburden your heart instead of your wallet by sticking to letter writing. And there's always e-mail.

Schedule Visits

Hanging with your long-lost chum is the least of the advantages you gain when you take this route. What's more is that you'll have your own personal tour guide to clue you into the customs of the natives. Top that off with free lodgings (do not even think of visiting a friend who does not have the decency to put you up), and you've got a utopian vacation the likes of which even Sir Thomas More couldn't imagine.

Nothing compares with the fun you can have when staying with a city-dwelling friend. Since your friend will naturally want to impress you with his/her city-slicker expertise, take advantage of it, and see all the sights you've only heard about. If you're the host, let your cares go the way of transistor radios, and have a great time squeezing a lifetime of fun into a week's worth of action. As long as you stick to a few simple rules of courtesy, everyone will be better off for having had the experience in the end.

Email and Snail Mail

The well-done letter needs to . . .

- Relate a tale of potential interest to the receiver.
- Involve the reader by means of questions, rhetorical or otherwise.
- Attempt to create the appearance of a conversation, as opposed to a monologue.
- Be legible.
- Be handwritten (handwriting permitting this).
- Be coherent.

It need not . . .

- Be free of spelling errors.
- Be embellished with the flowery language of Flaubert.
- Be grammatically correct.
- Be relevant to the fate of civilization, or worthy of insertion in a time capsule.
- Be filled with detail of Dickensian proportions.
- Be profanity-free.

Host with the Most vs. "This Host Sucks!"

The good host will . . .

- Sleep on the couch while you use the bed.
- Use his/her credit card to start your tab at the corner bar.
- Let you borrow anything in his/her closet.
- Not get peeved if your forty-minute shower uses up all of the hot water.
- Immediately dislike anyone who doesn't just LOVE you.

The bad host will . . .

- Think it big to loan you a sleeping bag.
- Expect you to cook, clean, and do windows.
- Borrow your clothes, and keep them as a security deposit.
- Stick an "off limits" sign on the bathroom door.
- Kick you out of the house if you begrudge your host an extra piece of sushi at dinner.

LONG-DISTANCE LOVIN'

You never thought it could happen to you; yet here you sit, enmeshed in a long-distance relationship. Before you start complaining and marking the days on your calendar with big red slashes, take a moment to consider the beauty of your situation. There are loads of happily married couples who, for occupational reasons, are forced to commute between their respective locales to meet for stolen moments of togetherness. Why are they so happy, you ask? Because distance does indeed make the heart grow fonder, keeping the union from lapsing into a tedious exercise in monotony. The secret of great relationships has always been giving each other space, and with long-distance liaisons, no one can be accused of being either needy or smothering.

Sure, you might get lonely; you might feel abandoned; you may even end up spending every weekend with a copy of *The Way We Were* and a half-gallon of ice cream. But consider the alternative: feeling lonely and abandoned, spending every weekend with a copy of *The Way We Were* and a half-gallon of ice cream. Play your cards right and you'll get to appreciate the freedom of exploration and the stability of a happy union simultaneously. Who says you can't have your cake and eat it too?

Of course, there is one minor glitch. Long-distance romances do require a certain amount of attention, effort, and commitment. It is all too easy to take your absent partner for granted. Any reason for involving yourself in a long-distance dalliance, other than a strong attachment, is seriously moronic. Why else would someone endure the kick in the wallet delivered by the phone bills and airfares? Be that as it may, there are many long-distance devotees who are only in it because they fear being alone. These desperadoes actually keep their distant partners on call as a mere safety precaution, often incurring the grave repercussions that come from toying with others' affections.

One recent grad tried to play the double agent and lost. She insisted that her college beau remain faithful to her while working in another city, while she lost no opportunity to scope the scene for any available stud.

I finally met this really gorgeous guy, Rob, at this bar where I was waiting tables. He was the bartender there, so I figured the situation was ripe for romance. When I asked him out, he told me that he wasn't in the habit of dating girls with boyfriends. I was totally floored. It turned out that my boyfriend, who is originally from Chicago, and Rob went way back and still kept in touch. I pleaded with Rob to keep my boyfriend in the dark, but he wasn't having it. Not only did he tell my boyfriend, who immediately broke up with me, but he turned everyone we worked with against me.

—MEGAN, DE PAUL UNIVERSITY, '96

Just because your sweetie is geographically challenged does not mean that your romance is kaput. Separate agendas do not separate lives make, so refrain from giving either yourself or your significant other a guilt trip if you find that all the attention is not centered on one person. Keeping things solid between you and your partner will take some effort. You may even decide to forgo the whole idea. Do remember that distance is one of the toughest tests of a relationship, but if it's meant to be, it can work.

Plan Ahead

Before kissing adieu and boarding your respective buses, try to establish some basic guidelines that both of you will be comfortable with. Topics like dating other people, time schedules, and personal expectations should be addressed. Appraise your circumstances carefully. Are you ready for a commitment to a person you'll rarely see? Does your calendar allow for extended visits? All these matters should be discussed before embarking upon a course of action. Concoct several hypothetical scenarios; then screen your partner's responses. His/her reactions might surprise you. Here are some to get you going:

1. You and your significant other have been planning to spend a certain weekend together, but his boss needs him to work overtime. What would you do?
    a) Get angry, and try to convince him to blow off his boss.

b) Get upset, but encourage him to do the best job he can.

c) Refuse to interfere with what you see as his decision and sulk in silence.

2. You meet someone you're attracted to and he/she asks you out. What would you do?

a) Tell all.

b) Keep mum.

c) Graciously say, "No, thanks. I'm in a relationship."

3. Your significant other relays his/her wild night with the boys/girls to you over the phone. What would you say?

a) "Oh, yeah? Uh hum. So everything's going fine?"

b) "Did you pick anybody up? Well, Joe/Sally saw you and said you probably *@!% the blond in the red shirt. What do you have to say to that?"

c) "How could you have any fun, what with missing me and all?"

Questions such as these may not be easy to pose or to answer honestly, but you have no choice other than to try. Remember, it was you who decided to take the long-distance challenge. Try not to give up so early in the race.

My college girlfriend and I were moving to different cities. We talked about seeing each other after the big move, but never got as far as actual details. I assumed things would remain pretty much the same. I could not have been more wrong. She called frequently at first, telling me how much she missed me. Great, I thought, business as usual. But soon the calls began to dwindle, and I was growing more and more frustrated. Whenever I tried to get hold of her, I would get the answering machine. I finally caught up with her, and ended up yelling at her for nearly an hour without pause. Then I realized that I was partially at fault. If I had gotten up the motivation, the courage, or whatever it was that kept me from analyzing our relationship while still at school, I would not have spent my first month out of college talking to an answering machine.
—DANNY, OHIO UNIVERSITY, '96

Living with Loneliness

Here's a basic formula: Avoid tear-jerking movies, romance novels, and sympathetic friends who love you best at your weakest. Ward off the urge to wallow in your sorrow. Hopefully, you and your honey weren't so cheesy as to designate a song your own, but if you were, abstain from playing it—in fact, forget it even exists. Listen to surfadelic rock while jumping around in your room. Thinking about your boyfriend/girlfriend should be kept to a stringent minimum; ten minutes per day should cover it. Any lovey-dovey pictures you two may have posed for should be removed and placed under lock and key. Why torture yourself? It's not as if you'll forget what (s)he looks like. Try to concentrate on other things—your job, your friends, the federal deficit—anything and everything except your pangs of loneliness and separation anxiety. With a little effort, these will soon subside and you'll be well on your way to long-distance heaven.

The Importance of Trust

Your long-distance relationship stands very little chance of surviving without the all-important element of trust. Not seeing your beau on a daily basis can lead one to become suspicious and resentful. It is not uncommon to feel stabs of jealousy when wondering about exactly what it is that your girlfriend/boyfriend is doing. Some frequently recurring musings include the following: Is (s)he cavorting with members of the opposite sex? Is (s)he so immersed in his/her new career that thoughts of you rarely enter into consciousness? Have his/her feelings toward you changed? It is entirely normal to entertain such doubts, especially during the initial phase of separation. You will, however, have to overcome these insecurities. Wasting your time worrying about that cross-country love's whereabouts may not only prevent you from having any fun but also sabotage your relationship.

When my long-term boyfriend, Mike, moved to Seattle for a job assignment, I became totally depressed. While Mike was constantly gushing about his job as a copywriter for an ad agency, I was working a dead-end job as a restaurant hostess.

The Dream Guest vs. "This Guest Sucks!"

The dream guest will . . .

- Treat you to one fabulous breakfast, lunch, or dinner.
- Listen to all of your stories and laugh at all of your jokes, even if your guest has already heard them.
- Answer your phone by saying, "_____'s residence."
- Shower you with extravagant gifts.

The bad guest will . . .

- Spread rumors about you to all of your friends.
- Seduce your lover.
- Answer your phone by saying, "_____ can't come to the phone . . . diarrhea."
- Rifle through your underwear drawer . . . just for kicks.

Foolproof ways to keep the faith alive:

- Focus on your good points. Self-confidence will obliterate any thoughts of his/her straying.
- Avoid administering the third degree. No one likes to be held suspect for crimes (s)he never committed.
- Climb a mountain. You'll be too worried about falling off to think of your relationship.
- Be honest. Don't lash out at your partner when feeling neglected. Owning up to your insecurities is often the best way to eliminate them.

Although we called one another often, wrote letters, and even visited from time to time, I became pretty jealous and possessive. He would tell me stories about all the cool new people he was meeting and the crazy night life out there; of course, this only increased my worry that he would meet someone new and forget all about me. I became very aggravated every time we spoke and accused him of sleeping around. I suppose he soon tired of my antics, as he told me that we should start seeing other people. I really can't blame him; I was distrustful and a general pain to be around. I am certain that had I trusted Mike, we would still be together.

—LAURA, UNIVERSITY OF MICHIGAN, '94

While your current relationship may not require your dealing with each and every one of the following problems, consider replenishing your warehouse of strategies— you never know what the future will bring.

Q: I want to start seeing other people. What's the best way to break the news to my long-distance steady?

A: Handle the situation with care. It is probable that you still love your boyfriend/girlfriend and don't want to lose him/her. On the other hand, you don't want to sneak around behind his/her back either. Your best bet is to come right out and say what you have to say. Try to break your news without breaking his/her heart. One key point: Give clear-cut reasons for what you are doing (i.e., you don't want to hide or feel guilty about your feelings, you think honesty is important, you have been feeling trapped). Should your partner grow angry, remain calm; put him/her on the offensive. Ask your partner what (s)he is willing to put up with. Ask yourself what consequences will your transgressions have on the relationship, and why? If your partner insists on breaking up with you, you'll be comforted by the memory of your mature and sincere conduct.

Q: What is the best way to keep in touch? Will phone calls and letters make the grade, or is there something else I could do to keep the relationship going?

A: Phone calls and letters are solid standbys, but if you want to save your relationship from getting in a rut, we suggest you engage the more creative methods of reaching out. Faxing or e-mailing love notes to your long-distance honey can be very romantic; it will keep every facet of your lives tightly intertwined. Another good approach is to tape-record a message and send it to your partner. This is superior to the letter-writing approach, since you can blurt out anything that comes to mind without having to write it down, and as everyone knows, the mouth *is* quicker than the pen. Added bonus: There won't be any misspelled words or paper wasted (have your sweetie tape his/her voice over yours and send it back) so it is environmentally sound, too.

Q: How can I tell if my long-distance girlfriend is no longer interested in me? Are there any telltale signs?

A: If your phone never rings, that's one. If she complains about the phone bill, you know you're low on her list of priorities. If she's in no rush to see you, who then *is* she excited about? Maybe she's trying to let you down easy, maybe she's just in the relationship out of habit, or maybe she's just preoccupied with some problems outside of the relationship. In any case, you're better off if you ask the big question yourself.

Q: I want to move in with my girlfriend, but am scared to relocate to a new city. Although I really love her, I have a great job in my hometown and I know my way around. In short, I am not sure about leaving. What if things don't work out for us? Is it worth the risk?

A: Before you can make the final decision, you have to resolve the fundamental questions still lurking at the bottom of your relationship. Since you are still perplexed about relocating for the sake of love, maybe you are unsure about whether you are truly in love. Have you had sufficient opportunity to find out how compatible you two are? Are you ready to forsake all others and live together? Does the prospect of being apart frighten you more than that of unemployment? Settle these issues, and the answer to your problem will become self-evident.

Twelve Steps to Self-Sufficiency

1. Tell your parents that you're an adult and expect to be treated as such.
2. Get a job.
3. Pay your own way.
4. Help your parents, instead of vice-versa.
5. Budget your time.
6. Realize who you are and what you want.
7. Wash the dishes right after you use them.
8. Abstain from playing ball in the house.
9. Wait two hours to swim after a meal.
10. Never run with scissors.
11. Remind yourself not to slouch.
12. Help the elderly to cross the street.

LOOSENING FAMILY TIES

It is now or never. The time has arrived for you to spread those wings and fly. You can't play mamma's boy/daddy's girl forever. This is not to say that your family should be abandoned, neglected, and forgotten, but you will have to establish a new rapport that better suits your new status as an adult. This means no running to daddy when Bloomingdales refuses to extend your credit line and doing your own laundry as well as the numerous other chores that will inevitably rear their ugly heads. Trying to solve your various problems to the best of your ability will make you the independent person you've dreamed of being.

One classmate came from a very close-knit family. While at school, he would call home at least four times a week, and made frequent home-for-the-weekend voyages. Furthermore, while many of his friends were taking off for road trips, the likes of which would make Kerouac proud, he would be packing his bags for another quiet vacation at home. After graduation, he found himself in a bind.

I wanted to explore the world, but I could not bear to part with my family. I realized that I was scared to be without my family, because they had always supported me. I feared that without them close by, I would be in some sort of danger. I realized that it was the fear of the unknown that was bothering me. Once I understood that I could not rely on my family forever, I began making more of an effort to be autonomous. I moved out of the family home, and rented an apartment of my own. True, my parents are not more than a half-hour's drive away, but I make sure that I am not there more than once or twice a week. It is the ideal arrangement; while I am close enough to visit, I am responsible for taking care of myself.
—DAVID, CORNELL UNIVERSITY, '93

I was totally freaked out when my parents came to graduation. They seemed so happy to see me, as if we'd been separated for eons. Since I only saw them two weeks prior, I didn't get what all the hype was about. When we went out to the big celebration dinner, I was given a plaque that read "WEL-COME HOME." It's not like I was lost in action or some kind of P.O.W. Then they started in about how my room was still just as I had left it and how great it was going to be to have me living at home again. I know I should have warned them in advance, but I just assumed they knew that I would be flying solo. We talked about my plans to travel with my friends and then rent an apartment together. It was difficult to watch their faces fall when I first told them, but my frequent calls and visits convinced them that although we were living apart, they still meant the world to me.

—LILA, KANSAS UNIVERSITY, '93

Staying Close

Considering what your parents will be going through—having their little lamb go out into the big, bad world and all—you should try to make the ordeal as painless as possible. If you plan on living close to home, make sure to stop in often, and not just around dinnertime. If you are moving to another city, call home, send letters, and visit on the holidays. Most important, keep your parents updated about what's going on in your life. Even if you have nothing extraordinary to relate, drop a line telling them how much you love them.

BATTLING IRRATIONAL FEARS

Just admit it. You're afraid, maybe even terrified, to part with the familiar and enter the world at large. It's all right. We're all cowards when it comes to change and upheaval. Hopefully, you have been dealing with your fears throughout your last semester at college, preparing for the uncertainty and doubts that lie ahead. But most of you have probably blown off these nagging reflections, in hopes that all your worries will magically dissolve. Believe us; they won't. Anxiety has a life and momentum all its own. If you don't promptly implement some form of damage control on your trepidations, you will wind up with a full-scale, grand mal panic attack on your hands. Don't start hyperventilating just yet. You've still got time to confront those ghastly fears.

Fear of Failure

How many times have you heard the phrase "By thirty, I'll have made my first million" emanate from the mouth of one of your arrogant friends? Yeah, right. While we may tease our friends for their self-promoting banter, all of us have something to prove to the junior high bullies, our parents, disapproving guidance counselors, and the world in general. Ambition is a glorious thing, provided you keep it in perspective. Only a handful of us are destined to become great leaders, famous celebs, or billionaires. The majority will have to find solace in rich family lives, rewarding low-profile careers, and a sense of self-respect. There *are* worse things. Everyone, at some point in their lives, has failed to live up to their own expectations. Usually this is because their expectations were too high. Still, falling flat on your face is never a pleasant experience, but neither is the regret that you could have been a success had you just tried a little harder.

Fear of Success

The flip side of the failure phobia is one of success. Don't laugh. Just think about how many times people have played second fiddle in order to escape the spotlight. Success has a way of drawing attention to everything you do. While many of us crave attention, others will do anything to avoid it. If you have a habit of shrinking from public scrutiny, you may become susceptible to the "you-take-the credit-instead" mentality. An effective way to battle the fear of success is to take pride in your work and flaunt your accomplishments. There is no reason why your talents should go unrecognized. If someone commends you for a job well done, you can respond with "I owe it all to myself"—sometimes it takes a more radical approach—or a simple "thank you."

Fear of Loneliness

Unless you're Ebenezer Scrooge incarnate, don't worry about ending up alone with nothing but a cat or dog to keep you company. While you may feel abandoned, don't start panicking yet. The majority of your friends probably moved on, or maybe you have just relocated to a strange, new city. Your family may even be giving you that space you so adamantly demanded. Any of these circumstances may be plaguing you, leading you to make false assumptions about the rest of your life. Keep in mind that this is probably just a temporary social drought and will eventually pass as you become more sure of yourself and your surroundings.

> *Everyone I met seemed really strange and nothing felt right. I tried hanging out with some of the guys from work, but they were into clubbing and house music; not exactly my scene. I felt cheated. I was supposed to have a great time in one of the hippest cities. What had gone so wrong? At this point, I was even considering moving back home. Meeting new people always came easy to me, so I chalked it up to bad luck and caught the first flight out of there. I'm glad to be home and everything, but I can't help thinking that had I tried harder, I might have actually made some valuable friends and experienced the good life.*
>
> —KEN, UNIVERSITY OF KANSAS, '95

In college, friendships just sort of happened. Fraternities and sororities provided one with a ready-made social life. However, a little extra effort will be required to avoid loneliness after graduation. And no feeling sorry for yourself when you get lonely; that is simply a waste of your precious time. Once you aggressively seek out potential chums, you will discover just how silly you were for ever doubting yourself.

Fear of Responsibility

The best way to keep fear of responsibility at bay is to take on more than you can chew. Ignore the aphorisms spouted by your cautious grandparents, and try your hand at the "beast-of-burden" routine. Practice taking responsibility by handling not only your affairs but also those of others. Volunteer to run all your friends' errands; take care of your and their financial matters. This strategy will not only win the admiration of all your friends but also prove, once and for all, that you can handle even the most demanding of schedules.

It's Scary Out There!

We polled one hundred recent graduates, asking them to rank their fears about the "real world" (one being the scariest and ten just mildly disturbing); see if yours measure up:

1. Not finding a job
2. Finding a boring job
3. Inability to pay the bills
4. Getting married
5. Not getting married
6. Living with parents
7. Losing touch with friends
8. Becoming an adult
9. Staying immature
10. Safety

CHEZ MOM

Chapter Two

HOW TO AFFORD LIVING WITH YOUR PARENTS

SOUP FOR ONE

No matter what notions your recently matured mind may have concocted, living with parents does not have to mean the end of the world. You are not a "loser," so stop worrying about where you live and start figuring out how to live well no matter where you are. Of course, as in any situation, you will be given many a reason and opportunity to get irritated, fly off the handle, or pack your trunks and shove off to clear your own trail. Should you choose to exercise the latter option to set yourself free, remember that on the average, most roommates register much higher on the nuisance scale than do parents. In fact, parents are by no means the ogres you may remember them to have been during your teen years. Let's not forget that their life with you was probably a few cherries short of a bowl as well. Now that the maturity gap between you has narrowed, you may even begin to admire your former guardians; and who knows, they may even turn out to be more fun than your friends.

However, it is completely understandable that within the scope of our crazy-for-rugged-individualism society, you may feel inadequate if you do not pull yourself up by your bootstraps and strike out on your own. While certainly a lofty ambition, going at it alone may also be foolish. Consider that for every self-made millionaire there's probably a million self-made bankruptcies. Given an alternative, no one in their right mind would voluntarily handicap themselves.

There is absolutely no shame in living with your parents. This is often the wisest possible variant open to you upon graduation. Why else would so many people be doing it? While we have been reared on the success stories of the '80s, we are faced with the reality of the '90s. That's right. No more big hair, big jewels, big boats, big parties, big shoulder pads, big spending sprees, big baby booming yuppies. These have all led to the inevitable big deficit and big recession.

THE BENEFITS OF MOVING BACK HOME

Put aside some of the drawbacks related to sharing living space with mammy and pappy and focus on what you stand to gain from this particular living arrangement. Yes, some people might actually choose this path; not everyone seeks refuge merely for financial reasons.

True, all parents are not created equal. Yours may not be likable or even tolerable for that matter. But unless you spent your childhood being force-fed Brussels sprouts while chained to a bedpost, give your parents some slack! You have very little to lose and much to gain. The family nest has plenty to offer in terms of comfort, stability, and solace. So, if your course was charted by necessity rather than genuine love and attachment, a trial period will probably confirm that given the choice you'd have probably crawled back anyway.

That Warm Fuzzy Feeling

Do you remember all those cozy nights watching television while wrestling with your younger brother for the remote, or when your older sister, in her haste to uncover the loot, crushed your foot during the scramble to open gifts on Christmas morning? Yes, these and many other equally fond memories can come to life once more. Living with your family will not be a care-free experience. But isn't that precisely the reason why we love our parents and siblings so much? The tough times, the fights, and the constant aggravation were part of the package deal. But that was way back when. And who could blame you—beset as you were by pubescent turmoil and teen angst? Look at you now! You are older and able to buy your own Christmas gifts; and you only hog the remote control on special television occasions. Yes, you are ready to reap the rewards of family living: the bountiful harvest of concern, affection, and boundless adoration.

When I moved back home, I was working full-time and couldn't afford my own place. I thought I was doomed to live a dull life. I was expecting to be constantly nagged, just like I was in high school, and given little freedom. My parents turned out to be pretty cool people. We ended up talking a lot; we even went shopping together. I guess I had them pegged all wrong. They were very curious about my job, hobbies, and pursuits. They even liked the independent films I took them to see. After a couple months, my parents told me how happy they've been since my return. I really couldn't have asked for more than that.
—CARL, UNIVERSITY OF MINNESOTA, '93

Activities You Could Do Only with Your Family

- Play hide-the-hairpiece with your senile Uncle Louie.
- Saw off the end of your grandpa's walking stick, and then watch the good times roll.
- Dress up like an alien, scaring the girdle off your grandma.
- Spike the punch at the family picnic.
- Wait till your dad brings some coworkers home for dinner, and then go into your Ruprick-the-Monkey-Boy routine.
- Offer to cook dinner for your mom, and just when she's about to get comfortable on the living room couch, tell her you were just kidding.

As with wine, there is a perfect conversation for every meal.

- *Meat and Potatoes.* This traditional, robust meal should be accompanied with talk of days of yore. Bring up memories of those happy childhood moments. Asking about your parents' recollections of you as a baby and their happy pre-child union should put everyone in the right mood.
- *Fish and Vegetables.* This light, healthy repast will have everyone thinking about outdoor activities, abandoned exercise regimens, and summer vacations. Use this time to recommend lively vacation spots or health tips that could benefit your parents—they'll be thrilled with your concern.
- *Ethnic.* Whether it's Mexican, Moroccan, or Malaysian food you're having, take this opportunity to impress your parents with the world knowledge you've accumulated in college. They will have an easier time swallowing their spicy fare while considering that all the money they've invested into your education wasn't a waste after all.

Home Style Cookin'

If you've learned only one thing in college, it was probably never to underestimate a home-cooked meal. While college may not have afforded you enough time to nuke a TV dinner, you'll be lucky to find the time to buy a TV dinner once you get out. Having a full-course meal on a regular basis, with mashed potatoes and real meat, is not something to scoff at. But don't get lazy! While you may be dining like a king, don't treat the chef like a humble servant. Offer to help with the side dishes—these are usually the easiest to prepare—or pick up some fresh bread on your way home from work. Setting the table and making sure everyone is accounted for are small prices to pay for your role as the apple of the family eye. Once everyone is gathered, enhance their good mood by introducing conversation topics everyone can partake in.

Maturity

Many are convinced that flying the coop is the only way to become a full-fledged adult. But this is simply not true. Granted, your parents have a knack for making you feel like an overeducated toddler. Maybe it's that old separation anxiety kicking in, maybe it's a fear of death, maybe it's just plain ignorance; but whatever the reason, the fact is that parents often make the mistake of treating adult children like, you guessed it, children. What your parents don't know is that your entrance into the adult world has transformed their little child into a mature companion. A deliberate reconstruction of your parents' outdated notions will be required if you ever hope to feel like a grown-up.

It will take a hefty portion of strength to resist being coddled and babied. Do not blame your parents for giving way to this instinct; it's all they know. You have to help them come to grips with the new you. No man is an island, and your parents' opinion of you *can* affect the rate at which you develop. Don't let this opportunity to earn your wings of adulthood slip through your fingers.

Rachel moved into an apartment with a few friends right after graduation. She thought this would be a step toward independence and maturity, but found that her subsequent move back home was much more helpful in affirming her adulthood.

I was wrong to think that sharing living space with room-mates would make me feel like a grown-up. It was actually more like college than anything—the late nights, the pile of pizza boxes littering the floor, the overflowing laundry hampers. I wanted my life to change after graduation, but my friends were hopelessly hung up on the past. I considered how much money I could be saving living at home and decided to do just that. I figured it couldn't be any worse than my present situation. I had a difficult time adjusting to the rules at home, but I soon realized that becoming an adult meant learning to compromise and assuming responsibilities. My parents treated me with respect and often asked for my opinion about certain household matters. Had I stayed in my apartment, it would have taken much longer to become the mature and secure person I am today.

—RACHEL, UNIVERSITY OF IOWA, '94

Eluding the Marriage Trap

If you're like us—terrified of tying our shoelaces because it reminds us of tying the knot—you stand to be amply rewarded for moving back home. Imagine the possibilities—a ready-made family, complete with younger siblings, aging parents, and Bruno the dog. You couldn't have asked for a better deal. The kinfolk need you. What would they do without your support? Sing this tune and any prospective suitors will quickly fall by the wayside. Maternal instincts can be easily exorcised by fawning over everyone around you. After all, don't your parents deserve a little pampering? Just think, you'll be providing both them and yourself with an invaluable service.

Things between me and my girlfriend were getting really serious after graduation. She wanted not only to move in with me but also to get engaged. I was getting nervous and uncom-fortable with the whole thing. I mean, I loved her and all—but marriage? I was definitely not ready for that. I knew my par-ents were having financial problems, so I came up with a plan that would put off marriage, keep my girlfriend at bay, and improve my parents' financial situation—I would move back home. Needless to say, it worked like a charm.

—LEWIS, UNIVERSITY OF WISCONSIN, '94

Keys to the Family Wagon

That safe and reliable caboose you mocked throughout high school will no longer be a laughing matter (once you check out the going rates for car insurance). Just look at those long lines, the mammoth proportions, the dab of rust on the left fender. Ahhh! a sight to behold. This heap . . . excuse us . . . this treasure can be all yours for the low, low price of a full gas tank. So what if you get a little embarrassed cruising through the streets; consider how much money you are saving. When in doubt or when about to go on a date, remember what your dad said: "This car is not old; it's a classic." Be grateful for having been allowed to maneuver this symbol of family togetherness.

Familiarity

Getting used to a different routine, to the clashing personalities at work, and to your fresh role as an adult will be difficult. One of the greatest advantages of living at home during this terribly unsettling time is the comfort of being around the people who know you best (and think you're the best to boot). While there is the danger of falling back upon pre-established childhood patterns, living with parents need not result in a full-blown regression. Remain focused on the goal of uncovering your dormant inner adult. You'll find that moving back home will go a long way toward giving that emerging adult the solid footing necessary to make a spectacular debut into the real world.

After graduation, I decided to get out of the family house. I bought the city paper and checked out ads for roommates. I went from person to person, and at the risk of sounding clueless, I'll tell you that each one was more bizarre than the next. After meeting one wacko after another, I ended my search for human life forms along with my quest to find an apartment. Used to be I thought my parents stranger than fiction; now they seem like carbons of Ward and June Cleaver. The whole after-college period was so strange and stressful that I felt really lucky to have this bit of normalcy to keep me grounded.
—DAN, TULANE UNIVERSITY, '95

WHO'S THE BOSS?

We are not going to insult your intelligence by telling you what you so obviously want to hear. No matter how you slice it, the house belongs to your parents. Paying room and board does not suddenly entitle you to a slot on the deed. So, as far as your parents are concerned, you are to abide by their house rules just like any other tenant. What did you expect, the rolling out of the red carpet perhaps? If warmth and kindness are a royal reception in your book, you won't be disappointed. But get greedy and you'll find your over-inflated I-just-graduated-from-college-worship-me ego eating humble pie.

Walking the Fine Line Between Tenant and Dependent

Your parents may be in charge, but be consoled; you will not have to put your life on hold or sacrifice even a shred of merriment to please your parents. Don't pull the old stand-off routine either; you'll be sorry in the end. You have everything to gain, while your parents have everything to lose. Consider their situation: While raising a bunch of noisy, ungrateful, and demanding children to the best of their abilities, they anticipated a period of peace and quiet in their twilight years. Did you actually think that they consented to your going to an out-of-state university out of sheer love for you? So now that you're back, don't get carried away and pull the "I'm running away from home" routine. You may just find that your suitcase has already been packed. Now is the time to solidify your personal growth in the eyes of your parents. Show them that you can follow reasonable rules like a rational human being. This means no tantrums, pouts, tearful pleas, or holding your breath until you turn blue. When you feel some demand is unjustifiable, present your case against it. If what you're doing is not harming anyone, you have the same right that all adults do, and that is the right to carry on. After all, these weary people are taking pity on your poor newly graduated soul. Make sure you don't step on any toes and never, *ever* forget that they call the final shots.

Establishing a Good Rapport

Atmosphere is all about vibes. No one wants to live with a bunch of angry people, least of all when these people's opinion

Valid Complaints

- Playing your music too loud and/or too late
- Tying up the phone lines
- Receiving guests at improper hours
- Eating so much that the rest of the family has to fight over your scraps
- Smoking in their non-smoking residence
- Buying a pet chinchilla that smells up the place

Invalid Complaints

- Wearing indecent attire
- Eating a nutritionally unbalanced diet
- Hanging out with the wrong crowd
- Working at an unsuitable job
- Staying out past your old curfew
- Sleeping over at your boyfriend's/girlfriend's house

really matters. So getting along with your parents cannot be stressed enough. Easier said than done? You bet! But nothing valuable comes cheap. You have to put everything you've got into this relationship. Taking your parents for granted was okay when they were legally required to support you, but now that they are doing you this gargantuan favor, be prepared to treat them with the same delicacy and tact that you would extend to any other similarly generous hosts.

When I found out that I would have to live at home after college, I was really mad. Most of the kids I knew were from affluent backgrounds and were major trust fund babies. They all got to have their own places, even without jobs. I had to wait in my old room until I got a job and saved up enough money to get my own place. I was so resentful that I took it out on my parents. I wouldn't talk to them and never helped around the house. I was always out partying with my friends and totally ignored my family. Finally, they decided to kick me out. They said they were tired of supporting me and that I was ungrateful. I was really taken by surprise. I started thinking about what they had said, and it suddenly dawned on me how immature I was being. Although I was worried that it was too late to remedy the situation, I went downstairs and sat down with my folks for a long talk. The more I listened, the more ridiculous my behavior seemed. I actually had no excuses to make. I explained what I had been going through since graduation and asked if they would give me another chance. They agreed. I put a lot of energy into getting to know my mom and dad as people, and I found that I was very lucky to have them in my life.
—ALLY, UNIVERSITY OF SOUTHERN CALIFORNIA, '92

It often takes a swift kick in the pants for us to realize that we are being less than gracious about imposing on our parents' good nature. Most of us still find self-absorption a fascinating pastime. But to get along with our parents, we have to open our minds to the possibility that they deal with issues unrelated to us on a daily basis.

LISTEN AND LEARN

Prick up your ears and listen to your parents. The art of listening is not an easy one to master. We often fall in love with the sound of our own voices, neglecting to notice the precious pearls of wisdom and gems of insight being dropped at our very feet. There is nothing wrong with wanting to be heard, so long as you are willing to return the favor. You'd be surprised at just how many interesting stories your parents have to relate. Tapping into the wealth of their experiences will most certainly be the fountainhead of your new and much improved relationship. You'll rediscover your parents and possibly learn a thing or two; your folks will feel appreciated and gratified for having raised such a considerate offspring.

The great listeners of our time will tell you that audience reaction has the power to make or break any speech. How many times have you gotten ready to say something meaningful, only to be interrupted by the all too aggravating "I know exactly what you mean," followed by an endless litany of a completely irrelevant experience? Such tyrannical egomania can take the wind out of anyone's sails, so by all means don't try it at home.

> Since childhood, I had felt incapable of talking to my parents. Once I moved back home, my social network dwindled and I became rather lonely. I could deal with the rudiments of interaction—"How was your day?" or "What did you do today?"—but nothing more substantial. One day my mother came home in tears; she'd had a fight with her supervisor and wanted to talk about the situation at work. I was kind of weirded out by the whole experience—my mother was not supposed to be looking to me for help. But after hearing about her problem, I realized that we had many things in common, including our inability to deal with authority figures. Because I had taken the time to listen to my mother's problems, my life has improved dramatically. It's great to have someone so interesting to talk to.

Take a gander at the following set of questions, and then let your parents rate your responses:

1. How did your parents meet?
2. Did your mother ever have any other offers of marriage?
3. What are the names of your parents' high schools?
4. How often does your mother wash her hair?
5. How often does your father shave? Does he use an electric razor?
6. What is your mother's favorite perfume, if any?
7. Who was your mother's favorite teen heartthrob in high school? Your father's?
8. If your father went on vacation to another city, what would he visit first? A tourist attraction or a museum? The shopping district or a picturesque park bench with a bag of crumbs for the pigeons?
9. What kind of getaway would your mother prefer? A European capital, a tropical isle, or a bed and breakfast in the country?
10. Did either of your parents take music lessons as children? If yes, which instrument?
11. What was the last book your father read?
12. Do your mother's literary tastes lean toward the romantic, the humorous, science fiction, or the classics?
13. If your mother could have any job in the world, which would she choose?
14. If your father could live anywhere on the planet, where would it be?
15. Did your parents agree on your name at birth, or did they end up tossing a coin?
16. Who was your mother's favorite musician when she was in college?
17. What foreign countries has your father traveled to in his lifetime?
18. Does your mother prefer French, Middle Eastern, Chinese, or Italian cuisine?
19. Did your mother vote in all of the last three presidential elections? For whom?
20. How old were your parents when they started dating?
21. What color are your father's eyes?
22. Did either of your parents play sports in high school? If so, which ones?
23. Who is your father's favorite actress?
24. What is your father's favorite ice cream flavor?
25. Did either of your parents own a pet while growing up? If so, what kind and what was its name?
26. What was your mother's favorite subject in school?
27. Where did your parents go on their last night out?
28. What TV show does your father stay home to watch?
29. How old are your parents?
30. Which of your parents got sick last? What was the matter?

Listening to your folks takes a little courage. Realizing that your parents are not some *uber*-beings, that they too have insecurities and problems, might make you feel as if the world is about to collapse in a little pile at your feet. Do not let this stop you from seeing the light. While you might feel burdened by some of their grievances, consider yourself lucky to have had this opportunity to familiarize yourself with your parents on a human level. This time of life is replete with some of the most crucial steps on your path toward maturity. Try not to trip all over them.

Relationships, whether between parents, friends, or lovers, require constant attention. Unlike a love interest or a new pal, you and your parents have a foundation already laid out. Your parents will not be giving you a hard time or trying to draw you into some silly mind games; in fact, they will encourage any attempt you make at solidifying the familial bond. They'll meet you halfway any day. Make sure you're prepared to do the same.

NEGOTIATION AND COMPROMISE

Negotiating is a delicate process that shouldn't be taken lightly. Try not to haggle over trifles, but be prepared to stand your ground on weighty matters. If you're having a hard time deciphering what is and isn't important, seek out the counsel of older friends who have already gone through the ritual. When all else fails, ask your parents what they expect of you. Asking them to lay down their cards early in the game may give you the upper hand. This tactic will allow you to prepare adequate rebuttals to some of their unreasonable demands. Each side will have to concede certain points, but in the end all will be more satisfied at having reached a unanimous decision.

SETTING GROUND RULES

Before you embark upon a life beneath the familial roof, you really should find out what will be expected of you and what you have a right to expect in return. The many issues that will surface while you share your parents' dwelling should be enough to make your head spin. Attempt to intercept them at the pass by anticipating and dealing with as many as possible, before they become bones of contention.

Chores Are for Bradys

Everyone remembers the fuss made over chores by the Brady Bunch. Let's face it. No one likes to have all of the work leveled onto their shoulders. That's right, not even house parents. Try a field study. After your dad comes in from mowing the lawn or finishes the dishes, ask him to vacuum the crumbs he left on the carpet the day before. You probably shudder at the mere thought! And with good reason. You'd see the results of built-up resentment immediately (recall high school chemistry: add some substance X to some solution Y and . . . kaboom! You're sitting at the nurse's office). Because everyone likes to feel important and necessary, performing a house function can help your self-esteem as well as the overall atmosphere in the home. The old adage "it is far better to give than to receive" is never so fitting as when applied to the work you can save someone, thereby giving them that elusive and unexpected moment of peace and quiet. We recommend tackling the chore issue head on. Sit down with your folks and outline the chores you prefer doing. Your selfless offering will astound and delight the ears of your adoring audience, while adding an extra increment to your own self-respect.

Lights Out!

As if! So sure! Who dares impose their stodginess upon a young reveler such as yourself? The unfortunate truth is that certain parents do expect to re-establish some nominal curfew rules. If yours try to throw the book at you (you know the one, it's called *My House/My Rules!*), don't panic. They're not the only ones who've got books to throw around. Here's Plan A: Go to the library and check out some self-help books that attempt to show parents how to best deal with their grown children. These will all be on your side. Curfews are definitely not part of a functional parent–adult child relationship.

In the unlikely event that Plan A fails, we direct your attention to Plan B. This latter strategy revolves around the aforementioned concept of compromise. However, maybe the Ps have a point: Sleeping *does* tend to get a tad complicated when some drunkard is slamming doors and watching TV at full volume in the next room.

There are chores and then there are CHORES. Choose yours wisely and you'll be in and out before Julie Andrews can finish an abridged rendition of "Superkalafragilisticexpialadotious."

Gold, Silver, and Bronze Medalists of the Easy Chore Competition

- *Taking Out the Trash.* It takes only two minutes. Bar none, it is the easiest chore to perform. Still, don't forget to affect the martyr as you state, "It's a dirty job, but somebody's got to do it."
- *Cleaning the Microwave.* This is another chore that elicits the "Yuk!" response—but not for you. Just remember the motto: No job too gross, or too quick. Well, microwave clean-up road tested at four minutes flat (and that's if you're a perfectionist!).
- *Grocery Shopping.* While this takes a bit longer (twenty minutes to one hour, on average), it does have the distinct advantage of being a fun little chore. You dress up, go to the supermarket, and thump those melons, all while keeping a keen eye out for eligible singles. Basically, it's a social errand that goes a long way toward filling up that free time you've been trying to kill.

Top Loser Chores

- *Washing Dishes.* This baby is more trouble than it's worth. It takes an unseemly twenty minutes and leaves your hands an unsightly dishpan red.
- *Cooking.* Unless you are a true gourmet, do not volunteer to feed the family. Cooking dinner denotes at least a half hour of solitary kitchen duty.
- *Vacuuming.* Vacuuming looks easier when Donna Reed does it. Barring the possibility that you require some serious muscular arm therapy, there is absolutely no reason why any rational adult should choose to push that heavy Hoover back and forth for upwards of an hour.
- *Mowing the Lawn.* If asked to perform this ungodly chore, refuse on principle. If you thought the vacuum was bad, wait until you get a load of this monstrosity.

If that's the case, your parents may confront you with the new house rules. You can ask, "Why the kindergarten treatment?" But don't be surprised to get a set of well thought-out reasons. As far as retorts go, "No fair!" is not going to cut it. You must first reason, then offer incentives, and last, but most certainly not least, veil your threats. The triple punch combination works sort of like this: Explain that since you've come home from college, you have not been feeling like yourself. Tell them you've been depressed and a little self-destructive. Next, elaborate upon how different and accommodating you plan to behave now that you've had some time to get the stress of the transition out of your system. Entice them into trusting you with promises of calls if you'll be late and being quiet as a mouse when no one's stirring in the house. If these tactics don't work, call on the final reserves. Squeeze out a tear or two (easy when you fathom the thought of your late-night soirees coming to an end), and proceed upon a sob story so pathetic as to make Harvey Keitel bawl. Talk about how you've been battling your self-destructive tendencies all of this time and how the parental compassion coupled with the ability to release stress with your friends has really been your saving grace. Apologize for having been self-absorbed, but make sure they understand how much you have had to deal with. After everyone has a good hug, turn over a new leaf. Try not to do irreparable damage to your credibility by resuming the old m.o. right away.

Smoking Policy

This varies from home to home, but going by the most recent polls, chances are that your house is a smoke-free zone. So what happens when you smoke but the owners don't? There is minimal dissension among experts on this point. The proper way to handle such a situation is to obey the Wrigley's Spearmint Gum commercials, and run right out to buy yourself a pack.

Yet if your house reeks of the smoke exhaled by your parents, while you are still forbidden to indulge, we are here to tell you that you have been going about your life all wrong. If your parents smoke, you should have informed them of your habit long ago. It was them who got you started, wasn't it? Just tell them about the theory of modeling—children mimicking their parents' actions—and let that guilty feeling gnaw at them for a while. Remain in the smokers' closet and you risk leading a life filled with the hypocrite's perpetual shame.

The Beauty of Headphones

Yes, everybody with any musical taste should love your selections. But by now you've had ample time to realize that most people are tasteless to the point of tackiness when it comes to the issue of tunes. Your parents, much as we hate to admit it, are probably no exception. So when you're grooving to unchartered frequencies in the privacy of your own room, don't get upset when you are labeled a noisemaker. What sounds like a terrific musical composition to you most likely comes off as the chaos of Bedlam to your folks. So what's a modern music lover to do? This is where we extol the virtues of headphones. If you don't want your practice of music appreciation confined to the car, you'll have to invest in a quality set. And then . . . did anybody say "Rumba!"?

Tying Up the Wires

While some of us have a healthy relationship with the phone, others are downright codependent. Those of you in the latter category know you have a problem, but you don't care. Do you? And why should you when the mere thought of receiver withdrawal sends you into delirium tremors? Since the phone is a nonlethal addiction, there really is no reason for you to quit using. Yet once you move home and have to share this commodity, problems may arise. In college you lived with roommates, and no one really had dibs on the phone. But now you're back to a place where you must bow out of many a conversation in order to let Mom deal with her clients or Dad work financial matters out with insurance agents. Clearly their grown-up concerns take precedence over your talking Paul into dining on sushi instead of tapas or discussing the latest trends in athletic footwear with Sam. If you are truly hooked, you may want to

A Mom Is Always a Mom

You know your parents still think of you as their little baby when . . .

- You wake up and your day clothes are neatly laid out on the bed.
- They insist that you look both ways before crossing the street.
- You ask your mom to buy you some Band-Aids, and she comes home with the Sesame Street variety.
- Your mom still makes those bothersome airplane noises to get you to eat.
- Your mom keeps referring to the new fall collection as back-to-school clothes.
- They show up at your office with bagged lunches.
- Your dad still shudders with pride whenever he happens to catch sight of your Little League trophy.

look into a separate line. We wish we had other alternatives to offer, but face it; it's either that or you white knuckle it through the conversations of others and learn to concede gracefully when long-distance relatives interrupt your stimulating chats.

How Much Longer, Papa Smurf?

If your stay begins to exceed a certain time, you may just start hearing the refrain, "How much longer, Papa Smurf?" Avoid the unwanted guest's pathetic destiny by deciding in advance how long you plan to remain the recipient of your parents' good will. Once you calculate the time it will take you to find a job, your own apartment, and whatever else you require to get started, share the info with the others. This way you will have a concrete goal to live up to. Beware: If you keep the cutoff date to yourself, you're likely to rationalize it away until you are well into your thirties.

Don't fool yourself. Your parents may love to have you around; but if your stay exceeds a year, trust us, your parting date will have come none too soon. The best way to get out of the house on schedule is not to fall into the vicious cycle of the talk show circuit. If you're living at home, without working nine to five, there is no use in denying that you are on intimate terms with Ricki, Springer, and Oprah. The ticket is to set daily goals for yourself. One day research a job market, and compile the killer resume on the next. Set up an appointment to "corporatize" your unruly mane and shabby chic wardrobe. Next thing you know you've got a job. Then you can start planning the big good-bye party and housewarming bash.

A QUESTION OF DOLLARS

Now you're ready to handle any minor problem before it escalates into an all-out catastrophe. Yet there are still a few issues that you may find a bit more difficult to deal with. One of these is the green stuff that does not grow on trees. You know it isn't called the root of all evil for nothing.

You probably hoped that the monetary dilemma would get settled as soon as you moved in and your parents realized how lucky they were to have you grace them with your benevolent presence.

You may be right, but you're much more likely to be wrong. There is no better time to get wise to this bottom line than when asked to fork over the cash by your parents. Shock of shocks! They who housed you all of these years, providing for your every need—notwithstanding that pricey pair of Nikes owned by everyone who was anyone in junior high—now want compensation? You betcha! And you'd better get an attitude adjustment if you actually expect your parents to put up with your free-loading fanny.

Money has always been regarded as a conversational no-no, the armpit of civilized discourse, if you will. Even negotiating a salary can make one feel like a money-grubbing sleazoid. It's a seedy business; yet you have no choice but to settle the matter as promptly as possible. No use postponing the inevitable when every minute counts. Imagine yourself racing against your parents to come up with the closing figure. The actual cost of your keep should remain strictly confidential as you round down the hundreds to arrive at a minimal yet somewhat feasible balance. When you're at the notorious bargaining table and ready to settle the score, there are only three things to remember: Underestimate, underestimate, and then underestimate some more. Sign and seal the contract quickly; they'll never know what hit them. Doubting these methods will do you no good unless your goal is to wind up in debtors' prison. When it comes to money, everyone's the enemy—parents are no exception.

Rent

The roof over your head, even if situated in the boonies, is a valuable commodity to some. Paying room and board is a small price to pay when you consider the free reign to be had over utilities, washer/dryer, cable, and even the power-stocked fridge. Consider it a show of respect, as much from you toward your parents as from them toward you. After all, you are an adult and probably have (or will soon have) a job. Your piddly contribution hardly measures a drop in your parents' fiscal bucket. While that extra hundred bucks every month may not be enough to secure their retirement, it is a sign that they view you as an adult with "grown-up" responsibilities. On average, the amount does not exceed $300. Nor should it, as some graduates get away with only $50. It all depends. Nevertheless, no matter what numbers you finally agree on, you can count on their being much lower than those you'd be offered by any other landlord.

Gas, Food, and Bills

Telephone rates are not what they used to be, but unless your parents are die-hard cheapskates, they probably won't raise a big to-do over local calls. If you're corresponding long distance, or steaming up the wires with Girl 6, prepare to own up and cover your share like the stand-up guy you are.

Electricity, water, heat, and cable should all be included in the monthly tab. If you're paying a very low amount, you may have to shell out a few extra bucks for some of these amenities—especially if you're harder than the rest of the fam on stuff such as the a/c and the old heat generator.

If you're going to be commandeering the family wagon, expect to fill up the gas tank at least once a week, depending on the frequency of your use. Tallying up the amount per driven mile and then presenting your parents with the breakdown may not be the most inspired idea. Don't nickel and dime around, save your balance statements for the stuff that will make a difference. Making yourself out to look like the penny pincher you really are will only make them wonder where they went wrong.

Used to be that after consuming the contents of the family fridge you would absolve yourself from guilt with the "I'm a growing boy/girl" line. Now that you're really grown, this tactic is obsolete. Reserving private shelf space or labeling your share of the goodies is also not recommended. Instead, do the family shopping once a week, or contribute a small but fair amount to your daily nutritional needs.

Begging for Spare Change

During these hard economic times, the temptation to borrow money may be very strong. If you find yourself avoiding tollways like the plague for fear of being short of change, consider hitting your parents up for a loan. Pestering them each time your out-on-the-town funds want replenishing is not the way to go about doing this. Those of you without a steady income should deal with the temporary plug in cash flow head on. Pick an amount that should see you through this rough impasse, and then present your folks with your promissory note. Your parents will be so impressed with your assumption of responsibility that they may even waive the interest rates. Dare to dream!

PUT IT IN WRITING

Once you've hammered out an agreement on the distribution of chores and wealth, make out a contract specifying the exact terms of the arrangement. This precaution can save you and your parents from wasting valuable time bickering over technicalities. If your contribution to the running of the household is ever brought into question, refer your parents to proviso no. 235, which clearly states that you are not responsible for cleaning up after your brother's mangy mutt, or doing the dishes if the count exceeds the agreed-upon number. A contract will also keep you from reneging on your promises and shirking your responsibilities, and, most important, away from the small-claims courtroom.

WHEN PRIVACY BECOMES A LUXURY

After a couple of months at home, you may very well find yourself pleading with the makers of Calgon to take you away. Living within a household can make time alone look as decadent and opulent as Don King's wardrobe. This is especially true if you have live-in siblings. Often times the only place you can remain undisturbed is in the bathroom—if you're lucky. But before you go soaking yourself into a prune-like state all for the sake of a few hours of solitude, take a look into some less orthodox means to arrive at serenity's blissful nirvana.

1. *Play hide (forget seek).* Just pretend you are not at home. This is easy to maneuver. Unbeknownst to anyone, you leave a note on the kitchen table alerting the inhabitants of your whereabouts someplace outside the home. Then you simply retreat into an out-of-the-way corner of the house. Odds are you will not be disturbed. On the off chance that you are discovered, plead that the note was a remnant from a time long gone by.

2. *Stock your room with provisions.* That little fridge you kept in your college dorm room need not go to waste. If you are living with your parents, you may just find you need it now more than ever. When the urge to sequester yourself behind a curtain of solitude takes over, this mini-appliance will serve you well. Read, sleep, write, or ponder the meaning of life in your room, without ever having to step outside to satisfy the baser instinct of hunger; the rest of the household will think you mid-slumber. You've heard the popular wisdom regarding sleeping dogs. Well, the same applies to children.

3. *Do not disturb.* While you may want to bypass the "Maid Service" sign, the flip side will go a long way toward helping your room remain a peaceful asylum.

4. *Do the Greg.* Remember the time when Greg moved into the Brady attic? Well, it need not be an attic for you. A basement would do just as nicely. Relocate your room to a seldom-used area of the house. If your room is one of a cluster, it will always prove difficult to be left alone. If, on the other hand, you are steps above or below the rest of the cohabitants, you will probably find yourself having to actually leave your room in search of the company you had been trying to avoid.

Parents Need Privacy Too

We've already established that *Homo sapiens* includes parents. Okay, so why then do we so often invade our parents' breathing space, thinking they wouldn't have it any other way? Parents need time to think, to be idle, to get away from you. Sure they love you, but can you blame them for wanting a wee bit of quiet time? Anticipating and respecting your folks' desire to be left alone will make them much easier to handle in the long run. Just because they're your mom and pop does not mean they are exempt from foul moods and sour tempers. If, after a long day of work, your dad comes in exhausted, barges into his room, and slams the door behind him, refrain from making any attempt at contact. Unless the house is on fire, any news you have to impart can wait until the next day. This approach will help you avoid the common household feuds, which often stem from too much contact.

Getting Along with Siblings

We remember them with fondness and love them from afar, but when at last we are face to face, we wait with baited breath for that golden moment when we can prod them with a fork underneath the dinner table. Getting along with siblings remains as nerve-racking as trying to find street parking in the city. It may be that you have a bad seed, an evil twin, or a black sheep in the family, but it is more likely that once reunited, you all simply regress. Falling into your childish patterns can be oh so tempting when confronted with those rapscallion brothers and sisters. Older or younger, their presence was probably a regular wellspring of irritation. Be that as it may, you have a new score to settle. Think of it as a challenge. Play how-long-can-you-be-in-the-same-room-with-your-sibling-without-shedding-blood. Have fun with it. Hopefully, you'll find that although you may not have always seen eye to eye in the past, it's never too late to lock eyeballs.

As with parents, siblings have to be reappraised every so often. Seeing them from a whole new light may be a bit hard on the eyes at first, but it will be worth it once you work past the initial discomfort. We can't all be bosom buddies with our brethren, and no one is saying we can. You can, however, live peacefully under one roof provided you follow the rules:

- Do not resort to the "I'm telling on you" routine.
- Steer clear of bathroom brawls over the hair dryer by investing in your own.
- Resist the urge to pillage his/her room, diary and all.
- Stay away when his/her friends come over.
- Play along when (s)he is caught in a bald-faced lie.
- Do not offer any bits of advice, even if you are older.

Sibling rivalry has been known to tamper with even the most loving of relationships. A certain degree of competitiveness can be healthy, provided it is vented in the proper spheres. If your sib and you are renowned in the one-upmanship arena, resist the urge when you're together. There are plenty of other places to play your hand. For instance, the competitive edge is often required at your workplace. Here's your opportunity to get ahead. If you're wasting precious energy fighting with your brother or sister and waging your battles on the home front, your family winds up the loser. Get that killer instinct out of your system in the corporate jungle.

How to Finally Win an Argument with Dad

Bargaining for one's fair share can rattle even the most astute of diplomats. If things heat up, as they very well might, these guidelines will help you keep your cool and remain focused:

- **Pause between arguments.** Allow your parents to mull over your statements. This will help the logic set in.
- **Don't interrupt your parents mid-harangue.** This belies fear and lack of confidence in your position.
- **Concentrate on one point at a time.** Digressions will keep you from making the necessary strides.
- **Back up your arguments with clear examples.** The argument that others your age don't have to baby-sit their kid siblings might work against you.
- **If tempers flare, count to ten.** This will prevent you from saying anything you may regret later on. If that doesn't work, beat a hasty retreat out of the lion's den until calm sets in.

STUDIO/SUNNY

Chapter Three

ON YOUR OWN IN A BRAND-NEW PLACE

DUMP

THE LOCAL SEARCH

We walk by apartment buildings on a daily basis, never stopping to think of the tenants within. Why did they decide upon that particular building? How many places did they look at before settling on that one? Finding a place to lay your weary head is no laughing matter. Sure, we've all seen those sitcoms, where struggling youths live in luxurious lofts and penthouses in some of our country's most prime real estate locales. Hopefully, you've noticed the insurmountable discrepancy between their incomes and their rent. Your first apartment will most likely fail to live up to your standards, but it may be that your standards are too high. For instance, you might have to give up space in the name of location, or vice versa. Some people love to be in the thick of things, thereby choosing a studio in a lively part of town. Others would rather live amidst gang warfare before settling on less than 1000 square feet.. It's these types of tradeoffs that will get you off the street, and isn't that what really matters?

If you're planning on settling in a city near you, consider yourself blessed. You'll encounter fewer obstacles than had you chosen to come in for a landing on unfamiliar grounds. Consider the advantages: no need to haul your cookies cross-country to screen an apartment dud, plenty of opportunities to test out neighborhood/resident compatibility, and no shortage of friends living in the area to give you valuable hunting leads. Shopping locally is simpler and cheaper, but not entirely carefree. There are truckloads of pesky technicalities that will need to be considered. But as with anything, securing a place to live seems harder than it actually is. Don't sweat it; getting started is the hardest part. Once you do, it'll be relatively smooth sailing.

> *Everyone I asked had their own horror story about finding a decent place to live. One guy told me not to even bother with brokers; another claimed that his saved him from a life on the streets. Some people said to avoid responding to too many ads; others extolled the virtues of seeing as many places as possible. I was becoming increasingly confused. All I wanted was a clean, well-lighted place to hang my hat. I had never expected that apartment shopping could be so complicated. After stalling for a while longer, I finally went out and did my own research, And I found a great place in about one month.*
> —TODD, DARTMOUTH COLLEGE, '93

Where to Live and What to Look for

Before you can start prowling for a flat, you must do a fair amount of soul searching. Deciding where to live and what type of place you're seeking will simplify the whole affair. How many times have you gone clothes shopping without the slightest clue as to what it was you wanted to buy? Did you, by any chance, end up with something to donate to charity later in the year? Where such a large investment is concerned, you cannot afford to be ambivalent. Your funds and time are scarce enough without going on a myriad of fruitless searches. If you know what you are looking for, your chances of finding it will be that much better.

Neighborhood

Mr. Rogers had it all figured out. He loved his neighborhood to the point of, literally, singing its praises. Hey, the man may have had something there. Where we live is just as important as the apartment we live in. When it comes right down to it, picking the right neighborhood can make or break your living experience. But in order to pinpoint your ideal zone, you will have to consider many factors and get a grip on the kind of lifestyle you plan on living.

Transportation

If your plan is to commute to and from work, check out the proximity of the nearest train or bus station.

Age of Residents

Some neighborhoods are bastions of the young and the restless; others are open campus retirement homes. Investigate the atmosphere of each hood before settling on one.

Nightlife

Living in the hub of activity can be very convenient for you night crawlers. One step out the door, and the city is sprawled out before you like a Thanksgiving feast. Mmmmmmm . . . you can hardly wait to sample it all. If you're the *Little House on the Prairie* sort, this option may not be quite your speed. Traffic, noise, and crowded streets will probably be more than you nature lovers can swallow.

Real Estate Lingo

Creative advertising is a part of life in the consumer lane. Learn to read between the lines, and you'll be saving yourself a lot of time and trouble. Make sure these catch phrases don't catch you off guard:

- "Rehab's Dream"—try nightmare
- "Up and Coming Neighborhood"—seedy part of town
- "Veranda off the Kitchen"—fire escape
- "Seconds from the Train"—put away your good china
- "Garden-Level"—notes from the underground

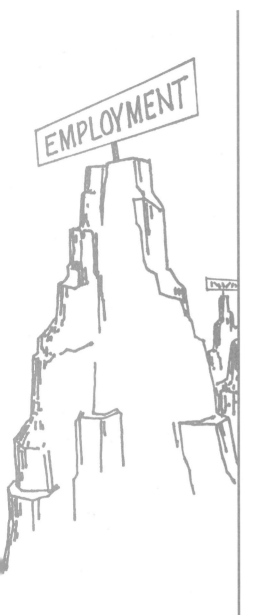

I moved to the city because all my friends could talk about was the proverbial fast-paced life on the edge—you know . . . the women, the parties, the high-profile jobs to afford it all. I was more than intrigued. But after living out there for a couple of months, frequenting the same bars and clubs, hanging out with the same girls I knew in college, and being stuck at a far from high-profile job all got old. I couldn't understand what all the hype had been about. I was paying huge sums of money to live in the city and not having any fun. I decided to relocate to another part of town, with cheaper rents and a laid-back crowd. Now this felt like home. I met new people and ended up commuting to my city job. Even though I still go downtown to party on weekends, inner-city living was not for me.

—TRENT, IOWA STATE UNIVERSITY, '95

Culture Club

Those of you with artistic inclinations should steer clear of the yuppie-blighted areas. There are plenty of neighborhoods that will satisfy the Bohemian in you. These areas are usually replete with art galleries, small theater venues, and trendy coffeehouses. An added bonus to the sheer thrill of living among this pedantic and off-beat set is that starving young artists tend to congregate in areas with lower property rates. Join these throngs and watch your savings and the good times multiply.

Other Conveniences

When choosing a neighborhood, check out how close you will be residing to the nearest twenty-four-hour convenience store, laundromat, supermarket, and bank. Trekking across town with a heavy hamper and an armful of groceries can be avoided by picking a spot close to everything.

You Must Pay the Rent!

Now that you know where you want to live, it's time to settle the rent dilemma. What can you afford? The answer to this question will limit your options considerably. Be grateful. This means less work for you. Review your financial situation and then come up with a figure that won't have you in debt after the first payment. We have yet to find a view or decor that would compensate for this wretched fate. Be prepared to alter your chosen locale if the going rates are steeper than you'd anticipated. If need be, make a run for the border. You'll discover that housing rates contain peaks and valleys even within a vicinity as small as four blocks. Also, remember to factor in the cost of utilities when calculating rent. Prices vary from building to building, and can make or break your efforts at sound budgeting. Setting a reasonable price limit will prevent you from giving into the temptation of signing a lease on a place you can't afford.

Start Your Engines

Now that the neighborhood and price range have been worked out, it's time to get your hands dirty. This leg of the trip will require pounding the pavement, consummating your phone skills, and networking know-how. You don't want to pick a place just because it was the first one you saw that happened to fit into your budget. Prepare to scope out a plethora of empty spaces. Seeing is believing. Once you spot that cozy fireplace or that inviting view, you'll wonder how you ever considered moving into that other dilapidated hovel. There are piles of resources from which to extract all the necessary info; pool these and you'll be strides closer to finding your new home.

Extra! Extra! Read All About It!

Head out to the closest newsstand and get your hands on the local paper. This is your best bet when it comes to setting up residence in a nearby community. The Sunday edition is a must-read. This issue is usually bursting at the seams and includes ads not listed in the daily. Some papers will organize apartments by location; others use the bedroom number system. Once you familiarize yourself with the format, you can begin to differentiate the winners from the losers. The former will usually list prices, exact location, and a concise description of amenities. If the listing is leaving too much to the imagination, you're probably better off staying in the dark.

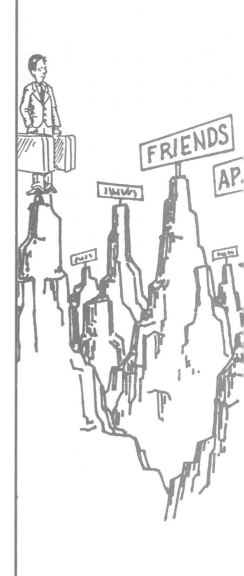

Rent via the Internet

Wayward home seekers like yourself swear by the Net. Cruise on over to the Internet and investigate these stellar sites for yourself:

- Rent Net
  http://www.rent.net/
- Web Rent
  http://www.room4rent.com/
- Apartment On-Line
  http://aptline.com
- Apartment Guides
  http://www.aptguides.com/
- Rent Check
  http://www.rentcheck.com/
- Rental Living
  http://www.rentweb.com

Strictly Hearsay

Word gets around, so be there when it does. The best pads are usually scooped up even before they go to press. Bother your pals, and tell them to inform any friends or relatives living in your selected vicinity to keep their eyes peeled for stellar vacancies. You wouldn't believe how high the turnover rate is for happening flats. Getting out fast when a new opportunity presents itself is, after all, why people choose to rent in the first place. Besides, you'll have less work to do once your new recruits get busy.

Thanks to my friends and relatives, I was set up in a great apartment that was much cheaper than those I screened on my own. It turned out that my best friend from college had an uncle who published a small-business magazine and rented advertising space to a real estate agency. They were constantly making deals back and forth, and this time I was on the receiving end. My friend's uncle set it all up, and I got the deal of a lifetime. I paid him back by working a couple of Saturdays on his publication. Considering how much money he saved me, it was well worth it. Had it not been for the help of good contacts, I would never have gotten such a great apartment.

—TRACEY, UNIVERSITY OF MIAMI, '95

The Pick of the Litter

You made all the calls and set up all the appointments. Now you're ready to appraise the slew of options lined up before you. Don't do the "I'll take what's behind door number three" thing—dumb luck and a cavalier attitude just won't cut it. It's the Inspector Gadget route that will take you where you want to go. It might look lovely when you get there, but be careful not to mistake flair for substance. Be ready to stay a while, ask questions about asbestos and termite inspections, and don't ever let yourself be pressured into making a decision. You're entitled to a good, hard look. If the landlord doesn't see it your way, (s)he probably never will, so get out while you still can. Knowing what to look out for should speed up the process.

Size

Make sure the place is large enough to house that four-poster bed you wouldn't dream of parting with. You should also measure the door/hallway dimensions prior to lugging your oversized couch up five flights of stairs only to realize that there's no chance of squeezing it through. Room sizes should be evaluated in terms of how often you will use them. If you have a habit of sleeping on the living room sofa, don't worry if your bedroom is the size of a closet. The kitchen is cramped, but the dining room is of robust proportions? Don't be such a stickler; it all balances out in the end.

Light

No matter how much money you spend on sunglasses just to elude the light of day, try living without it for a week. It's not easy. Humans, like plants, need light, and plenty of it. Never go looking at places at night. Generally, windows facing east get morning light, those facing west are heated by the strong afternoon rays, and those facing north are sometimes left without sunshine. But windows looking south will leave you basking in warm rays all day long.

Noise

Noise is a major concern if you're checking out city spots. Living on or off of Main Street does have its advantages, but the din is definitely not one of them. Open the windows in each apartment, and give a good listen to the sounds of the metropolis.

The Super

Find out if your super will be living on the premises. Disasters are just waiting to happen: broken pipes, radiator leaks, gum in the keyholes, and other late-night lock-outs. Having a super next door will save you hours of trouble and heartache.

Finding a place that's right for you requires that you know what you want and how to get it. Everyone has different needs, budgets, and lifestyles, yet all these factors play a crucial role in the selection of an apartment. Don't expect to find a place in a week's time; some people have become aficionados by virtue of having spent months

Ask the Realtor . . .

Having this list of questions by your side will keep you focused during a Q & A with a realtor:

- Are pets allowed?
- Will I be charged for repairs, or are they included in the rent?
- Is there a storage area?
- Is there a garbage chute on my floor, or do I have to carry garbage to some particular area?
- Have any of the neighbors been cited for noise violations?
- Aside from me, who will have keys to my place?
- Is there a security system?
- Has anyone ever been evicted from the building?
- When was the apartment last renovated?
- Will the apartment be painted before I move in?
- What is the parking situation? Garage or street-side?
- Are there laundry facilities on the premises?
- Has anyone in the building reported sightings of cockroaches or rats?
- Is the water pressure high or low?
- How much is the security deposit?

scavenging around for an appropriate dwelling. In the meantime, you can always live with parents, with accommodating friends, or at a youth hostel. But whatever you do, don't settle on the first place you tour. Home is where the heart is; so find one suited to house yours.

A FAR-OFF PLACE

Let's say, for the sake of argument, that you've had it with the old digs. Tired of the same old vistas, you've decided to move on up in the world, out of the old hood, out of the old tri-state area for that matter, all the way across miles and miles of land to an altogether different city. A word of caution to all you free spirits: If you don't want to wind up on the street, find your new home prior to leaving your old one behind. Trust us when we tell you that there is no mind-boggler like the one resulting from the attempt to zero in on an oasis amidst an unfamiliar desert.

Travel Section

No respectable bookstore or library sets up shop without a travel section. You just march right into that bastion of literature and park yourself next to U.S. Travel—A,B,C, ahhh there's D . . . we've got Denver. Wait, there's one, there's two, three . . . what is going on here?! How many Denver books could one person possibly have the tenacity to look through? The trick is to skim them all first; some you'll nix right away; others you'll take right up to the counter and bring home. Make sure you take along a roomy bag, as you may have to pour over a score of volumes to get a sense of where it is in Denver that you want to live. If you're at the store but cash poor, take up several hours of bookstore residence (it's free) as you scratch your notebook chock full of notes on that future home.

Newspapers

While looking through your various travel books, make sure you find out what newspapers the city has to offer. Then find your local out-of-town newspaper source. Try to find the paper that best suits your needs, as the rag trade is structured around different audiences.

In Chicago, for example, you've got the *Tribune* and *Sun-Times*, which are both mainstream papers. If, on the other hand, you're looking to find something of a more peripheral nature, your best bet is *The Chicago Reader*, a funkier and smaller paper, read most often by the vogueish city swingers. Find the right paper for your needs and you'll be on the right track soon enough.

Use the information you gained through all that guidebook perusal to locate the area in which you want to live. Imagine, for example, that you have decided that the yuppie lifestyle is all that matters in life. From the travel books, you've learned where the high-end shopping is and where the affluent youths congregate—there is your neighborhood! Now that you're in business, you can start looking at For Rent Classifieds located in your ideal spot.

Real Estate Brokers

If you're looking from afar, a broker can be your best friend. That is, unless the apartment you get is a lemon, in which case the broker becomes a lifelong nemesis. Of course, this latter development need never happen if you play your cards wisely. The first thing to do when dealing with these flat finders is to come up with a list of necessities. Have this list on hand when you contact the brokers. By this phase of the process, you should have already gathered all the information you need. The issue of rent goes without saying. Pay careful attention to the broker's reaction when you explain your wants and your income. If you hear a loud and resounding cackle, chances are your dreams are bigger than your wallet.

A word of caution about brokers: Some will charge you a nothing-to-sneeze-at-type fee; others collect their bread and butter directly from the landlords. If you're like us and loathe to part with a dollar, we suggest you find out which category your personal apartment shopper falls into. As you've probably realized, many of these people are straight out of *Glengarry Glen Ross*, born losers out for a fast buck. Whether those bills are coming from you or from the landlord is of no consequence. All they see standing between them and several hundred bills is an empty dotted line. Some dapper shyster may try to swindle you into the quick fix, but stand firm. Do not fall prey to pressure tactics. Use many different apartment locators; this way you'll get a feel for who you are dealing with. Since a broker is not your only link to shelter, consider using a friend or any other possible connection (parent's friend, distant relative, old acquaintance, friend of a friend, etc.) to help you out with your future place. But if you do find a professional who's got the goods on the model space, don't pass it up only to save a month's rent worth of tokens. *Do* make sure it is worth the splurge by asking to have pictures faxed or mailed, by having a friend scope it out, and, finally, by making a list of that particular apartment's pros and cons. Of course, the optimal way to make sure your future habitat is picture perfect is to make that sojourn and see it for yourself.

The Preliminary Site Visit

Before you sign a year or more of your life away, make sure you know what's in it for you. It may be wise to plop down that wad of bills at the ticket counter and buy yourself a round-trip, economy class ticket to destination Brand New Town. It's always a good idea to have several options in mind before you get there, just so you can shop around. You don't want to make that final decision only for lack of alternatives.

After really putting my broker through the wringer, I finally settled on a place. Still, something told me I should see it. I couldn't imagine trusting a total stranger, or even the friend who double-checked for me. It turned out I was right. When I got to the building, I liked it. The neighborhood was great, and the courtyard was also pretty nifty. The apartment itself was not at all disappointing. It seemed as though I should have saved the cash and trusted the others. Since I had nothing better to do, I took a walk around the area. And what do you know? Two blocks down, there was a "For Rent" sign. I decided to look into it. They showed me the flat, and I was blown away. It wasn't any better than the place I had been ready to snag, but it was considerably cheaper—no broker's fee either. You could say that that was when I officially broke with my broker.

—ZOE, UNIVERSITY OF TEXAS, '94.

The Letter of the Law

Let's face it; the only thing fine about legal matters is the font size. Although you would rather shell out your last dollar than read through pages of boring legalese, the lease is one document that you really can peruse without the aid of hired help. Read through it to make sure that your landlord's idea of the rent matches your own, that Fluffy will not have to meet with any untimely injections, and that you will not be evicted for not being a good sport on Halloween. These and other equally minor but potentially disastrous details could easily mean your downfall.

Don't be afraid to ask your landlord about anything you deem worthy of suspicion. If you don't like what you're told, don't worry. Help is just a phone call away. Whatever breed of person you are, if you're going to rent, you've got a renters' union standing behind you every step of the way.

The Tenants Association

These people work hard to make sure you get what's coming to you. If you and your landlord are at odds, this group may be the only friend you have. The tenants association will stick up for your rights and not charge you one thin dime to do so. That there, fellow graduates, is true friendship. Picture this . . . your drain has been clogged for over a week, you haven't been able to shower, and your landlord keeps promising to fix the problem. But alas, nothing gets fixed. Meanwhile, you smell like an open can of sardines in yesterday's trash. Have you no legal recourse? Is yours but to do and die and never stop to wonder why? Of course not, you're an educated adult. You know there's a tenants association just waiting to help you. In fact, this type of situation is the association's forte. You'll learn all about your power to withhold rent if the landlord is not keeping up with repairs. You may even find that you can pocket some of that withheld dough for compensation. This little union is a regular gold mine of helpful hints; make sure to call upon its resources should you ever find yourself up the creek without a paddle.

Big Bad Broker—Buyer Beware!

As we've already alluded to, *some* brokers are real meanies. They may look like friends and act like long-lost relatives, but look closer and you'll see the eyes of wolves beneath the wool of their sheep's clothing. Here are some tipoffs that your broker is hungry and has a broiled pigeon, bearing a striking resemblance to you, on the mind:

- "I've got two couples just waiting to get their hands on this baby." If this were true, the broker would be wasting precious little time talking to you.
- "It costs more, but it's well worth it." Chances are that any apartment outside your price range is out there for a good reason. You just don't happen to make enough dough to afford such reasoning.
- "I'll just take the requisite 10 percent of your price range limit and we can get going."

If you walk away with only one pointer from this entire chapter, remember to pay nothing until you've seen the rental agreement.

The Attorney

Friends for hire? Advocates for rent? Mercenaries? Whatever you call them, attorneys are professionals who get the job done. They will aid and abet you in solving any dilemma, be it big or small. The only problem is that they'll give you their expert advice, but then take all of your lunch money in exchange. "What about that pro bono stuff I've heard so much about?" you may be asking. Well, you can just forget it. If you can afford to eat without food stamps, you're much too well-to-do for a freebie.

MOVE IT OR LOSE IT!

Anticipating a move to a new apartment can be as thrilling as devouring the whole mixture of cookie dough before baking. Unfortunately, it could also leave your stomach just as queasy. Your entire life is about to change and you can't wait to get started. There is one minor problem. You and your valuables will somehow have to survive the relocation in one piece. There will be tons of little details to look after, and many unforeseen difficulties may arise. But none of it, no matter how harrowing, will be insurmountable. It's all in how you look at it. Think of it as an adventure, and you won't get overwhelmed when something goes awry; and something always does. Going with the flow and being ready for anything will make your move go much smoother.

Prepare for Takeoff

Preparation is the name of the game. If you're not aware of this, then all is lost. We're not just talking packing here. There are a slew of other contingencies to take care of before you can skip away footloose and fancy free to your new destination. You'll need one month, at the very least, to tie up your mess of various affairs into a neat little bundle. Careful planning is your only means of completing the relocation intact, so get started as soon as possible.

Breaking the News

Whether it be family or friends, don't wait until the last minute to let them in on your plans. Others might be affected by your move, and you never know how until you break the news. This small courtesy may also score you a few going-away parties and plenty of presents to boot. This is one opportunity you don't want to miss.

> *I had a hard time finding a job in my hometown, but was finally offered one in Dallas. I didn't want to worry my parents, so I kept everything to myself. Then one day, my Dad comes in with this big, goofy grin on his face, telling me that he just convinced his boss of twenty years to give me a job with his company. Great, I thought, now he tells me. I had accepted the offer in Dallas, and there was no turning back. When I finally told my Dad, boy was he mad! He had worked really hard to get me that job, and now had to apologize to his superior. I should have said something sooner, but I didn't want to ruin my last days with the family, which is precisely what ended up happening.*
> —ROD, CALIFORNIA INSTITUTE OF TECHNOLOGY, '96

Out with the Old, In with the New

This is the time to go through your stock of collectibles to decide what exactly you can and cannot live without. Consider the size of your new place when rummaging through your wares. Will it hold that raggedy old couch, or how about that bookcase you bought in college? You won't be needing many of the items you just couldn't bear to surrender in college, so don't go getting sentimental. A good rule of thumb: The more you toss, the less trouble and expense you'll have to go through on moving day.

Next, pick a weekend and place a garage/rummage sale ad in the paper, specifying where and when the festivities will be held. Now comes the fun part: pricing. Make your kitsch as reasonably priced as possible. There is no reason why that old lamp bearing your college insignia should go for twenty bucks. While the Kennedy cigar case may have gone for a couple hundred thousand, no one will buy your worthless lamp for twenty, no matter how adamantly you insist on its being a collector's item. If you

---

Preparing for a Move

The Week Before:

- Finish packing.
- Get ahold of your new set of keys.
- Compile an address book with telephone numbers of family and friends.
- Collect all your dental, medical, and insurance records.
- Cancel the utilities.
- Return all library books.
- Set up a bank account in your new city.
- Confirm your travel reservations.
- Pick up your clothes from the dry cleaners.
- Verify the starting date of all utilities at your new home.

The Day Of:

- Close and lock all the windows and doors.
- Turn off all the appliances.
- Make sure to take your new keys, your airline tickets, snacks, and proper identification.
- Check all the closets, cupboards, and storage areas for forgotten items.
- Turn off all the lights.

have leftover merchandise, contact a charitable organization to pick it up at no charge. You'll do a good deed, and get a tax deduction to boot.

Move Yourself or Hire a Professional?

This depends as much on the quantity as well as the quality of your stuff. It is much cheaper to move yourself. If you're low on funds, you may not have a choice in the matter. Moving companies can charge exorbitant fees, so be prepared to haggle if you find yourself in the unenviable position of needing their assistance. And by all means, shop around. There are plenty of movers just waiting to get their grubby little hands on your goods. If the expense turns out to be heavier on your budget than the weight of all of your crates and boxes combined, opt for the "anything they can do, I can do better" approach. Back spasms and cramps are part of this bargain, so don't start whining when the going gets tough. If you're lacking in the muscles department, recruit a beefy comrade or leave the heavier stuff behind.

Involve Your Friends

Every little bit of brawn helps. Offer to pay them a small fee, or just take the whole group out to lunch. If they still refuse to comply, start in with the guilt trip. Make it clear that this will be your last chance to bond before the big send-off, and that someday, maybe not today, maybe not tomorrow, but soon and for the rest of their lives, they will regret not having taken this golden opportunity to pay their last respects and achieve that much-sought-after sense of closure. Before you can say swindled, your friends will be jumping at the chance to lend a helping hand.

Man's Best Friend

Whether it be a dog, cat, turtle, or rat, your pet will require special care during the move. Those of you driving should make sure that your animal comes equipped with a favorite toy and plenty of food. If you're flying the friendly skies, call ahead to secure a space. Before heading for the airport, visit the vet and request copies of all the health records. (Don't forget to call first so that the wait at the office won't leave you and Fido stranded at the terminal.)

I decided to drive my dog, Leroy, out to my new pad in Portland. The trip was thirteen hours long, and I was sure old Leroy could stomach the voyage. I happened to forget his food at home, and had to buy another brand of dog chow along the way. Leroy got totally sick, and kept yelping in the most heart-rending way for six hours straight. When I pulled over to let him have some fresh air, Leroy ran off in another direction. Besides the food, I also neglected to adorn him with the proper tags. So I wound up driving up and down the streets of this strange town, yelling "Leroy" out the car window like a madman. Finally, I spotted Leroy in an alley. Instead of the adventure I thought it would be, the trip turned out to be a total washout.

—BORIS, ARIZONA STATE UNIVERSITY, '94

Packing Your Bags

You may not be aware of this, but there is a knack to packing. It's a tad more complicated than just tossing your stuff into old boxes and duct-taping them shut. Putting the wraps on your fragile items, stereo equipment, and books is not as easy as you might imagine. First you must assemble all the necessary supplies—various sized boxes, tissue paper, bubble pack, tape, scissors, and so on. Then there is the matter of storing your belongings in such a way as to ensure their molecular cohesion—and you thought the hard part was over.

Packing Savvy

Collect all the packing materials and get to work. Start by layering foam or paper at the bottom of every box. Then place all the heaviest things first and then the lightest things on top. You can fill in the empty spaces with more paper, or use clothing and towels for padding. Delicate items should be wrapped individually to prevent damage. Store these in small boxes, and, once again, fill in the gaps

Common Packing Faux Pas

- Jamming too much stuff into one box, making it impossibly heavy to carry
- Forgetting to mark the boxes
- Using printed newspaper for cushioning, which can easily stain your belongings
- Not packing items firmly enough in their boxes
- Neglecting to inventory the items
- Postponing packing until the last minute
- Forgoing the moving insurance

with foam or paper. If you're packing dishes, wrap each one separately and buy a cushioned dish-pack carton to place them in.

Whether you are an avid reader or just a textbook sycophant, make sure you don't lay all of these monuments to human knowledge in one basket. When we moved out of our college pad, we made the mistake of piling our books into one big box—as you may well imagine, a tow truck couldn't move that baby. After struggling with the monster for about an hour, we had to unpack the box and start from square one. Divide your books among the many boxes you're planning to transport. It will do wonders for your back and keep the much-warned-against hernia from becoming your grim reality.

Keeping Track

While packing, don't forget to keep a log of the location of each item and where it will go in your new home. In their haste to pack all their worldly possessions, most people give little heed to the hassles of unpacking. No one wants to centerpiece their first weeks at a new place with the grand event of searching for necessities. Writing it all down will give you the freedom to unpack quickly.

All Aboard!

Moving day can be a mad whirl of frenzied activity. A variety of things can go wrong—the moving crew might be late, important items may be misplaced or forgotten, fragiles may be shattered. Everyone has his/her own woeful tale to relate about the mishaps that seem to be inherent to this fateful day. One of our friends forgot to confirm her flight reservations and couldn't get to her new home to meet the movers. The moving service stored her stuff for a week, and when she finally did arrive on the scene, she had a hefty bill waiting to greet her. Had she prepared a list of things to do the day before and the day of the move, relocation would have been a breeze.

Moving to a new place should be an exciting experience. While it is important to coordinate and plan ahead, don't get sidetracked by the formalities. Recall why you are relocating in the first place—to expand your horizons, explore new territories, and start afresh. By taking care of the details and making sure things don't go astray during the move, you will be giving yourself the freedom to concentrate and fully appreciate this rare event of a new age dawning in your life.

A BRAND-NEW TOWN

You've really done it! Look at you now. You've forwarded yourself and all your material accoutrements to a brand-new city. You tell the cabby to slow down, as you make all the appropriate OOHS! and AHHHS! You're just so gosh-darned excited to be there that you don't even care whether the driver thinks you're some corn-fed, red-necked bumpkin fresh off the tractor trailer. You have every right to revel in the moment. There are few experiences in life that will match the sheer exhilaration of moving to a new town on your own. There are oodles of new stuff in store for you—a new job, new friends, a new apartment. Whatever happens, and anything can, your life will never be the same.

This pleasant reverie may usher in yet another, far less comforting, set of thoughts. After the initial glee passes, you may find yourself wondering, Will I ever learn to get around? Will I make new friends or end up a lonely, old nobody? or What if I hate my new job and want to go home? Before you go booking the next flight out of there, you should realize that if you didn't entertain at least a few doubts and apprehensions, you would be one sick puppy. Feeling overwhelmed is part of the adventure, so embrace the uncertain future while you're young enough to have one. Pretty soon you'll have responsibilities, kids, a life insurance policy, a retirement fund, a thirty-year mortgage, and an investment portfolio that will have you so grounded, you'll be feeling six feet under. True, you haven't the first clue as to where you're going or where you'll wind up. But isn't that precisely what makes life livable? Knowing exactly what will happen from day to day is for the birds. Your mission, on the other hand, should be to milk this exhilarating time for all it's worth.

Make Yourself at Home

The first few days at your new home will be best spent unpacking and establishing your presence. You will be running many errands and may have to forgo any expeditions into the promised land. There will be plenty of time for such excursions later. You probably wouldn't have any fun doing the town with the unfinished business of building a comfy nest hanging over your head. It's always a good idea to have some stable footing, before heading out to explore uncharted territory.

Unpacking

Make sure to meet your movers at the scheduled time to oversee the unloading of the goods. Movers tend to get sloppy at this stage, especially if your watchful eye is nowhere in sight. Giving them the old evil eye should keep them and your cherishables in check. If you're moving yourself, don't put off unloading your possessions. One friend of ours did so, and two years later he was still making constant trips to his truck in search of the required items. Moral of the story? Unpacking is much like removing a bandage—it's much less painful when done in one fell swoop.

Once you've gotten all that baggage inside, you may feel entitled to a break. Be wary of this temptation, as you may lose sight of the fact that you've only scratched the surface of the moving-in process. Everything in its rightful place is the essence of order, and now is the time to establish it. Dishes, clothes, and the myriad of knick-knacks will have to be arranged and organized. If you've decluttered before the move, and somehow managed to trash certain basic necessities, now is the time to replenish your stock. Head straight for the nearest Wal-Mart and equip yourself with a whole new set of wares.

Interior Design

Just because you have everything put away where you want it does not mean that your place is primed for living. It's those little personal touches that make an apartment a home, and that's exactly what you need to weather the new-kid-in-town ordeal. Plants, lively colors, funky prints, and sensual textures can jazz up even the dullest of flats, and won't require that you shell out the extra dough for an affected interior decorator. In order to be the chick/chuck magnet you've always imagined you'd be, your lion's lair should roar with flair and aesthetic appeal.

You must first obtain clearance from the management if you want to paint the walls or strip the carpeting to expose the original wood floors. Some landlords provide their new tenants with a redecorating fund, so be sure to inquire about the standard procedure. We strongly urge you to bypass that white-washed, one-flew-over-the-cuckoo's-nest wall look. Painting each surface a different color will designate your pad the official palace of funk. Try texturing the walls by using a sponge on a fresh coat of paint to further diversify the look. But don't go overboard by painting dots, stripes, or animal prints along the surfaces—you'll end up climbing the walls in no time. Next, go hunting at the flea markets for old furniture and off-beat textiles. You never know what you'll find, and you can save a fortune. Keep an eye out for dilapidated wood items such as bookcases, dressers, tables, and chairs. Buy special wood paint in bold colors or pastels, and transform these woebegone relics into paraphernalia of the shabby chic fad sweeping the nation. Old couches can be rejuvenated with brightly colored fabrics and a staple gun. Wrap some sprightly patterned material around a rod and you have instant curtains.

Contacting Service Companies

No one should have to spend their first days in a new home sitting in the dark or shivering to death. And while you should have contacted the electric, telephone, and gas companies before setting sail, there's no use crying over spilled milk. Upon arrival, arm yourself with the local yellow pages and march straight toward the nearest public phone—or just pull out the old cell. You'll be in hot water heaven soon enough.

Greeting Your Neighbors

At one time it was a big deal when a new resident moved in. The neighbors would pile atop the welcome wagon to bring you

---

Address Changes

To get your affairs in order prior to the big move, you'll need to compose an address change list. This will only take a moment's time, and should include the following:

- Bank
- College bursar's office
- Credit card companies
- Magazines and newspapers
- Voter registration
- Finance agencies/college loan offices
- Car registration
- Post office

Outfitting Your New Digs

Those of you who sold most of your belongings by way of a garage sale will need to shop till you drop. Discount stores are your best bet for acquiring the following necessities:

- TV set and VCR
- Alarm clock
- Furniture
- Lamps
- Kitchen appliances (big and small)
- CD player
- Pots and pans
- Mops and sponges
- Iron
- Hair dryer
- Hangers
- Garbage can
- Crates, shoe rack, and closet organizer
- Vacuum cleaner, hand vacuum, and feather duster
- Blankets, pillows, and sheets (You'll be happy to know that most stores do carry the Superfriends variety.)

cherry pies, care packages, and fruit baskets. A cup of sugar? No problem. A coffee chat? Not without a slice of cake! Hospitality is not what it used to be. But, frankly, who needs all those calories anyway? So you'll have to knock on a few doors before anyone deems you safe enough to enter. It's okay. Put on your most endearing scout face. Also refrain from encountering their eyeball in the peephole. No one likes a practical joker, especially one they don't know very well.

Be sure to get off on the right foot with your neighbors. Suppose, for example, that you misplace your keys. A friendly neighbor could lend you the use of his/her couch while you wait for a spare. On the other hand, say some bloodthirsty psycho chases you up the stairs (purely hypothetical), and, instead of coming to your rescue, your neighbors cheer as you face your maker—all because you have been nothing but a nuisance since day one. Had you been a more agreeable neighbor, your life span would have been considerably longer. But in all seriousness, neighbors are invaluable for helping each other out of some sticky jams. Build those bridges before it is too late. You only get one chance with neighbors. Usually the first meeting is the one that sets the tone for the duration of the residence. So be a cheery little go-getter from day one, and you won't ever have to endure those deafening elevator silences.

> *When I moved into my place, I was exhausted from the flight and could barely get my stuff put away. When my next-door neighbor came a'knocking, I was too exhausted to keep up my end of the conversation. I tried to be polite, but she just wouldn't quit talking. All I wanted to do was sleep, and I finally asked her to come back some other time. She had every right to be slightly miffed, but making me sleep in the hall after I misplaced my keys was going too far. It's been pretty much a cold war ever since. She won't even ride in the same elevator with me.*
>
> —SANDRA, UNIVERSITY OF INDIANA, '93

If you're lucky, you'll end up with some stable neighbors who'll quickly become your friends. They can go a long way toward acquainting you with the new city, taking you to parties, and making all the proper intros. Believe us, you'll need all the help you can get when you're first settling in, so don't go stealing their newspapers just yet.

Locating the Nearest Doctors and Hospital

It's no wonder healthy comes before wealthy and wise. Cover your bases as quickly as possible by finding a reputable doctor and hospital in your area. Have their telephone numbers on hand at all times. The best place to keep them is somewhere in your wallet. Say the unthinkable happens—that's right, you fall and you can't get up. Most likely your mommy won't be there to bail you out. Make sure emergency numbers are clearly and distinctly written at an accessible area near the phone. If you get really paranoid living alone, get a bathroom phone. If anyone asks, just tell them there are phones in all the swankiest European bathrooms. Add authority to your assertion (which is, by the way, true) by throwing the term *peasant* at the busybody.

The Key to the City

Even your initial stroll down to the corner coffee shop can make you feel like an American in Paris. You will probably suffer from a mild dose of culture shock upon arrival. Everyone does when they move to a new city. Many have said that although they visited the town prior to relocating, once they docked, it was a totally different cup of java. Much of the disoriented feeling has to do with the anxiety of moving. You'll want to do too much at once and learn the ropes as soon as possible. While we admire your zeal, it may cause you some unnecessary stress. Take it slowly. Don't be afraid to get lost (with the exception of certain neighborhoods). And, above all, don't expect to master the city in a matter of weeks. Exploring is the fun part. Stretch it out for as long as you can.

Charting Your Course

Don't leave your city map at home for fear of coming off as a common tourist. Your bravado will not help matters. Warm up to the idea that you don't know it all, and then study those coordinates until the sun comes up. It's either that or you ask every passerby to point out the proper directions. Once you take to the streets—in your quest to locate restaurants, grocery stores, nightclubs, and other pertinent sites—you'll be hard pressed to find a guide more valuable than the average map.

Subscribing to Local Newspapers

When it comes to unearthing the town's best-kept secrets, trust the journalists to do it for you. The people from the city paper have a nose for the stuff. They are, in a sense, the truffle pigs of any metropolis. Up to date and full of the city's vital statistics, this resource can get you off on the right foot. If you're looking to cover the basics, look into the city guides and your chamber of commerce. Yet, if you're looking for the real scoop, look no further than the local press.

Adjusting to a new city can be a harrowing experience, but don't despair. The hardest thing a young person like you can do is to uproot and face the future alone. After you've braved the big, bad metropolis, you'll find that you've gained enough strength and confidence to reckon with an army of obstacles. This is what's known as character formation, and after you get settled in your new city, you'll be tough as nails—that's right, a regular Van Damme.

Streetwise

Some people are born with it—that certain attitude, a determined strut. No hooligan will bother to mess with these boulevard brainiacs. Why should they, when they have you to push around? Look at you! With your purse flying off your shoulder and your wallet peeking out of your back pocket, you are a walking billboard, screaming "TAKE ME FOR ALL I'M WORTH!" For shame! You should know better. The city streets are mean by definition. You'll need to develop an awareness of your environment if you ever hope to feel safe in it. Practicing your defense methods in everyday situations will help you prevent or win out any foul play.

Crash Course

While you may consider your Mustang a safe asylum, your place to crank up the volume and forget the outside world, you may still be a target for unexpected attack. Many incidents of car-jackings are reported daily. One way to prevent becoming a victim is to always keep alert at stop signs and traffic lights. This is where the armed buzzards, their talons aimed directly at your gray matter, descend upon their prey. You halt at a red light, and Whammo! Some eight-year-old gang banger is flashing a firearm in your face and demanding that you kindly get the #@*% out of your car. Prevent this action by keeping a hawk's eye out for any suspicious loiterers. When you stop at intersections, make sure there is space between the front of your car and the back of the car before you. Car-jackers usually look for someone whose vehicle is sandwiched in and immobilized. Leave sufficient space to peel out of there if you get danger vibes.

Always be wary: Someone may not want your car, but if your windows are open and your purse, briefcase, or whatever, is lying on the passenger seat, what makes you think some of these unscrupulous characters would think twice about appropriating it? So, lock your doors and keep your windows at a level through which no unwelcome arms can reach.

Walking the Streets

Pedestrians are most vulnerable at night. If you have to walk alone at night, make sure you take a well-lit path. But you really should avoid going solo after sundown. Even if you're Mr. Macho Man, it's always a good idea to take a cab if you find yourself burning the midnight oil at the office. However, if you are going to pound the pavement at all hours, try to do it in an assertive manner. Don't fidget or look scared. Assailants can identify the smell of fear, even through that mist of cheap cologne. If you think you're being followed, don't hesitate to run into the street, or a store, or to yell at the top of your lungs.

Get Your Facts Straight! Here are some stats on the most popular destinations of today's young travelers:

NEW YORK CITY

Weather
Average July high: 85°F
Average January low: 26°F
Average annual rainfall: 40 inches
Days receiving some rain per year: 121
Average annual snowfall: 29 inches

Economy
Cost of living index (average = 100%): 221%
Job growth since 1995: +0.7%
Forecast job growth till 1999: +0.8%

Crime
Property crimes yearly per 100,000 people: 5,008
Violent crimes yearly per 100,000 people: 1,641

Miscellaneous Observations
This is a city with exorbitant medical costs and commute times—little wonder that no one drives there. Never mind those "fashion mecca" and "American theater capital" aspects; all your money will be tied up in doctors' bills and gasoline or public transport investments. Still, if you must go chi-chi, this is the only place to be.

City Match (continued)

LOS ANGELES

Weather
Average July high: 76°F
Average January low: 45°F
Average annual rainfall: 12 inches
Days receiving some rain per year: 35
Average annual snowfall: 0 inches

Economy
Cost of living index (average = 100%): 118%
Job growth since 1995: +0.3%
Forecast job growth till 1999: +4.0%

Crime
Property crimes yearly per 100,000 people:
4,927
Violent crimes yearly per 100,000 people:
1,498

Miscellaneous Observations
Since public transport leaves much to be desired, the freeways are clogged most of the time. This is one place where your car is your Siamese twin—thus, the smog. So consider the traffic question carefully before you pack your bags. Yet, if fun in the sun is your idea of heaven, you'll probably be a happy little L.A. goer no matter what the air-safety index.

CHICAGO

Weather
Average July high: 84°F
Average January low: 17°F
Average annual rainfall: 34 inches
Days receiving some rain per year: 123
Average annual snowfall: 40 inches

Economy
Cost of living index (average = 100%):
107%
Job growth since 1995: +0.7%
Forecast job growth till 1999: +3.8%

Crime
Property crimes yearly per 100,000 people:
5,485
Violent crimes yearly per 100,000 people:
1,800

Miscellaneous Observations
While it's no more windy than many cities, it's most certainly more frosty. Many commuters take the train (mostly lawyers), but others choose to cater to gridlock. Yet the cold does have some advantages. If you're looking for affordable, big-city living, you're in the right place. No glam scam and no thonged rollerbladers; just a big city with a smile and a small-town feel.

BOSTON

Weather
Average July high: 81°F
Average January low: 23°F
Average annual rainfall: 43 inches
Days receiving some rain per year: 128
Average annual snowfall: 42 inches

Economy
Cost of living index (average = 100%): 139%
Job growth since 1995: +0.4%
Forecast job growth till 1999: +3.7%

Crime
Property crimes yearly per 100,000 people:
3,773
Violent crimes yearly per 100,000 people:
687

Miscellaneous Observations
Boston is the smallest big city of record. Big surprise, but getting from point A to point B by car is no easy thing here either. The atmosphere is very argyle, even when no one is wearing any. Cobblestones, brownstones, and wrought iron fencing are everywhere you look. If you wanted Harvard, but it wouldn't have you, instead let Boston's historic landmarks make you feel part of an ancient tradition.

SEATTLE

Weather
Average July high: 75°F
Average January low: 33°F
Average annual rainfall: 39 inches
Days receiving some rain per year: 160
Average annual snowfall: 15 inches

Economy
Cost of living index (average = 100%):
107%
Job growth since 1995: +1.2%
Forecast job growth till 1999: +10.0%

Crime
Property crimes yearly per 100,000 people:
5,856
Violent crimes yearly per 100,000 people: 542

Miscellaneous Observations
A state without its own income tax? No wonder people are flocking here. Home of the corporate avant-garde, Microsoft and Starbucks, Seattle has no shortage of jobs, with an unemployment rate lower than the national average. Yes, traffic is impossible, but with the great mountain view you'll have from your car window, who cares?

MIAMI

Weather
Average July high: 90°F
Average January low: 59°F
Average annual rainfall: 60 inches
Days receiving some rain per year: 129
Average annual snowfall: 0 inches

Economy
Cost of living index (average = 100%): 110%
Job growth since 1995: +2.1%
Forecast job growth till 1999: +6.6%

Crime
Property crimes yearly per 100,000 people:
10,925
Violent crimes yearly per 100,000 people:
1,914

Miscellaneous Observations
Models, actors, and Madonna all call Miami
home. While it's not for the family values
crowd, it certainly calls out to those with a
penchant for wild nightlife and scanty dress.

SAN FRANCISCO

Weather
Average July high: 74°F
Average January low: 41°F
Average annual rainfall: 21 inches
Days receiving some rain per year: 67
Average annual snowfall: 0 inches

Economy
Cost of living index (average = 100%):
174%
Job growth since 1995: +0.7%
Forecast job growth till 1999: +5.1%

Crime
Property crimes yearly per 100,000 people:
5,083
Violent crimes yearly per 100,000 people:
916

Miscellaneous Observations
The mountains, the ocean, the trolley cars, and
the Golden Gate Bridge! What more can you ask
for? Only to be able to afford it all. With property rates the highest in the nation, it is only
the select few who get to call this city home.
Still, if you can score a job, head out fast. It's
a great town, with laid-back, Haight-Ashbury
appeal. Oh yeah! It's also easy on the eyes.

Home Alone

It's just you and the *Love Boat* tonight, so who could be at the door? Why, it's some guy in a tool belt, demanding he be let in to fix the leak in your bathroom. Now, you know you don't have a leak, and you're almost as sure that the guy with the tool belt is packing more than pliers and a drill. What do you do? Fight the instinct to crawl under the bed or to imitate a rabid dog's bark in the hopes of scaring him off. Our advice is to just go along with the gag without opening the door. Thank him for coming, but civilly explain that you couldn't possibly have him in tonight as you're having company. Dead bolt the doors as you keep up the banter with the maniac. He'll probably retreat once he realizes he's not scaring anyone, and that you're not alone. If he's the persistent type, a real wise guy, you may have to get rough with him. Inform him that you're calling the ambulance, so that they can pick him up after you've blown him away with your .38 magnum.

The Cash Dispenser

No one should risk visiting the ATM after hours. That's just asking for trouble. If your cash stash is running on empty, make an effort to replenish by daylight. Those cameras won't do you any good as you're staring into the barrel of a gun. If you're accosted, don't pull any fast ones. Hand over the money, no questions asked. And don't go pushing that little red "in case you need assistance" button. The teller can't help you during a stickup.

Parking Lots

Many a culprit has been known to lurk in these areas, lying amidst the cars for you to come along. If you have to cross an abandoned lot at night in order to get to your vehicle, solicit the aid of a friendly security guard. Or take Ted Roosevelt's advice and walk softly, big stick in hand. Always park beneath street lights, and don't wait until nightfall to claim your wheels. If you hear the ominous tread of footsteps gaining on you, run the other way, and always have your keys primed for lock insertion—this is no time to fumble.

Enjoy the Ride

You've just come back from your new job, played nice with your neighbors, locked all your doors, and realized that you've yet to kick back and relax since the big upheaval. This is not by any means an uncommon epiphany. Treading the rocky road of relocation can make one forget about the beauty of downtime and stability. Migration exhilaration can be addictive. Kerouac tried to glamorize the whole thing, but don't you follow his hobo butt. Remember *Easy Rider*? Heed its timeless warning. Now that you've got a place, try to set aside some time to enjoy the comforts of home. You'll be that much more energized when it comes time to exploring your surroundings. And, by all means, don't forget to go out and have fun! Maybe you're unsure about stepping out Lone Ranger style, but that insecurity shouldn't stop you from having a life. If going to bars alone makes your stomach flip-flop, take in a movie. The best thing about moving to a new place is that nobody knows you. Go ahead and do whatever you want—after all, who have you got to impress?

RUMINATIONS ON ROOMIES

You've no doubt had ample opportunity to sample a large array of roommates by now. Hardly anyone gets through college without getting stuck with some schmo for a bunk fellow. You know, the one who tries to chat you up while you're studying for midterms, thinks that gossiping and giggling are perfunctory pre-bedtime activities, and then eats all of your late-night Twinkie stash without so much as a second thought. Okay, some perks may have come out of all this communal living. For example, you met Janice who really cracked you up with stories of her trumped-up sexual exploits, or Bob who always fixed you up with the choicest dates. So, you take the good with the bad, chalk it all up to experience, and proceed to make wiser and better-informed decisions in the future. Now, it is possible, although highly unlikely, that one colossal dud has ruined your chances of ever finding true happiness in a room-sharing situation. If it takes going over the pluses and minuses of housemates all over again, then that is just what you must do. If

You Know You in the Wrong Neighborhood When . . .

- Iron bars adorn every shop window.
- You hear three different police sirens in a matter of five minutes.
- The bee that went buzzing past your ear turned out to be a bullet.
- You see a Rolex salesman on every corner.
- Pretty women are a dime a dozen, literally.
- The landlord asks you if you're packing, and when you say no, he mugs you.

you find that roomies beat out solitary confinement, then it's high time you got right back on that horse.

The Upside of Sharing a Dwelling

Economy

The rent for a two-bedroom flat is usually only one to two hundred dollars more per month than for a one-bedroom flat. Can you do the math in your head, or must we explain that that's about half of what you're paying to live alone plus another fifty or one hundred dollars. Quite a difference. It may be hard to imagine if you're still in college, but many of you will be hard pressed for sufficient coin to feed the parking meter at some point in your near future.

Companionship

Don't ever underestimate the value of a sound ear. Who doesn't need to complain once in a while? Unfortunate as it may seem, we have yet to encounter anyone who has nothing to gripe about. With a roommate, you no longer have to leave a message on the machine of every distant acquaintance to ensure a speedy response. Housemates will not only lend you an ear but also take you out to celebrate "the news" as well. And as nothing is more pathetic than eating and drinking alone, a roommate's willingness to split a pizza and unwind with a few beers at the corner pub can really lift your spirits, or keep your good mood from plummeting.

Safety

While the old adage of safety in numbers may not apply at a British rugby match, it is definitely true when referring to occupants of a dwelling. Those cat burglars prowling the street know to stay away from a home occupied by five strapping youths. By sharing space, you automatically up your odds of disarming an attacker. When picking a roommate, keep in mind that a burly one is more likely to take interlopers straight out of commission, even if only by making them think twice before using your domicile as their personal Wal-mart.

Emergencies

Think of your roommate as a spare tire or a substitute mom or dad—someone who will be there should you become temporarily incapacitated. For example, you could be pulled over for speeding and then taken to the police station. If you live alone, who can you call? Most friends prove unreliable at such times. A roommate, on the other hand, knows where half the rent is coming from. (S)he has a vested interest in your getting to work the following day, on time and in one piece. (S)he may also fear your powers of retaliation—Aqua Velva in the Scope bottle, for example, if (s)he fails you at such a key time.

The Downside

Private Lives

After a few months of space sharing, that "P" word may just fall out of your vocabulary. Privacy suffers a horrible blow when you take on a housing partner. You will find that the sharing of privacy, which goes hand in hand with a roomie, may catapult you straight into the "we" mentality. If you are desperately trying to find an answer to the age old question Who am I, this arrangement may not be your bag. Yet, often times, adversity brings out strengths we never knew existed. Grappling with the loss of solitude may bring a whole new you to light. If that new person turns out to be sneaky, calculating, and, above all, resourceful, so much the better.

Putting Up with Others

Everything won't always go your way. You may have to trash some of your nasty habits, and insist that others follow suit. "Why should I put up with having to pick up my dirty socks" "Why should I put up with Sara's raucous overnight romps?" "Why should I put up with the aroma of Jack's chocolate chip cookies when I'm trying to lose a few pounds?" These are just a sampling of the household disputes you will have to settle if you want to derive the benefits of sharing a place. If this is just too much for you to handle, then maybe you should live alone. Dealing with people isn't for everyone; maybe you'll find happiness in the company of numerous pets.

Splitting a pad two, three, or even five ways is no day in the park. You've got to look carefully to find the housemate who's right for you. As it is necessary to know what you're after before you begin any search, the first step is to decide who it is you want to live with.

The Friendly Commune

Here is a traditional roomie situation. You and your closest pals decide to go in on a place, and the good times are set to roll. While it's true that such arrangements rarely leave time for the dreaded dull moment, the stress that comes from keeping that college crew together can be hazardous to your health. You may grow apart or just find that you hate one another's guts. The more years you have invested in the relationship, the more difficult it will be to watch it deteriorate. While living under one roof with bosom buddies may seem easy, you'll have to be tactful, cautious, and extra considerate to keep the old ties tight.

Gender Bender

Thinking of going coed? Do you want to learn what it's like to live with a real man or do you want a cross-dressed buddy? Any of you guys out there still thinking that a woman will add that feminine touch to your cruddy sofa? Appreciating gender differences is one thing, but don't go picking an opposite sex roommate based purely on stereotypes of cleanliness or hopes of nymphomania. Here's the final analysis: Sharing clothes becomes more difficult, and while you get the skinny on a love interest's sullen behavior from someone who's been there, you must learn either to lower that toilet seat or to keep those used feminine napkins inconspicuous.

Smoke Alarms and Vice Squads

Whether you put your body through hell on a daily basis or are a model of purity, you probably don't need a second mother telling you to slow down or loosen up. You are who you are and you do what you do for a reason, be it ever so stupid; you have accepted it as part of what makes you unique. Thus, to set up a harmonious shop, you must look for someone with similar predilections. While interpersonal differences and contrived conflicts make for a popular MTV series, don't try to recreate an at-home dramatization. Without the expert camera crew and sound technicians, your household turmoil will not be anywhere near as entertaining.

Warring Factions

While some of you may not give two monkeys for political issues, there are always the activists and the true believers to complicate matters. If you fall into this latter category, you know full well you cannot coexist with anyone who takes lightly what you hold dear, much less with those who hold it in contempt. So come roommate-hunting season, be careful out there. All you who are lackadaisical when it comes down to the issues dividing the nation, beware of the activist, any activist. When all you really want to do is curl up with Stephen King and a cup of joe, the activist will try to rope you into rallies, frown upon your apathy, and insist that you rock the vote in his/her platform's favor. Activists must be doubly watchful for anyone who disagrees with their ardent belief systems. Demand the truth up front and eliminate the opposition from the get go.

The Odd Couple

Avoid this denouement like yesterday's sushi, as sharing space with someone with vastly different standards is as unsavory for the slob as it is for the neurotic. And while you may think you hold the record for going the longest without cleaning the bathroom, your roommate may just be the type who lets sandwiches fester under sofa cushions. This coupling will leave you playing the part of clean-up patrol. All this time you thought of yourself as good cop, when maybe you should have minded that hint about your last

It can happen to the best of us. You meet the guys from downstairs and the couple from across the hall. Several signs lead you to believe that they're normal. You hang out, find there are interests in common, and the next thing you know you're planning picnics and nights out on the town. BEWARE! STRANGER DANGER! Too much, too soon can lead to eviction, grand theft, police involvement, and even all-out fisticuffs. **A tight group of neighbors is the devil's playground!** What?! You scoff? Well, take it from someone who's been around an apartment building or two, these things are prone to happen. Ignore our sage advice, and you can expect the following:

- People sneaking through your windows, while you're at work, to use your bedroom as a cheap motel room

roomies' home experiencing sudden roach encroachment. The fact is that whether you view yourself as a cleanliness junkie or a litterbug, the subtle variations on each theme are of staggering proportions. Try to match wits with an equal and you'll always feel right at home.

Fashion Sense

Call it flair, call it pizzazz, or call it a personal style, but someone's aesthetic sensibility a.k.a. taste will nonetheless seem tacky if it does not match your own. How to find that well-coordinated match? Here's a clue: Buy a variety of *House and Garden*-genre magazines and leave 'em out on the coffee table. Explain that you're thinking of redecorating the outfit. Engage those applicants with housemate potential in brainstorming sessions. Should you find a meeting of the minds, feel free to broach weightier issues.

Sexual Orientation

No matter how hip you think it is to engage in deviant sexual practices, do you really want your home taken over by a dominatrix? What if your new roomie sheepishly hands you a paddle, telling you he's been a naughty boy? These things have been known to happen. Sounds like a dream come true, you say? Well, then just chalk that fetish up as a roommate requisite. Watch out for things like high leather stilletos, metal-studded chokers, and an excess of chains, especially if an all-out pervert is the last thing you want in a roomie. Ask about piercings; anyone who volunteers information about jewelry-defiled privates is a definite no-no for you straight-laced young Republicans.

Differences of Night and Day

Surprise! While you may think your nine-to-five route is the only way to go, there are oodles of kids out there who work the grave-yard shift. Some wait tables late into the evening, and others pull all-nighters as security guards in corporate buildings. Whatever they do and wherever they do it, it is not so much a concern (unless of course you're one of those white-collar job snobs) as how you'll feel when the only sign of life that has emanated from roomie for the last several weeks is a deeply disturbing snore.

A Character Study

Hopefully you're a quick character study. You'll need to be in order to get right past that if-you-let-me-live-here-I'll-be-your-best-friend facade to the mean, brutish, and short truth always lurking beneath. You must decide what characteristics you absolutely cannot abide. Say you arrive at the conclusion that impatience and trickery are to be nixed at all costs, you must then come up with a plan to test your live-in prospect on honesty and patience. Calm your test-anxious nerves; no one's said anything about Scantrons. The exams we have in mind are much more subtle. Test the prospect's patience by tapping your pen for the duration of the interview. If you see signs of barely pent-up rage, class dismissed. To quiz for roguery, begin a discussion about an offense such as shoplifting. Maybe they'll feel freer about opening up about their thieving selves. Either that or they may look at you funny and clutch at their purses. Try to test but not alienate; you wouldn't want to let a perfect score get away.

WORD UP!

So now that you know what you want, the only question left is what are you willing to do to get it? We're not going to lie to you. As there's no shortage of methods to help you get the word out and achieve that dream of roomie paradise, you may find yourself pretty busy. You may not want to go to any such lengths, and decide that whoever has the funds has the room. But that is just the type of devil-may-care attitude that will land you right back in the heat of roommate-search hell two months down the line—and that's being optimistic! While in college, you may have been voted Mr. Laid Back or Ms. Easy Going, but life on the outside has a tendency to stress out even the most relaxed people.

The person you may allow under your roof is potentially much weirder than anyone you'd been exposed to in school. Remember, the older people get, the stranger they become. Also consider that you no longer have the mutual yearning for higher learning and the

Melrose Place on Crack (continued)

- Falling in lust with the dork above you for the sole reason of proximity
- The girl in 2B borrowing your sweater (cashmere), and, after a falling-out, refusing to return it
- Halloween candy being tampered with
- Noise warnings whenever music is audible
- Late rent notices being stolen off your door, until the final eviction notice is posted
- All the untainted residents steering clear of you, maybe even moving out
- Loud stomping noises and plaster falling from the ceiling (your only weapon against which is that tired broom handle)

shared need to cram for finals to bond over. So, even if you're not in the market for a new friend, you should make at least a half-hearted effort to attract a compatible roommate. The best way to succeed is to lure as many prospects to your den as possible.

Selling Yourself

Advertising—it's everywhere you look. Our culture has propelled it into an art form. Now, if you do like Andy Warhol, maybe you can make your spare bed into a vied-after commodity. So, how do you plan to make your ad stand out? How do you make sure it appeals to the desired audience? And you thought it was easy to come up with an ad campaign. While a piece of cake it certainly isn't, neither is it beyond your university-honed expository skills. Just follow our basic formula and you'll have a line of housemate wannabes knocking down your door.

Writing the Ad

While it's important to be clear about the rent and the locale, that you'd rather sleep with a plastic bag secured snugly over your head than live with a smoker or pet owner should not be the gist of your promo.

Pay careful attention to vocabulary here. If you haven't stored a warehouse full of appealing adjectives, the trick is to go for the thesaurus. But you don't really need to do a lot fancy word work to get your point across. Play up your assets, as well as the apartment's, such as the gleaming hardwood floors, Euro-style kitchen, view of the lake or park, and ten-foot ceilings. In short, whatever it is that made you put down the deposit to begin with should entice some response if plugged into your little commercial.

Placing the Ad

Once you've penned your campaign, it's time to implement. Where will your target audience be? Are they behind the pages of the city paper, or are they scanning the smaller community news? Maybe they're too busy to browse classifieds or are fly-by-the-seat-of-their-pants kind of people. It stands to reason that your marketing strategy depends on your market.

Major City Newspapers

This will draw in a mainstream crowd. The corporate world comes here for the hard-hitting info. If you're looking for just such a roommate, this is where you get off. One disadvantage is that the cost of placing your ad here is a bit on the pricey side. But after keeping it in for a week, or even just a one-shot deal for the Sunday edition, you should get enough responses to keep you sifting till pay dirt.

Community Newspapers

More eclectic, sometimes even eccentric, these readers want to know what's going on in their neighborhood in terms of good times and leisure. It's not as expensive as the big boys, but you may get a fair share of people who howl come midnight. So be careful out there, and pay close scrutiny to the telephone phase of interviews.

Billboard Flyers

You've seen these phone-number-fringed ads plenty of times. Are you the type to stop and take a number? If yes, you probably know that these speak straight to those who are always on the lookout for whatever it is they want. Maybe they don't go out of their way to get it, but keen powers of observation ensure they never come up short. These guys/gals are also willing to take chances and explore out of their usual spheres of experience. If you're looking for someone on the impulsive and adventurous end of the spectrum, look no further than the billboard or shop window. Big plus: FREE ADVERTISING!

Roommate Matching Service

Get your listing in with these people, and you'll surely wind up with someone who's got discretionary income to throw around. Most of the time, if you have a free room, it won't cost you a red cent—the bedroom seeker pays all costs. And you find someone who's relatively safe (Charles Manson and the like are usually blackballed from services) and somewhat compatible, since interviews are conducted to match up like-minded roomies.

The Roommate Screen Test

The following six questions will get you past the interview small talk in no time. Why waste your breath on unsuitable candidates?

1. Have you ever killed a man?
2. Have you ever been institutionalized?
3. Are you a crack addict?
4. Do you get irrepressible urges to flash unsuspecting strangers?
5. Do you have a 666 tattooed anywhere on your body?
6. Do you have any affiliation with the Ku Klux Klan?

Word of Mouth

Imagine you're at a party and being what is termed *social*. Suddenly you hear your name. This is called the cocktail party phenomenon—through the din of your own conversation and countless others, you hear personally pertinent information. If you're in the market for a bunkmate, this can work for you. Pick up on signals that others are looking to part ways from the family nest, the love shack, or the roommate from hell. Then strike up a conversation, give them your spiel, and see where it leads you. Hey, you already have a circle of acquaintances in common; this could be the beginning of your own *90210: The Post-College Years*.

Too Close for Comfort

After the flurry of the move, the elation of the roomie honeymoon will subside and you'll have to acquire the skills that make life with roommates tolerable. How often is it the case when you meet someone that you think they're one way, only to learn that they're keeping that other, less favorable but distinctly more pronounced persona under wraps. And with good reason, you think. Let's face it: You're probably not the upbeat healer of all woes that you pretended to be, either. Consistency is the hobgoblin of small minds, and neither you nor your roomie could pull off that *Rebecca of Sunnybrook Farm* act for long. The corrosion of the facade is usually catalyzed by some minor transgression—like when you forget to wash the dishes (for the seventh straight day) and the new housemate tosses every last one out the window. You could knock 'em silly, but this would only exacerbate the situation. And think about how dull life would be if everything was what it appeared. Dishes are made to be broken, as are the illusions you and your flatmates have about one another. It's never too late for a heart-to-heart. Handle each problem as soon as it presents itself and you'll be singing kumbaya before you know it.

Scrub-a-Dub-Dub

Cleaning is one of the most tedious chores around. All that mopping, scrubbing, and spraying is probably not how you envision an afternoon well spent. If you're into whistling while you work, then come on over to our house. Actually, if you're one of those compulsive cleaners, you'll be the love of anyone's life, and the matter will be settled. But if you're less than enchanted by the prospect of sweeping up after your roomfellows, you may have a problem. Say you're the only in-house tidy. Are you to be held responsible for the spring cleaning? We think not. Let Snow White play out her fairy tale cleaning for the seven dwarfs; you've got better things to do. Assign each cohabitant a weekend of clean-up duty—and levy heavy fines on all those who balk.

Splitting and Paying the Bills

There comes a time in everyone's life when an envelope bearing the utility company's logo arrives in the mail. This missive will probably get thrown around, passed from hand to hand, and end up buried underneath a stack of papers on the kitchen table or in some obscure drawer. Soon another letter will follow, and then another; but now it will be inscribed with THIS IS YOUR FINAL WARNING in bold, red, we-mean-business capitals. And still no one pays attention. Until, all of a sudden, the lights go out, and the chorus begins. "I thought you were supposed to pay that bill!" "Why do you think I left it out for you?!" And so on, back and forth, until . . . well, we won't go into details. Suffice it to say, it's not a pretty picture. A home is somewhat like an office; it must have the accounts payable and receivable departments. Somebody has to pore over the bills, split up the costs, collect the funds, and write the final checks. It's a boring job, but if someone doesn't do it, you will all go down. If nobody volunteers, try splitting the work. Is Mary a whiz with numbers? Logic, and her own pride, would then have her calculate the amount owed by each roommate. Is Sid the bulkiest and surliest of the bunch? Ah ha! You've got your repo-man. Putting everyone's skills to work will ensure that your credit rating stays as good as gold.

The Rules of the Kitchen

Just because you're in culinary school doesn't mean you have to sweat over the hot stove every chance you get. By now you should all be able to satisfy your own grazing appetites. That's not saying you can't treat your consorts to an occasional dinner every once in a while. Hey, they may even return the favor. The problem with cooking for others is that they may come to expect at least a bite-sized portion of your every concoction. Even your baloney sandwiches won't be safe once you start feeding your housemates. So go ahead and offer up your lasagna for the tasting, but be ready to strike should anyone trespass onto the garlic bread.

Groceries should never be shared. Someone always ends up with the short end of the salami stick, and that's when things could get messy. Writing your name on your food is also off limits. It's troublesome, often unsanitary, and terminally tasteless. So what to do if you absolutely must have a fair share of the pie? Dividing kitchen shelf space is your only option. Designate your cabinet and hoard your food without reeking stinginess. This approach can work provided you don't have the kind of roommates who pillage your supply when your back is turned. If this happens, your only chance is to let them know you're onto them. Either leave notes in your cupboard, eat their food right back, or just say "I'm onto you." If this doesn't put a stop to their midnight raids, then you may have to go the old-fashioned route: Tell them to cease and desist under threat of physical violence.

Sex and Other Indoor Sports

Mom may have warned you not to play ball in the house, but most roommates won't really give a damn. The libido thing may cause more than a few raised eyebrows, though. How comfortable will you be with your multiorgasmic, or just plain loud, partner when you find out that the walls have ears? Think of your poor sexually frustrated roomie! Is a little consideration too much to ask for? If you're nodding an enthusiastic yes, how about showing just a little decorum? Yes, even in the heat of passion. If your roommate is indoors, a good rule of thumb to follow is to keep the sexual vocals at least a quarter of a notch below music level. Ahhh . . . the sound of music is never so sweet as when providing you and your bed buddy with the rhythm to while the night away. Needless to say, dead-bolt all doors when recruiting the kitchen table or much of the roomie's gourmet condiments as toys or props. Make sure no one's the wiser, and no one will get hurt.

Can't We All Just Get Along?

The politically correct camp will have you thinking that effort and awareness can bridge all gaps of understanding. The aging flower children of the '60s will duly stress that love, peace, and happiness are all we need. Both groups, however, are forgetting one vital fact: Conflict can be a very positive thing if it is handled properly. You and your roommates are going to have the occasional spat, pillow fight, or even an all-out brawl. This may be a healthy outlet to some of the pent-up frustrations that living in close quarters can produce. Don't take every little confrontation to mean that you and the crew are incompatible. That's just not the case. The way in which you settle the trivial household rivalries can establish a coping pattern for the future. If all parties can sit down and calmly discuss the problem, then you're in good shape. But if no one can get past resentment long enough to engage in civil discourse, consider your living arrangement null and void. There is no guarantee that you and your mates can live harmoniously. Sometimes the chemistry is all wrong. But when it works, and everyone does their "bestest," living with housemates can be one long slumber party.

FORMING NEW FRIENDSHIPS

Leaving college life behind is probably hardest felt on your social calendar, especially if you then move to a new town. One day you're high as a kite, running amuck with your pals, and engaging in every conceivable high jink. The next, you're skulking around restaurant windows and gazing longingly at the carefree groups within. What happened? Well, you've graduated and must begin your quest for friendship and good times anew. Easier said than done, right? Not necessarily.

Go back a few years, maybe even to high school, and try to remember how you roped your chums into hanging out with you. The common interests, the Greek system, the similar fashion sense,

The best thing about a part-time gig is that it's going nowhere. You know it and you don't give a snail's antler! This is not your time to impress the bosses but to giggle behind their backs with your coworkers.

- Tend bar at a happening boîte. Did you ever see *Cocktail?* Enough said.
- Wait tables where cute guys/gals hang out.
- Work at a coffee bar.
- Be a restaurant host/hostess. No one sees easier money.
- Work in high-end retail sales. Look down your nose at the customers and watch commissions rise. As your laughter propels you all the way to the deposit window, someone will actually be thinking (s)he showed you!
- Work as an usher. See your favorite shows, movies, concerts, or operas, for no money down.

and many other factors may have facilitated the camaraderie. So now that you're on your own, a born-again-loser, if you will, what measures will you take to rectify your sorry situation? Whatever you do, avoid investing in a MY NAME IS DESPERATE tag or placing an ad in the paper. There are more dignified ways to find new friends. In the meanwhile, get yourself a big-screen TV and give it a name. There is your new best pal. The television is a great temporary way to combat loneliness. You can laugh at the stupidity of others and come up with clever put-downs for talk-show participants—all this in the privacy of your own home. Of course, we don't recommend that you limit your interpersonal interaction to yelling at an inanimate box. Remember that this is just to get you through the tough times. The initial period, before you've devised a game plan or before it has gone into effect, is always the toughest. If you lose your sense of humor, there's no telling which antidepressant you'll end up taking.

Being a stranger among strangers could get very lonely. But look on the bright side: It beats being a stranger among we-picked-our-noses-in-first-grade-together friends. Just because you're not surrounded by a rowdy bunch of partiers does not mean that you're not a self-contained party unit. Yes, you can find amusement in the single-file line. Don't be so conventional; fun isn't all about other people you know. Many have even said that others are what hell is all about. So stop feeling sorry for yourself; someone out there envies you—even if it is only a dead existentialist.

Me, Myself, and I Kind of Fun

You are a fascinating and multidimensional person. Don't take our word for it; see for yourself. Tap into your many sides by taking advantage of your time alone to learn a little about what you enjoy doing. What is your idea of a good time? If you're at a total loss, we've come up with some leisure activities that may help you while away the solitary hours without boring you to the point of looking forward to the morning commute.

Clearly, lack of popular support does not have to eliminate you from being a candidate for an active lifestyle. You're trying to lead your life, not a cult. So go do your own thing, whatever it may be, all alone. You just keep mum about the fact that you had little choice in the matter, and your independence will win you tons of esteem from the many who can't even venture into the bathroom without a bodyguard. Following are some suggestions.

Shop Till You Drop

This pastime is actually better when done alone. Consorts only get in the way. Discover the model in you as the salespeople arrive in droves at your dressing room door just to get a peek. Imagine how much time and dignity you'll save by passing up shopping with friends who come along only to drag you through one department store after another, and tell you that the sole reason that sexy salesperson gave you the eye was to collect on the Armani suit commission.

Anyone Say Tetris?

Who needs companions when it's man against machine? The arcade is a great place to enjoy hours of pure adrenaline, all by your lonely. Do you think that Mario Andretti wanted for friends behind the wheel of his speed racer? Neither will you when you deposit your fifty cents into the Indy 500. Go ahead and monopolize it. The hand-eye coordination you'll achieve will really impress your friends—once you get some, that is.

Cinema Paradiso

You can't beat an old-fashioned night at the movies for one-and-lonely-style amusement. Of course, you'll see people there with their friends. But you have to stop and ask yourself the question, Do such group movie excursions add or detract from the movie-going experience? Film viewing en masse is an emphatic no-no! First of all, you never truly get down to what you think of the flick, and second, you get annoying whispers from all sides because theaters have the mysterious effect of turning many people stone deaf. When alone, you don't have to get caught up in the insane laughter of others or miss vital lines of dialogue while reciting the movie to the hearing impaired. And, finally . . . you buy the popcorn, you eat the popcorn. Fancy that!

Crosswords, Solitaire, the Internet, and That Ain't All

There's no end to the fun you can have at home alone. And we're not talking about being glued to the tube like a coma patient to life support either. Crossword puzzles and games of solitaire are stimulants for the mind, and if you manage to complete them without anyone's helpful hints, you'll feel ever so accomplished—it will be like graduating all over again. Avoid getting discouraged early in the game. Because all puzzles are not created equal, work your way up to the *New York Times*' Sunday challenge. (Hint: The puzzle gets progressively harder Monday to Sunday, anyway.)

While parlor games are old reliables, if you want to be on the cutting edge of solo adventures, trade that couch-potato hat you've been wearing for the new and improved mouse-potato style. That's right, the computer you may still be afraid of is the modern single's best friend. Plug into the Internet and you'll have occupation enough to last till the end of your days. Chessmaster will rival you if you lack a partner; America Online will talk you out of committing suicide when you're down; and the World Wide Web will supply you with the latest news on your favorite celebrities, health trends, books, and much more. Now, how many friends have you had that will do all that?

To Be or Not to Be?

Drama classes not only are fun but also will help you break out of your shell, as almost no one signs up for one of these courses with a friend. Drama classes are nothing but group romps—improvisations, charades, oh! the fracas you'll get into. If you're yet to have many a story to tell your grandchildren, you'll soon have a journal full.

While I knew that most of my college friends weren't planning to follow me home after graduation, I was sure that making new friends or bonding with my old high school group would be no big deal. I was dead wrong! It was pretty awful at first; I felt like a complete pariah. My phone calls to high school friends went unanswered, and I had no clue as to how to befriend random people on the street. Nor, may I add, did I particularly want to. My mom suggested I take a course or something. I had always thought being an actress sounded like fun, so I decided to participate in a popular local acting workshop. I met most of my current friends there. Everyone was so cool. Every night after class let out we all went out together for drinks and just had a blast. If I hear that anyone's lonely, I immediately recommend taking such a class. It really did wonders for my social life.

—TIANA, VANDERBILT UNIVERSITY, '93

Play Catch-up

Make wise use of the extra free time you've got on your hands. It'll be a while before you have this opportunity again. That's right, you're not going to be sitting around, twiddling your thumbs for long. Look at this as a chance to catch up on all those things you've been meaning to get to but always bailed out of because of the lame "who's got the time?" excuse. Since the answer to that query is now self-evident, go ahead and complete your personal portfolio by engaging in any, or all, of the following "self-improvements."

The Body as Temple Ideology

Time was when you couldn't tear yourself away from the phone long enough to complete one set of sit-ups. And what do you have to show for that socially flurried period of your life, except a telltale beer belly? Repair the damage the good times wrought by immersing yourself in a healthy lifestyle. You can pick up any one of a thousand sports, buy yourself a Soloflex or Stairmaster, or just spring for a ten-dollar Jane Fonda video (some of you guys may find Cindy Crawford a more motivating guru). In truth, team sports are a great way to encounter new people, jogging will put you into direct contact with great-legged date ops, and even working up a sweat at home will provide the endorphin rush necessary to boost your flagging ego (a major turn-on for friends and dates alike). So tie up those laces and ready, set, go!

Those of you having a hard time figuring out where to move can finally breathe easier. No two cities are exactly alike, and there are so many to choose from. Finding a compatible town can be just as arduous a process as finding a suitable mate. The following information should get you packing in no time.

These communities are full of young, hip cats like yourself—it's bound to be a jolly good time:

1. Portland, OR
2. Ann Arbor, MI
3. Madison, WI
4. Seattle, WA
5. Ithaca, NY
6. Boulder, CO
7. Miami, FL
8. Providence, RI
9. Austin, TX
10. San Francisco, CA

The Work Ethic

Maybe workaholics are not the jolliest bunch around, but they're certainly the most financially solvent. While the diversions of your life are temporarily on the back burner, concentrate on work to gain future peace of mind. If your present job does not provide you with overtime pay, maybe you'll want to stay late anyway—if only to maneuver your way into a speedy promotion. Or you could consider a part-time position that seems like fun but will also buffer your bank account. Such jobs are not hard to come by. Take one of your weekends (which are all probably free anyway) and go from shop to store, asking if anyone needs part-time help. Or you could let your fingers do the walking by calling every place where you imagine the employment to be a source of amusement and money. Note that nowhere did anyone mention stress: Part-time jobs are purely for recreational purposes.

Illiteracy Is an Ugly Thing

Remember all those books that were recommended to you? Surely somewhere amidst the pile of paper cluttering up your drawers, there's a reading list you sincerely meant to start at some point in your life. Well, stall no more. We urge you to push your literary skills to new heights; your vocabulary will thank you for it—in more ways than one. Explore the world of classics, read up on your favorite historical period, peruse the pages of a suspense novel, or just keep buying a steady stream of self-help manuals. The point is to delve into whatever it is that gets you through the solitary night. (Note: Steer clear of "throbbing thrill hammer" type romance novels, which will leave you feeling more inadequate than ever.)

Lending a Helping Hand

You know that if it feels good, you've just got to do it! There is no satisfaction like the kind you can gain from giving back to your community. No one's saying you should put on candy-striper fatigues if you despise doctors and hospitals, but how about being a Big Brother or Big Sister to some disadvantaged kid? It'll only take one day out of your week, and you'll have a great time. You could also spend some time at an AIDS hospice, a runaway shelter, a halfway house, a suicide hotline, and so forth. If your situation looks bad, there's no better way of getting some perspective than to encounter people who have real problems to worry about.

Choose or Lose

Decisions, decisions, decisions! Picking people to befriend is probably one of the most difficult choices you'll ever be faced with. As no two individuals are exactly alike, you'll have a harder time choosing a friend in which to invest than a stock listed on the NASDAQ. As soon as you think you have it all figured out, another equally—if not more—appealing prospect rears its lovely head. What's an indecisive person to do? Most of us fall into one of two categories: (1) We throw our hands up in disgust and decide to stick with what we know. (2) We rub our hands together in anticipation of investigating the possible advantages presented by the new option. You could just decide to stick with like-minded folk, but haven't you been doing that long enough? Making friends in college was a snap. You either bonded over a keg, a cappuccino, or a textbook. Regardless, you didn't have to search high and low for, or even give much thought to, what kind of people suited you best. Whatever came your way was good enough.

Now that you're friend-free, it may be a good time to reflect upon your past relationships. Were they good investments? Ask yourself why or why not, and then proceed not to make the same mistakes again. Go out and pin down a whole new set of buds, using the wealth of your past experience as a guide. Once you take this initiative, you'll not only find that your assertiveness quotient has skyrocketed but also that you are finally clued into why you want friends and what you expect from them.

I was really glad to meet someone with whom I got along so well. We shared a lot of the same opinions, and I just assumed that Jim would be as much of a partier as I am. I soon realized that while Jim was no dummy, he was a real dullard. He never wanted to do the city thing or anything new, for that matter. We went for drinks a couple of times, and I was disappointed to find that his usual, corner bar hangout was really boring. But Jim was content to just sit with his

Popular Destinations (continued)

As for all you insatiable cow tippers, there is no lack of small towns to terrorize. If you're convinced that Green Acres is the place to be, check out these paragons of small-town bliss:

1. Essex, CT
2. Steamboat Springs, CO
3. Lebanon, NH
4. Brattleboro, VT
5. Pierre, SD
6. Middlebury, VT
7. Monroe, WI
8. Bath, ME
9. Bedford, VA
10. Williamstown, MA

beer and watch the same old show. I quickly made up my mind that while we got along at work, this was not friendship material. Jim was happy in a rut, and unless I was going to join him in it, I had better move on.

—CLAUS, NEW YORK UNIVERSITY, '95

Claus was wise not to invest energy in a friendship that was obviously going nowhere. There are plenty of people out there who share your idea of the good life, so why waste your time trying to change someone who does not fit your mold?

Beauty and the Beast

Some say looks don't matter, but what do you think? Studies have shown that people equate beauty with goodness, sometimes even with intelligence. While we'll grant that having an attractive love interest around is important, why do we crave the platonic company of gorgeous friends? It may be the old guilt-by-association mentality, but most likely it's another way to snag a cute date. Even if you have a face that could curdle milk, attractive friends can up your success rate in the sexual arena. You know the scenario: One guy is hot as hell and the other is a dead ringer for Alanis Morissette. Your friend is already making a major play for the beefcake, and you're stuck looking over the other one's head. Eventually, he starts trying out his jokes on you, making you laugh, and all of a sudden he's perfect for your older sister!

So there *are* advantages to having good-looking friends. But being as superficial as you were in high school is ill advised. Now that you are no longer bound by the pledge of popularity to associate only with the terminally cool crowd, you can judge people by something other than their appearance. Try hanging out with someone who's not exactly styler of the year; you'll find that to compensate (s)he may have developed other unique qualities and interests. And notice that not one person walking by the two of you has stopped to give you a dirty look, or give you the biting "nice friend" put-down. Do you know why that is? Because in the real world, people have enough problems to worry about without concerning themselves with what some stranger's friends look like. The rules have changed since high school. Have you?

Family Background

This may not seem like a noteworthy consideration, but factors such as birth order and how we interact with our parents can determine how we deal with others. If you're an only child, ready to serve and protect the underdog, be wary of older children; their pioneer pride won't tolerate accepting such assistance. You sneaky youngsters, who've learned all about how to size up situations and manipulate people, steer clear of your own. You'll be onto each other in no time, and sparks won't be all that will fly. If you hail from a family tighter than the Swiss Robinsons, look for the same attitude in your friends. People who come from such environments tend to value loyalty above all else. On the other hand, if Papa and Mama were both rolling stones, and having to often fend for yourself you turned out to be somewhat of a Lone Ranger, don't try to befriend the homesick. Your codependent friend is liable to become clingy and possessive, so unless you're ready for Tonto, you may want to forgo such entanglements for those that will give you space to ramble on your own.

Political Platform

Many a battle has been waged because of political dissension, be it between presidential candidates or lifelong chums. It stands to reason, therefore, that when selecting new friends you should try to gauge where they stand on the political spectrum. Making friends on your political wavelength can improve the quality of the friendship. You'll be going to the same rallies and supporting the same causes. What more can you ask for? Think about it: Do you really want a friend who will splatter a stranger's multithousand-dollar coat with red paint just to prove a point? Maybe a smidgen too militant for you? What if you were the one to make a splash and were looking to get bailed out? This would be a good time to have friends who don't consider you a freak for being anti-fur.

Everything was going fine. Tara and I hung out, hit the bars, and studied together. All hell broke loose when I got pregnant halfway through the school year, and I decided to get an abortion. It seemed like Tara and I agreed on everything, so I never even bothered to ask where she stood on certain issues. When I asked Tara to accompany me to the clinic, she totally flipped out. She started barraging me with talk-show lines, like "if you can't handle the responsibility you shouldn't be having sex." I couldn't believe it; instead of supporting her friend she was supporting a "movement." After that blow-out, we couldn't even stand to be in the same room together.

—MARCI, UNIVERSITY OF MICHIGAN, '93

So whether you're politically nonchalant or a staunch lobbyist, find someone who shares your views or lack thereof. This maxim, of course, does not apply to law students. If you want to perfect your debate skills, polarized viewpoints become an asset. Just be subtle when appraising someone's global perspective; inquisitiveness is one thing, the Inquisition is another.

Ethnicity

Go the American way, and create your own personal melting pot. Those of you from rural or small communities probably went without the requisite dose of multiculturalism. No time like the present, we say, to get familiarized with people of all races and ethnicities. While we're not advocating going out with the expressed purpose of befriending a minority member, we do recommend that you view such friendships as much a possibility as same race/ethnicity liaisons. With your newfound tolerance and awareness, you'll be all set to handle any type of individual and will never again be called an inbred, backwoods ignoramus. People are more alike than different, so get off your ethnocentric, xenophobic soapbox and see how the other half lives.

Wealth

Cash-friendly pals are often the most popular. Doubt that, do you? Okay then, go out into the street, start throwing handfuls of bills around, and see how many instant friends you'll have made. Being friends with the rich does have its perks. Just ask Kato Kaelin. Moneybags will drive your butt around town

in his/her swanky new Jag, comp most of your meals, and let you crash in his/her centrally located duplex. Not bad for a small town kid, eh? Yeah, yeah, don't get too excited. You know what they say: If it sounds too good to be true, your benefactor is probably Mrs. Havisham in Pip's clothing. When you least expect it, (s)he will start reminding you of how much (s)he has done for you, and asking you favors right and left. Next thing you know, you're beck-and-call boy/girl. Playing Annie to someone's Daddy Warbucks can be damaging for both parties. Once your sugar buddy cuts off your allowance, it'll be pretty clear that you were only in it for the money.

Getting Acquainted

Potential chums lurk in the strangest places. Most people meet others at group-oriented events, where they can form relationships in a casual manner. Classes were a major friend fest in college; you could gripe about the teacher and the insane workload, and cram for tests together. Now that your scholastic career has come to a close, you'll have to find another leveling and unifying force. Once you decide what you enjoy doing, you're bound to stumble upon others who share your predilection.

Even as we write, prime meeting areas are abuzz with new recruits just waiting for your presence to brighten their world. Choose one of the following thriving locales, and your days of solitary confinement will be a thing of the past.

The Water Cooler

Why work when you can be enjoying the company of fellow gossip mongers and procrastinators? These afternoon chats can often extend way past happy hour right into coworkers' living rooms. Here's the perfect common denominator—your workplace. Time to check out who's wearing yesterday's outfit, your boss's long dictation sessions with the temp, and that gorgeous someone in marketing. Such yummy talks can easily substitute lunch. Before long, you'll have a friend for life—and all because you were doing your job.

The Sweat Shop

Health clubs are a great place to meet your new circle of friends. Everyone is looking for a little guidance around the Nautilus, so adopt the fitness guru persona whenever you spy someone who looks lost. Even if you don't know what you're talking about, faking it won't do you any harm. Just make sure you don't endanger any lives by spotting someone lifting hundreds of pounds over their head, when all you can muster is a nickel-sized dumbbell.

Women are always bonding in the locker rooms of aerobics classes. Go right ahead and make yourself at home. But before you do, brush up on your nutrition and nonfat cooking jargon. Health-conscious women want to know you're one of them before taking you aboard the friend express. They will avoid Twinkie-toting comrades like the refrigerator after dinnertime.

Most gents prefer the weight room to prancing in the aerobics corner; so if male bonding is what you're after, just follow the grunting sounds. Emitting enough noise to make Monica Seles sound silent by comparison, you couldn't miss the big boys even if you tried. Once you find the place, prepare to take on the role of new kid on the block. If you pretend you know what's up here, you'll either end up a laughingstock or a punching bag, neither of which will win you any friends.

Pigeon Feeding

Park your seat on a park bench and feed leftover lunch scraps to the neglected pigeons. This practice not only is therapeutic and educational (no need for the nature channel when you've got a loaf of stale bread) but also will help you meet people. Parks are full of idle and relaxed visitors, most of whom are more than anxious to strike up a conversation. Avoid those engrossed in a book or other reading material—these are do-not-disturb signs. If you spot others throwing crumbs to the pigeons, entertain them with your pigeon-feeding theories. But don't forget to let the other feeder speak. There's more than one way to nourish a pigeon, and others are just as eager to share their methods.

Continuing Education

Going to classes will have you killing two flies with one swatter: You will acquire whatever new skills you desire, and you will make necessary contacts while you're at it. You computer-phobes may want to check out some courses designed for the information-age challenged. Tired of throwing money away on ready-to-eat food? Enroll in a cooking course at the local community center. These courses are reasonably priced and full of people who share at least one of your goals. Oh, the fun you will have. And when you've completed all those assertiveness training, public speaking, and self-defense seminars, you'll have not only made enough friends to fill an auditorium but also transformed yourself into a regular New Age Renaissance person.

Poetry Readings

You cannot go wrong at these venues. Just snag a remote table so that the poets won't hear you snickering at (or tearfully lamenting) their verse, and feast your eyes on a captivated public. Amateur poetry can try the most tolerant of souls. Nonetheless, such gatherings are an easy friend score. It's not at all challenging to approach people at this most vulnerable time, since they'd be grateful for any feedback you could muster. Honesty is not the best policy, so be prepared to offer ersatz praise. If you're not prepared to compromise your artistic integrity, you've got no business being in the friend racket.

Getting Past Shyness

How can you be Happy when you're forever cast in the part of Bashful? It's not that hard once you get a grip. Listen, we're all intimidated by the task of approaching strangers. But when shyness interferes with your ability to make friends, you are teetering on the precipice of the social phobia abyss. This problem can have its roots in an assortment of causes—low-self esteem, depression, or just plain misanthropy, to name a few.

A negative self-concept is, however, a difficult problem to overcome. Try to get to the bottom of what is causing you to bash

---

Stage Fright

You'd never know by looking at them now, but even the most suave personas of our time have suffered from an occasional bout with stage fright. These famous folks got over it. Maybe they can inspire you to do the same.

- Barbara Streisand
- Jean-Paul Sartre
- Marlon Brando
- Michelle Pfeiffer
- Natalie Merchant
- Cindy Crawford
- Michael Jordan
- Pope John Paul II
- Conan O'Brien

yourself; there are so many more deserving objects for your censure passing by everyday. Realizing that everyone has flaws and focusing on those instead of your own may just do the trick. The key to gaining confidence is a delicate balance of disallowing the possibility of personal faults and exaggerating the defects of others. But you'll have to really concentrate. How else are you ever going to have fun and laughter if not at someone else's expense? You'll see, it's ever so entertaining.

Watch Them Squirm

The first step to overcoming any fear, whether it be of people or of spiders, is to confront the anxiety-inducing agent head on. You should hang around people, on their every word and gesture to be exact. But hush! Don't speak! This way you'll soon see how silly people are as a group. Pick up on those telltale mannerisms that give away the nervous wreck beneath the smooth veneer. This exercise will exhibit, like no other, that everyone has weaknesses when it comes to socializing. Keep track of all the ridiculous things people do when they feel scrutinized and self-conscious. Once you're ready to strike up chatter, you'll be much better at detecting signs of insecurity in others and will, as a result, grow more comfortable with yourself. Remember that power is energy that can neither be created nor destroyed; so when someone is deflating before your very eyes, all that energy is not being squandered—it's heading straight for your ego. And lord knows you need it!

Makeover Madness

Those of you afflicted with chronic shyness may be in need of a whole new look, one that will get you noticed. Granted, that's the last thing you want, but it's the only way for you to get comfortable in the spotlight. Once you're accustomed to getting the attention you deserve, you will realize the benefits of being the life of the party. There is nothing better than having all eyes on you; just ask the neighborhood flasher. Your metamorphosis doesn't have to involve anything too radical, like blue hair and a pierced tongue. One dramatic alteration can greatly change your self-image. Try bleaching your wheat-colored tresses to acid blonde, or your mousy brown mane to raven black. One trip to the hair salon may be all you need to uncover your bold and boisterous nature.

A Star Is Born

Lie down on your couch, put on some relaxing music, and get ready to direct your own movie. Cast yourself as the most energetic and popular character. Then . . . ACTION! Watch yourself as you glide glibly through every scene and line of dialogue, expertly leading the supporting cast. You should try to pick everyday situations, such as work, going to a party, or being introduced to a new person. Once you visualize yourself handling these commonplace scenarios with the ease of a professional, you won't have any trouble shining in your re-enactment of these scenes off camera.

The Value of Networking

Make a mental list of all the qualities your ideal friend should possess. You probably won't find any one person who can live up to all your standards, but that is exactly why doctors recommend establishing a network of pals. Skim through the list after each acquisition, and mark off all of the qualities each new friend possesses. You'll soon find that your search for the perfect companions has culminated in success.

Those who make networking their top priority know that good networkers will never be abandoned in their time of need. Building a solid system of casual acquaintances is sometimes just as rewarding as having one bosom buddy. It all depends on your lifestyle and what you seek out of interaction with others. There are those who need to reveal their innermost feelings and thoughts and are, thus, incapable of finding satisfaction in the often impersonal tone of casual friendships. Others cannot begin to stomach even a mere hint at a long, weepy confession, and eschew the intimate friendship in favor of a large network of "pals." Time is also a consideration. If you've got hours to spare, building solid friendships with a few people won't put you out. But if time is pressing, you may have to spread yourself thinly among a group of associates who require minimum maintenance. If this is your case scenario, don't despair; there are plenty of benefits to being networking savvy.

Utilitarian

Networking is the perfect solution for a busy graduate's financial woes. If done correctly, it will ensure that you have someone to turn to should your car get towed, your taxes need filing, and your hair need trimming. You'll never have to pay your way again, if you make a concerted effort to chat up anybody who comes your way. A friend of ours, Emma, has wired the town so well, that she can leave home sans American Express card with two dollars to her name, and still come home manicured and well fed—with the same two dollars still burning a hot little hole in her blazer. If she needs a ride to the airport, she knows just the limo driver who'll give her a shotgun lift while an unsuspecting customer is paying full price for riding in the backseat. Half the waiters in the city are good for her free lunch. A happening ensemble? The friends she's made in department stores make sure she never goes last season. Some would call her a con artist; others would call her a very resourceful young lady, but most just call her to follow through on her promises. That's right, you'll have to shell out favors galore (e.g., running errands, baby-sitting, helping out come moving day) if you want to get the necessary kickbacks. And like Jan Brady found out, reneging on your promises can make you the least popular kid on the block.

That's Entertainment

Who could complain about being connected to a syndicate of busy acquaintances when all it takes to tap into party central is one two-minute phone call? If you're spending long hours at the office, you'll be thanking your personal savior for sending you a merry throng of excitement seekers. Your connections will give you the low-down on where to go come quitting time in a span of time shorter than your average commercial break. Who cares if you have no idea what these scamps are doing throughout the day? Why bother with the minutiae; just tell me where the party is! Once there, you exchange the required amount of small talk and get introductions to the hottest attenders. Now is that too much to ask for? We think not. Just be prepared to make your own share of phone calls whenever you're hip to some wild soiree—more is always merrier, and it is the least you can do.

Creating a Network

Given that you know no one, building a network of companions can be quite a chore. You're starting from the bottom, but that's exactly where all the greats began. Much hand shaking and baby kissing will be involved, so look alive! Eventually, you will be the toast of the town, and all eyes will be vying for your attention. Just remember where you came from, and don't forget those who helped get you to the top. With a little clever maneuvering, that pinnacle of success—where every bouncer is a buddy and every waiting crowd makes like the Red Sea to let you through—will soon be yours.

Miss No Opportunity

It is all too easy to walk through our days, never exchanging a solitary word with a human being. But, it's just as easy to greet and strike up conversations with a variety of friendly strangers. Let's take the grocery clerk or the doorman. Or how about the train conductor or the mail clerk at your office? What? You think talking to the periphery is below your station? A college-educated intellect such as yours can't be seen associating with the hardworking, blue-collared pillars of American society? If that's your attitude, you don't deserve the gains associated with the cultivation of such friendships. Just think about it. Say hi to your grocery clerk on a regular basis, and say good-bye to being fifty cents short of the much-needed cereal at the checkout. Still not a believer? Then let's take the doorman. Get on his good side, and he'll be letting your friends park in the loading zone for hours at a time, giving you the keys for late-night parties in the pool area, and letting you rifle through the lost and found to your scavenger heart's delight. It doesn't get much better than that; so before you ignore yet another invaluable associate, consider what you'll be missing out on by stifling those few friendly words.

Friendship Hazards

You know it's time to put a friendship out of its misery when . . .

- **Your every conversation begins and ends with "I'm bored."**
- **Your birthday has gone unrewarded for two years in a row.**
- **(S)he has slept with your ex on more than one occasion.**
- **(S)he has run out of amusing things to say.**
- **Your shoulder is perpetually wet from his/her tears.**
- **Your time together has become nothing but a parody of its former self.**

Mnemonic Devices

People just love to hear you say their first name, even if you're reading it right off their name tag. When you remember someone's name, that person feels important enough to have been worth your notice. If it takes so little to impress the majority, why not take advantage of your memory's capacity to store such vital data. Whenever you are introduced to a new person, select one distinguishing trait and parlay it into a nickname. For example, Linda with the scraggly mane is a.k.a. Linda Limp Locks. Can you guess where Dandruff Dave comes from? See how easy it is? Now it's time to create your own pseudonyms. Everyone will love you just a little better for having cared to remember their names, as long as you keep your method hermetically sealed.

Pick a Card, Any Card

Business cards are the bread and butter of the networker's existence. If you are presently without a job and have no means of obtaining these small but powerful promos of "self" at the company's expense, go out and buy your own. It's a worthy investment, since any copy shop can print you up way more than you can use for way less than you can afford. Business cards have come a long way, and they can speak volumes in your favor, provided you select or create the right one. When deciding on the layout, text, and color, keep your personality in mind. Laura Ashleyists will have no problem procuring a floral motif; the bold, in-your-face color scheme is always available for the biker in you; and the "I'm too sexy for myself" crowd can get any number of print shops to create a masterpiece of a calling card set, with a picture of themselves emblazoned on each one. Steer clear of creating a negative impression with a bad card. We met a guy who actually had a large first-prize ribbon on his card. Can you guess what came to mind every time we looked at it?

Society Maven 101

You are now ready for the advanced course in friend finding. Your goal at this juncture is not only to have people to hang with but also to charm them into flocking to you. You will be the center of an entire entourage if you follow our well-thought-out advice. Maybe you will be faking it for a while, but if you find that a strategy works, you will use it so often that it will actually come to personify you. Don't worry about being something you're not; that's not a consideration. You pick up traits all the time; it's just that usually these are incorporated into your personality unconsciously. Just imagine how many undesirable characteristics you've picked up from others along the way. From now on, you will master your fate and literally be whoever you choose. There are several basic strategies that will take you a long way toward creating your own social circle. Find the ones that suit your taste and personality, and then incorporate them into your social routine. But before you do, we warn you about the power that is in your hands. The saying "be careful what you wish for" goes double for you because with our methods as your tools, you'll most surely get exactly what you seek.

The "I Couldn't Care Less" Approach

Do you know what the vast majority of twentysomethings have in common? The answer is desperate insecurity, low self-esteem, and a much higher concern for what others think than for what is going on upstairs in their own building. Don't get mad at us. This may be a sweeping generalization, but isn't that always the case with truth? If you don't accept us as authorities, just look at what the advertisers are doing. If the product is geared at our age group, they try to tell us that everyone is using it. If this is not proof conclusive of our self-conscious status, then just try to come up with a counterargument.

Now that you're clued in, capitalize on this "I wouldn't join any club that would have me as a member" mentality. This may go against much of what you stand for, but we are in fact proposing that you appropriate all the snob characteristics you can get away with. Once you start, you'll have to be able to back up your position. Here's how you do it:

1. Go on and on about the wild times you're having and the many parties to which you're invited. The grass is always greener on the other side, so pretend you're on that side and watch how many people come to join you.

2. Always keep a cool and standoffish attitude so as not to appear in need of company. People will believe that you have something to feel superior about and try to get into your good graces.

3. When making plans, insist on following your own agenda. People will gladly yield control over to you if you just take it. This way you won't look like a follower and hanger-on; instead you will present the leader-of-the-pack image you are trying to hone.

4. Whenever someone has an idea for an evening outing, pretend it's old hat to you. This technique will make clear that you know your way around a good time. Your new friends will only be sorry that they didn't meet you sooner.

5. Always end phone conversations with the pretext that someone's at the door. It'll look like there's a line forming just to see you.

6. If you must invite someone out with you, pretend that it's just an offhand proposal. It gives the impression that what you'll be doing is so much fun, you could go with or without the invitee's company.

7. Fill your datebook with scribbles. When asked to commit to a date, leaf through it and say, "Okay, I guess I could cancel on Jack/Jill, since this sounds like more fun." This tactic also makes the other person feel like they've won some kind of contest by getting to hang out with you.

8. Should someone call you, take their number and get back to them after you get off the line with one of your many acquaintances. Who cares if they're all imaginary; they won't be for long.

The "You're So Cool, Tell Me All About Yourself" Approach

The antithesis of the foregoing tactic will also work, if you can stomach the huge quantities of sticky sweets your mouth will be turning out. If you're no stranger to puckering up and making nice, then this is a sure thing. As we said before, people don't have self-esteem to spare. Many will adhere like glue to anyone who gives their vanity that much-needed stroke.

Give Me an *E* for Energy!

If you had pompom wishes and cheerleading dreams in high school or college, but found that your peppiness just didn't cut mustard, you're not alone. By now you're probably relieved that you were denied this dubious honor. As you've most likely already learned, sometimes rejection is just a blessing in disguise. Nevertheless, our third approach to becoming a friend magnet is to exude vitality and overwhelm people with your contagious spirit. If you were so fortunate as to have been handpicked to sport the school colors in acrylic and have your way with a megaphone way back when, then your hard work should finally pay off. Often those of our demographic are steeped in an apathy so profound that, in fact, it would take a cheerleader to pull them out. Let the first law of physics serve as your authority: An object at rest tends to remain at rest, an object in motion. . . . So you see, if you succeed in extracting someone out of their Garfieldesque existence, nothing short of cardiac arrest will make them go back. So your friends gain a life, and you get applause. Everyone is happy!

Open the Window and See Who Flies In

Another easy way to get friends is to disclose. That's right, we're talking personal information here. People usually have something they want to get off their chests. You share your secrets, they share theirs, and pretty soon you've got 'em right where you want 'em. After the dirty laundry is aired, this type will be dying to be your friend. Why? Two answers: (1) they fear blackmail, and (2) they fear rejection.

While you may be thinking that these are not exactly the best ways to begin a beautiful friendship, see how many converts you draw in with a "Hi, my name is Lonely Friendless. What's yours?" approach—then get back to us.

SETTLE DOWN

Chapter Four

THE DATING GAME
(AS YOU'VE NEVER PLAYED
IT BEFORE)

WORK THE SCENE

The dating world as you knew it no longer exists. The college wonder years were a carefree time when dating was simple. Relationships were things that just happened—no planning, no background checks, no resumes or business card exchanges. You found someone attractive and chances were that you already had friends in common. If you attended a small, private university, dating was most likely no different from what it had been in high school. Yet, as we've all learned, even the most casual of dates requires a certain amount of courage, calculation, and ingenuity. Out there, in the real world, the proper combination of these elements is your only chance of dating success.

The real world dating realm has proved extremely problematic for even its most seasoned veterans. To prepare for what lies ahead, be ready to change your outlook and learn from those who have come before you. This section was designed to provide you with an advanced course in dating strategies and tactics not featured in your school's curriculum. True stories and dating advice from people who have "been there" and "done that" will substantially improve your chances of getting an "A" in Dating 101.

A WHOLE NEW BALL GAME

The best analogy for what you will soon encounter is the switch from a minor to a major sports league—or, in your case, from college to pro ball. The rules have changed, and before you can play, you must acquaint yourself with the subtle yet all-important differences. As a rookie, you'll most likely be kept in the dark as a ritual of initiation. Mistakes are a rite of passage, but in heeding our warnings, many of these can be easily avoided.

The contrast between college and real-life dating is stark. While almost anything passes for a date in college, the real-world arena demands the implementation of a more formal and stylized approach. For instance, people have to be more responsible after graduation; holding down a job alone necessitates planning in advance. The following two scenarios should clue you in to some other distinctions.

The College Date

7:00 P.M.

- College Girl takes thirty-minute shower—motivation: to ensure that her roommates go without water.
- College Girl carefully removes her precious Caboodles Makeup Organizer and begins her ritual makeover.
- College Girl enters closet and proceeds to stare blankly at her wardrobe for the next twenty minutes.
- College Girl changes three times, only to wind up in her sorority sweatshirt—after all, it is the best sorority on campus.

9:00 P.M.

- College Guy begins the evening with a trip to the liquor store—motivation: afte-hours keg party.
- Upon return, College Guy throws dirty clothes in closet, in case he gets lucky.
- College Guy runs hand through hair, returns to closet for a soiled but comfortable flannel, and checks the look in the mirror.
- College Guy leaves for bar with six friends.

9:30 P.M.

- College Guy has been spotted haggling with the bouncer over the $2 cover charge.
- College Girl has fallen asleep in her closet.

10:00 P.M.

- College Guy is working on his second pitcher.
- College Guy spots College Girl, who has finally made it, and pours beer in her plastic cup without asking.
- College Guy resumes his game of quarters.
- College Girl pretends to appear offended, for the benefit of her ever-vigilant sorority sisters.

It's a Date

In college, it must be a date when . . .

- **You make eye contact.**
- **Beers are on him/her!**
- **You're cheating off of one another's exams.**
- **You exchange hellos.**
- **You're wearing the same school shirts.**
- **You second his/her response in class.**
- **(S)he apologizes, after stepping on your toe.**
- **You're tapping the same keg.**
- **(S)he asks you to watch his/her laundry.**
- **You're at the same place, at the same time.**

In the real world, it must be a date when . . .

- **You go out to dinner and a movie.**

11:00 P.M.

- College Guy shoots pool, intermittently emitting noises of disappointment and elation just loud enough to catch College Girl's attention.
- College Girl has spent the last hour nodding and uh-humming to her friend's comments without hearing a single word.

12:00 A.M.

- College Guy makes the grand gesture; he tells College Girl that he's having an After Hours at his place and that she should spread the word.
- College Girl consents.

1:00 A.M.

- College Girl and College Guy leave bar together.
- Partygoers follow in tow.

The Real-World Date

6:00 P.M.

- Reality Man returns home from work and heads straight for his free-weights—motivation: to impress Reality Woman (she has received rave reviews from his friends at the office).
- Reality Woman is on the phone with her friends, telling them about her blind date—motivation: to inform others of her whereabouts as a safety precaution.

7:00 P.M.

- Reality Man has showered, shaved, coordinated, and completed his breathing exercises.
- Reality Man confirms reservations by calling all four restaurants.
- Reality Man calls Reality Woman.

- Reality Woman has revamped her office look into a dramatic evening ensemble.
- When Reality Man calls, Reality Woman demands that they meet at a restaurant with valet parking.

8:00 P.M.

- Reality Man saunters toward the bar.
- Reality Man looks for the woman in fuchsia. One flower is seen hanging limply from his hand.
- Reality Man waits at the bar.

8:15 P.M.

- Reality Woman has been seated for the past twenty minutes. She has almost gone beyond her two-drink limit when Reality Man finally shows up.

9:00 P.M.

- Reality Man and Reality Woman sip cappuccinos.
- Reality Man asks if Reality Woman would see a movie with him later on.
- Reality Man stalls; she's not interested and looks forward to completing her marketing analysis at home.

10:00 P.M.

- Reality Man picks up the check, but asks Reality Woman whether she's comfortable with his paying.
- Reality Woman is not attracted to Reality Man and insists on paying half.
- Due to budget constraints, Reality Man accepts.

10:15 P.M.

- Reality Woman feigns an upset stomach.
- Date comes to a close.

In college, I got lazy. I met guys in classes, through my sorority, and at bars while hanging out with friends. We would spot a group of guys and just begin talking. If I liked a guy, I would just tell a friend, and she'd set us up for a sorority event. The whole scene was very casual, as opposed to now, where everything is so planned.

—STACY, UNIVERSITY OF DELAWARE, '96

This is embarrassing to admit, but I was a total ass when I graduated, thinking I was master of the game. It turned out that I did not have the first clue about how to meet girls. I had gotten so used to seeing groups of girls on my fraternity doorstep, that I totally forgot about the role effort plays in dating. I soon realized that, once out of college, most girls could care less what fraternity I belonged to. Money also became an issue. Seems like most girls won't even go out with you unless there is a dinner involved.

—JASON, UNIVERSITY OF COLORADO, '97

Where the Boys and Girls Are

Getting yourself to the right locale is crucial if you ever hope to meet someone. Don't delay; get right over to your chosen hot spot and scope out the premises from top to bottom. Make sure you're familiar with the layout of the place. Once you're ready to score, you'll feel comfortable enough to make your big move.

Above all, wherever you go, have a good time! Don't get so bogged down in your quest to meet a soul mate that you forget what's really important—the here and now. If you're really enjoying yourself, others will sense it. People think fun is contagious, and if you're the one emanating those good-time vibes, watch out! You may very well end up blowing half your salary on little black books.

Take this quiz to find if you're ready for the real world of dating. Warning: You may discover that your zest for rock climbing is simply an attempt to avoid facing another more difficult challenge—OTHER PEOPLE.

1. You went on a great date and had the time of your life, yet you're not quite sure if your partner felt the same. What should you do?
   a)   Consider calling in a week's time.
   b)   Wait for him/her to call; it is his/her turn after all.
   c)   Decide to ask him/her out again. What do you have to lose?

2. You and a very attractive person are alone in an elevator—the clock is ticking. What should you do?
   a)   "Accidentally" push emergency stop.
   b)   Cast side-long glances, while watching the floors light up.
   c)   Strike up a conversation—about the weather.

3. You've asked someone out, only to be turned down. Later in the week, you spot the culprit at a club. What should you do?
   a)   Hide in the bathroom; then make a mad dash for the back door.
   b)   Ignore him/her.
   c)   Act friendly; (s)he was probably just having a bad day.

4. Your date loved the new Jim Carrey flick, but you'd rather die than see it again. What should you do?
   a)   Change the subject.
   b)   Rip the movie to shreds, and then make fun of your date's taste in film to anyone who'll listen for the rest of the night.
   c)   Agree vehemently; you want to make a good impression.

5. It's your first date and you want to look your best. What should you do?
   a)   Go with an old standby.
   b)   Add a new accessory to a comfortable but attractive ensemble.
   c)   Run to the nearest department store for the latest look.

Scoring

Give yourself the following number of points for each answer:

1.	a)2	b)1	c)3		3.	a)1	b)2	c)3		5.	a)1	b)2	c)3
2.	a)3	b)1	c)2		4.	a)2	b)3	c)1					

What the Numbers Say About You

If you scored more than 12 points, consider yourself risk-taker extraordinaire—you know what you want and can't be bothered with what others think. Get out the giant Yellow Pages and start dialing for dates.

If you scored 8 to 12 points, you've got the winning combination—you're able to express yourself without alienating others, and you're a born leader with the diplomacy skills necessary to actualize your goals. Start your dating network by calling friends of friends.

If you scored 7 or under, there is really no excuse—after searching for your long-lost spine, practice acting assertive, even if you feel anything but. If others believe you, you must start to believe yourself. Ask yourself out in the mirror, and take it from there.

Coffeehouses

It used to be that coffeehouses were only for the bespectacled intellectual set. They were too busy pondering the futility of existence to notice anyone. Today, coffeehouses are for the fun, eclectic crowd. They come in to check out the scene and load up on caffeine before heading out on the town. This is the optimal place to map out your evening itinerary and squeeze in a quick game of chess. Your mission: Challenge someone to a game of backgammon, chess, or checkers. Impress him/her with your expertise. Cappuccino brings out the philosopher in all of us, so use this opportunity to unleash your views on the crisis of postmodernism.

Nightclubs

Nightclubs are a little too loud for truly scintillating conversation, but you will definitely score points with body language at this venue. Trendy crowds come here to see and be seen; attire is all important. Gals should avoid revealing too much; check your exhibitionist tendencies at the door. If you must be noticed, let your dancing speak for itself. Guys should keep a low profile, at first. Once you've set your sights on someone, be bold and ask for a dance. If the object of your desire is swaying and tapping to the rhythm, (s)he is probably anxious to dance but just hasn't been asked.

Bookstores

Bookstores are a popular place to meet like-minded individuals. Head straight for your area of interest, park yourself, and wait to see who shares your affinity for cyber-mystery novels or vegetarian cooking. You will already have something in common, so topics of conversation shouldn't be too hard to come by. Ask if the book you're considering is worth the read. If (s)he hasn't read it, ask him/her to recommend something else. Now switch roles. Muster your innate eloquence and expound upon the brilliance of your favorite title. Your enthusiasm is bound to get a response. Take the hint and suggest a more detailed discussion over dinner.

Health Clubs

For those in need of a sneak preview, health clubs are a great place for locating dates. You'll have the ultimate excuse for ogling unsuspecting strangers—your health. It's sad but true that only a select few work out for health reasons. If all we wanted was fitness, we'd all be sweating to the oldies with Richard Simmons. Fortunately, no one has to know why you're really there. So, girls, don't let a full make-up job blow your cover. Less is more here, and we're not just talking about your pressed powder. The health club is one place where you can let it all hang out, provided not much does.

Art Galleries

Art galleries are the ideal place for those whose art acumen is up to par with that of the often loquacious patrons of these establishments. Conversations can be extremely amusing, especially if you find yourself involved in a heated debate with an equally ignorant individual who is also familiar with the requisite vocabulary. Much like a game, the one who convinces the other of his/her art expertise is the champ.

Pool Halls

The game of pool is no longer for men only. You'll find all walks of life chalking their hands, sharpening their cues, and spewing mouthfuls of invective after lousy shots. Be brave. Ask if you could play the winner of a game in progress. Then spend the next hour rooting for the one you're after. If you are hopelessly inept, sign up for a lesson or two. Who knows? Your instructor might captivate something other than your interest in the game.

Putting Yourself on the Line

We know what you're thinking. You're thinking that lines are phrases meant for the baby-blue-polyester-leisure-suit-clad-baby-boomer of the '70s, and not for a hip cat like yourself. But, lines are used everyday, and if used well, they are very hard to notice. Opening lines fall into these three uninspired, but immensely appropriate, categories: the good, the bad, and the ugly.

Let's save the best for last and get the ugly out of the way. These lines range from the sleazy, "Is it cold in here or are you just glad to see me?" to the cheesy, "When they made the alphabet they should have put 'U' and 'I' together," to the overused, "Was your father a thief? He stole the stars from the skies and put them in your eyes." Ugh!

A bad line is not so much an affront to a person's taste or intelligence as it is a lame comment that fails to promote further conversation. For example, if you tell someone (s)he is attractive, you'll probably meet with one of three responses: a "thank you," an "I know," or a scornful sneer. This approach lacks imagination, sincerity, and effort. You'll need to hit at least two out of three to penetrate the wall of defenses separating you from your dates in the real world. But once you do prove worthy of notice, the hard part will be over. You might even be able to relax and, yes, be yourself.

It's rare that experts concur, but all agree that the best lines are the ones appropriate to the situation at hand. For instance, any line delivered within the sacred confines of a church will come out sounding vulgar and misguided. Proper timing can mean the difference between painting the town red and spending another night watching HBO. Situations made for love arise every day; it's up to you to take advantage of them.

Situation: In line at the bank
Strategy: Toss your coins

This strategy is equivalent to dropping a hanky, but much more revealing in this day and age. You have nothing to lose—as long as you don't drop any quarters. As (s)he joins in the scramble to retrieve your loot, open with this gem: "A penny for your thoughts." (S)he's bound to crack a smile.

Situation: Bar
Strategy: "Survey Says!"

When you walk into a bar, it never fails that the one person you're interested in is busy chatting with a large group of friends. When this happens, it's time for the trusty notepad. Assume your most dignified air and walk right up to the group, under the guise of taking a survey for an article you're writing. Come up with a creative title and ask away. Single out your target for a more informative one on one.

Situation: Restaurant
Strategy: Slip 'em a note

You're both having lunch with friends; unfortunately, it's at different tables. How can you cross paths without involving a waiter and a glass of wine? Scribble a message, making sure to include all the vital stats (e.g., phone number), and deliver it yourself. Keep the conversation brief: "I thought you may want this" says it all.

Situation: Grocery store
Strategy: Make a little mess

Get in the same aisle and reach for the sky, or at least the highest shelf. You'll probably topple some merchandise in the process, but that's the point. If that special someone doesn't try to excavate you from the rubble, (s)he's not worth it. If (s)he does, laughter will be the only opener you'll need.

Situation: On the street
Strategy: "Where am I?"

This strategy instantly makes him a knight in shining armor to your damsel in distress, or allows her to finally find that one special guy secure enough to admit he's lost. (S)he need not know that you're asking to be pointed in the direction (s)he's already going. Strike up a conversation as you stroll.

Looking Romantic

Approaching others requires skill and calculation. But keeping their attention, once you've got it, is an art form in its own right. The most subtle cues can make or break a situation. Learning how to make your eyes and body work for you will keep an open door from slamming shut. Following are the four stages of eye contact:

Stage 1: Mutual Recognition
After choosing the apple of your eye, prepare to deliver some quick and well-timed looks. Staring too long or too

hard might scare off your target. Pay attention to what (s)he's doing. If (s)he shifts position or moves to the other side of the room, refrain from making further contact. A quick aversion of the eyes or no response should encourage you to continue, but proceed with caution.

Stage 2: Interaction

You've successfully implemented the use of your eyes, and (s)he is looking back, waiting for your next move. What now? Should you go over and close the deal or continue the visual volley? Be patient; you're still being assessed. Let your eyes linger a while longer; build up the tension.

Stage 3: The Conversation

Let your eyes and gestures do the talking. At this stage, you can even attempt an enigmatic smile. Don't be too eager; an air of mystery will sharpen your target's interest. In fact, take this time to ignore your target altogether. His/her anxiety to uncover your true intentions should peak right before the next stage.

Stage 4: The Confrontation

Resume looking at your target. By this time, it is safe to assume that (s)he is bursting with anticipation. Satisfy his/her curiosity and introduce yourself.

(Every) Body Knows

Often, while your mouth is saying one thing, your body is bent on conveying something else entirely. Nonverbal messages have a way of transmitting information without your consent. Understanding your body's unspoken language will help you take full charge of your life.

Body Positions

Make sure your body reflects your attitude. Crossed arms and legs express anxiety and fear. If you want to appear inviting, relax your limbs. Also, do your dear mother some justice and take her advice—"Don't slouch!" While slouching screams insecurity, the proper shoulder position (squared) will exude confidence.

The Walk

Pay the utmost attention to your strut. It worked wonders for Travolta. Why not you? An appealing walk is sometimes all you need to get noticed. And make no mistake about it. A bad walk can detract from overall appeal, and actually turn people off. So if your walk needs some work, try practicing in front of the mirror—it's only silly when you're caught in the act. Our advice: Lock your door.

Touching

Provided you're looking to start something up, a "barely there" brush of your hand or body can set off an explosion. Act casual when touching others; you'll seem less forward and aggressive. Just enough to keep them wondering should do the trick.

Avoidance Tactics

Remember that the name of the game is taking the plunge, and now that you're an old hand, you'll be much quicker at spotting others giving it the good old college try on you. Getting a date is, after all, a two-way street. You won't always be required to do all of the work. So what do you do when the most gorgeous human specimen walks over to you and says . . . anything at all? Well, at first you'll probably do the victory dance in your head. Then you'll rack your brain for conversation, and, be it a comment on the weather or a critique of *The Celestine Prophecy*, you'll definitely come up with something. But what happens when, after striking up this brilliant conversation, you notice that your new friend's idea of a Herculean feat is an utterance involving anything over two syllables? "The hell with intellectual equality," you'll most likely tell yourself. Then it dawns on you that your potential dream date has not heard a word you've said. Suddenly the prince(ss) is a frog, and you're not in the market for warts. What can you do?

1. You plead a full bladder, and then beat a hasty retreat out the nearest back exit.
2. Select an attractive person and identify him/her as an old college pal. Rush on over and have a good laugh at the boor's expense. (This also doubles as a meeting strategy.)

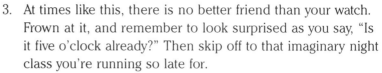

3. At times like this, there is no better friend than your watch. Frown at it, and remember to look surprised as you say, "Is it five o'clock already?" Then skip off to that imaginary night class you're running so late for.

4. "Is that spinach in your teeth? I would just hate it if no one told me. No, a little to the right, now higher. Looks like it's really jammed. You'd better check that in the bathroom." As soon as the back is turned, you make like a banana and split just in case (s)he comes back mad.

5. If you've no intention of leaving, just call it an "out" and send the batter back to the bench. How? Well, a good start would be to wax poetic on the beauty of anyone other than the annoying person at your side. No matter how dense, (s)he'll soon get the message and clear out—satisfaction guaranteed.

You've Got a Date!

So you followed our advice, studied the technique, and voilà! It's all paid off; you have completed your mission and found your first real date. Now that you're an expert at getting yourself into and out of any situation, you may inadvertently fall into the pit of thinking you know it all. Hang on . . . we're about to throw you a lifeline. Or should we say a telephone cord?

Pre-First-Date Phone Call

He is on the phone. It's true; the guy you charmed on the elevator the other day has actually called. You may want to chat, hear his life story, or tell your own. Our advice: Step on the brake and come to a screeching halt, even if you have nothing better to do than channel surf. If you're wondering at our reasoning, you still have a lot to learn. There are only four simple rules to adhere to, and once you do, you'll be glad you did:

1. Keep the conversation to a bare minimum. You'll have plenty of time for chatter when you're face to face. Bear in mind that after all that time spent divulging your best material on

the phone, you may get stuck with nothing left to say on the date.

2. Utilize call waiting. Make sure to take all of your incoming calls. Excuse yourself for a moment to let the third party know that you'll get right back to him/her. People can tell that you have another call by that telltale clicking noise. They expect you to get it; let it go and it's a sure sign you're either a pushover or just plain desperate. Trust us; there is no less alluring cologne.

3. Do not leave a message on an answering machine. At this point of your dating cycle, there is no more abhorrent instrument of torture than an answering machine. In no case should you ever leave a message prior to the first date (unless of course you are calling to cancel). Trust us; nothing is so urgent that it cannot wait until the other person is home and available. Extra hint: Do not call more than twice; if you get a machine on both occasions, try the next day. With some of the newfangled phone systems of the '90s, people can tell you have called even when you don't leave a message (i.e., the dreaded "caller i.d."). In any case, it's much easier to explain that you don't talk to machines on principle than why you sounded like a blathering idiot.

4. Use the direct approach. And lastly, please, whatever you do, don't "beat around the phone." You know what you enjoy— food, movies, or beverages—so why, at the crucial moment of date planning do so many of us suddenly forget? A survey of singles showed that by far the most common answer to "What would you like to do?" is some variation of "I don't know; what do you want to do?" Rule of the phone: Whoever asks first has the right of way—not to answer that is. So, if you know yourself to be indecisive, weak-willed, and spineless, beat 'em to the punch and leave all that pesky planning to your date. Of course you may have a miserable time watching *Police Academy 13* and dining at McDonald's, but since you didn't have it in you to pipe up for Burger King, you deserve it.

Dating Dos

- Dress comfortably. If you're preoccupied with what you're wearing, your mind won't be on your date.
- Be prompt. It's not fashionable to be late for a date.
- Show interest in your companion—likes, dislikes, friends, family. You get the point.
- Talk about yourself. Revel in the sound of your own voice and express your personality.
- Be polite. Miss Manners doesn't have a daily column and a book series for nothing.

Dating Dos & Don'ts

The time of the rendezvous is upon you. Pat yourself on the back. You've done very well to have come this far. The date itself is one fleeting encounter that can make a lasting impression. You're on display, along with your eating habits, taste in clothes, and overall savoir faire. Yes, even if you've disregarded our painstakingly compiled bits of wisdom and gabbed on the phone until blue in the face, this is still as crucial a first impression as you're going to get for the entire duration of your relationship.

The Gift of Gab

In the game of chess, one can make all the right moves but still wind up losing the game. The dating game follows a similar format. Showing up on time in an attractive ensemble is important, but to clinch your triumph, you'll have to become skilled in the ways of thought-provoking conversation., A few great openers are all you'll need to establish a lively rapport. Here are a few suggestions:

- "So who are your favorite movie stars?" If any of those listed match your own physical profile, you'll know he/she is interested.
- "Do you like to travel?" If so, go on to trade tales of traveling adventure until the sun comes up.
- "Which career do you see as the absolute ideal?" If he wants to be a comedian, this guy most definitely craves attention. But if she's dreaming of carpentry, right off the bat you know this is one girl who likes to work with her hands.
- "Have you read any good books lately?" Literature is always a fascinating topic, assuming you're an avid reader. *Mad Magazine* does not qualify as literature (and if you think otherwise, consider disregarding this topic altogether).
- What would you do with a million dollars?" Everyone loves to talk about imaginary money.

The first guy I went out with after college turned out to be a real loser. When I met Julian he seemed pleasant enough. He was older and pursuing a career in dentistry. He called to set up our dinner date. We decided on 7:30. He called promptly at

7:30 to let me know that he was running late. Then again at 8:00, and 8:30. Finally, at 9:00 P.M. he showed up. I was so hungry and angry by this point that I pressured him into taking me to the most expensive French restaurant in the area. I proceeded to order with reckless abandon, as he droned on and on about new techniques in oral surgery. After the lavish meal, Julian began fumbling for his wallet. When the check arrived and he still couldn't find it, I told him to wait while I went to the ATM. I haven't heard from Julian since.

—LIZA, NORTHWESTERN UNIVERSITY, '95

I finally got up the courage to ask this hot girl to the annual company picnic. Hoping to impress all my coworkers, I was looking forward to showing her off. I guess Elaine was thinking the same thing. She showed up in the shortest pair of shorts I'd ever seen and a t-shirt that left nothing to the imagination. I hinted that maybe she would like to change, but she insisted that her outfit represented the height of fashion. When we got to the picnic, Elaine got really wasted and struck up a risqué conversation with the conservative wife of my boss. She ended up falling into the nearby pond. The next day at work, the whole department was abuzz with stories of my date, and I am still trying to get over the embarrassment.

—JASON, YALE UNIVERSITY, '94

My best date was with a girl who had just moved to town. Although I found her physically attractive, it was her attitude that was most appealing. She didn't expect me to spend tons of money, and actually suggested we go to the beach. When I picked her up, I saw that she had packed a picnic lunch. During the entire conversation, she never mentioned an ex, or the words date *and* relationship. *I felt that she was truly enjoying the moment. When I splashed her with water, she didn't complain about her hair or clothes being ruined, but actually began a water fight with me. I called her the next day and we've been together ever since.*

—ANDREW, UCLA, '93

Dating No-Nos

- Don't show up in sweats. Grunge is for mosh pits—not candlelit dinners.
- Don't leave your wallet behind. Even if you're not buying, it can't hurt to keep cash on hand. You never know when you might have to jam.
- Don't be an open book. A little mystery goes a long way. No one need know about the relationship you've developed with Prozac, aside from your therapist.
- Don't talk about your ex. (S)he's probably not talking about you.
- Don't be a lush. You'll only embarrass yourself.
- Don't act nervous. It's all right to feel anxious, but as a wise man once said, never let 'em see you sweat.

Dating No-Nos

Gregg and I met at a party of a mutual friend. We hit it off right away and decided to go out together the next night. When he picked me up, he apologized for being five minutes early. He also presented me with a chocolate rose, which was perfect because I don't care for flowers but love chocolate. He took me to an elegant restaurant, asked me loads of questions, and laughed at all of my stupid jokes. The kiss good night was especially steamy.

—AMY, KANSAS UNIVERSITY,'94

SETTLE DOWN OR WORK THE SCENE?

Where do you stand? If you view relationships as akin to prisons or insane asylums, read no more of this segment. Your choice is loud and clear. But if you feel that a normal person possessing the capacity for rational thought may actually want to pledge fidelity to another, then read on to find out if you're (a) ready, (b) willing, and (c) sufficiently mature.

Never Having to Say "I Do"

Maybe you've watched too many episodes of *Seinfeld* and *Friends*. Maybe you're still recovering from living with nagging parents. Regardless, if you are hell bent on staying single, living on your own can be a very rewarding experience. This may not be the best time to commit yourself to another person. You'll be hunting for living space and a job, as well as trying to establish yourself in the real world as an entity to be reckoned with. If, along with all this, you still have time to worry about building a lasting and stable relationship, can we please borrow your weekly planner? For most people, there is a very strong case to be made for living single. Just make sure that your choice to remain footloose and fancy free is based upon solid and well-thought-out reasoning.

There are many good reasons for staying single. Here are some of them:

1. *Learning about yourself.* This exciting and unpredictable stage of your life is ideal for getting to know the one person

you've been steadily avoiding—yourself. Taking the time to listen to yourself is a worthy investment, so don't be stingy. Buy a journal and try to limit your interaction with voices from the not-so-distant past.

2. *Starting a career.* Setting your sights on finding a fulfilling career is an acceptable reason for avoiding relationships. Long hours at the office might interfere with a standing commitment. Of course, there are ways to maintain both; but it's always a delicate balance, and many people prefer not to partake in the juggling act.

3. *Meeting new people.* Getting out there and talking to different people from all walks of life can become pretty difficult—not to mention hazardous—especially when there is a significant other at your side getting angrier and angrier at being ignored.

Likewise there are some poor excuses for staying single:

1. *The grass is always greener.* If you're the type who's attentive to everyone but your date and never satisfied with what's before you—your eyes are always scanning the room for something better to come along—learn to appreciate what others have to offer by grazing in your own pasture for awhile.

2. *Fear of failure.* While it's true that the divorce rate is currently at an all-time high, don't let this dismal prospect determine your decision to stay single. The breakup of Donna and David, your college buddies who you always thought had a great relationship, does not mean that you are bound for failure. Living single should not be used as a means of escape but as a time to build a foundation of self-awareness, which you'll use when building solid relationships in the future.

Steady and Ready

During this time of change and upheaval, you may find yourself craving stability and comfort. Rather than reach for your old security blanket or favorite stuffed animal, you might consider settling down with one person. Sharing your living space and saying "I do" are both pretty much the same enchilada. Each involves a great deal of compromise and tolerance. Take some time to analyze your motivation; it might not be an open-and-shut case. Here are some invalid rationales:

1. *Lonely heart*. Never let your fear of being alone steer you into a commitment. Living with or marrying someone who is wrong for you can only enhance feelings of loneliness and isolation. Be patient; don't let your desperation get the best of you.

2. *Money*. If Anna Nicole-Smith did it, why shouldn't you? After all, if people are stupid enough to give you their money, don't they deserve to be taken for all they're worth? If this is your attitude, be ready to encounter some surprises. Nothing comes cheap, especially not happiness. Trite but true, you'll only be cheating yourself in the end.

3. *The condom broke*. Yes, it happens to the best of us. You take all the necessary precautions and then . . . WHAMMO—you're with child. Committing to someone for the sake of your unborn baby may backfire. If you are determined to have the baby, look to your family for support.

4. *Pressure from all sides*. Your parents, your beau, and even your own friends are convinced that it's time for you to tie the knot. You'd rather tie a noose around your neck than settle down, but you are losing the fight. You feel that it would be easier to give in. Our advice: Don't do it; hold your ground. Be polite but firm; it's your life after all.

And here is one valid rationale:

1. *Love*. You have been smitten by the love bug and there is no cure—you're caught, hook, line, and sinker. The relationship has been put to the test and it's passed with flying colors. Both you and your significant other are ready to face the music of chance and you're willing to do whatever it takes to make your union a lasting one.

LOVE ON THE RUN

Finding time for dating is easy—when you're in college. Go to class; don't go to class; do your laundry; hide your laundry. Shirking your responsibilities to follow Cupid's urging was not something you lost sleep over, except when pulling all-nighters. Then along comes The Job. After staring at your computer screen or sitting hunched over your desk for an eight-hour stretch, you'll be hard pressed to find your libido at the end of the day. Losing your wind is only part of the problem. Even if you're a raving lunatic and eager to pursue every liaison you encounter after work, you may still find that time is no longer on your side.

Time Sabotage

Remember how you used to roll your eyes each time your parents said "seems like only yesterday you were taking your first steps"? Well, don't be surprised if you catch yourself in the midst of spouting some eerily similar statements. You can't turn into your parents until you've had kids, but you'll soon learn that you don't necessarily have to be senile to lose a firm grip on the concept of time.

Work, devouring one-third of your life for its own selfish profit, is the real villain. Sleep (and you'll need the full eight hours) takes another third. What then is left for you? After doing a few simple calculations, you may decide that the eight remaining hours are plenty for each day's amusement. But wait—cooking, eating, exercising, and even taking the most basic of sanitary precautions all combine to leave you with only a few precious moments to seek romance and love. So now you can appreciate the evil of wasted time. But do you know how to avoid it?

Here are some suggestions for making the most of your hectic schedule:

1. *Breakfast of Champions.* Instead of globbing an endless stream of hair products upon your defenseless mane, try running to the nearby bakery for a nutritious breakfast. Strike up a conversation with a cute guy/girl about the morning TV anchor's misguided fashion sense. Breakfast is the most important meal of the day; put it to good use.

Now that you are one with your rationale, you'll have to decide which lifestyle matches your personality. Are you a taker or a giver? How do you deal with compromise and rejection? Figuring out if you have what it takes to stay single or get hitched will put you on the right track.

1. Your boy- or girlfriend is away on business almost every weekend. How do you feel?
   a) You are thrilled.
   b) You are upset and spend your weekends waiting by the phone.
   c) You are disappointed but use the time to catch up with old friends.

2. You and a group of friends are deciding where to eat dinner. You want Italian; they're set on Thai. What do you do?
   a) Insist on Italian. You are not about to waste your money on sprouts and bamboo shoots.
   b) Agree to Thai. If your friends are big fans, maybe you should join the club.
   c) Consent to Thai but complain throughout the whole dinner.

3. An old flame pops into town and wants to meet for drinks.
   There is just one hitch: you're already involved. What do you do?
   a) Go anyway—"What they don't know won't hurt them."
   b) Decline because you don't want your boyfriend/girlfriend to get jealous.
   c) Accept the invitation by saying, "We'd love to be there."

4. Your sister asks you to baby-sit her two-year-old but you have a date. What do you do?
   a) Pretend you didn't hear her.
   b) Agree to help, and reschedule your date.
   c) Baby-sit but tell her that she owes you one.

Scoring:

If you selected option a three or more times, you should run from any and all relationships. You won't have a difficult time escaping; your stubborn and selfish ways will keep most people at bay. If option b was your most frequently picked response, you are compatible with neither lifestyle. You're bound to run into problems whether you're in a relationship or hanging out on your own. How can you forge your own path when you're too busy following the crowd? If you selected option c three or more times, you can rest assured that any relationship you're in will be a success. Compromise isn't synonymous with sacrifice; but you probably already knew that.

2. *The trick of the "train."* Too many of us view our commutes as a time to catch up on current events, the latest novel by Danielle Steele, or a new business proposal. Too few of us take advantage of the fertile meeting ground presented by the train/bus/whatever your public transport of choice. Use this time to acquaint yourself with the other passengers. The little old lady sitting next to you may just have a gorgeous grandson waiting for you to come along. If you spot someone you find attractive, make a note of his/her stop. Next time you'll know just how much time you have to get a phone number.

3. *Commuting by car:* How many times has a beautiful someone pulled up right next to you, only to roll quickly out of your life? You sit there wishing the cars in front of you would magically disappear so that you could flag him/her down and yell out your phone number, thereby giving off the disturbing impression reserved strictly for psychos? Hopefully, you're just a little too suave for that kind of scene. Instead, keep a large piece of cardboard displaying your phone number in your car. Flash it at anyone you deem worthy. This stratagem has become quite the thing in L.A.; pioneer its popularity in your hometown.

4. *On the job.* Suffice it to say that dating people you work with is not always a good idea. But what about the thousands of available specimens lurking behind the walls of your company's premises? They are fair game. The elevator is ideal for meeting people in your building. Make sure to ride up and down several times each day.

5. *The lunch hour.* Don't waste this precious hour cooped up in your cafeteria with the same haggard faces. Pound that pavement and discover the world just waiting outside your office door.

SETUPS, PERSONALS, AND DATING SERVICES

Too many of us are convinced that to do something right, we must do it ourselves. That's all well and good, as long as we don't ignore

Lunch Hour Getaways

1. Pack a picnic lunch and take it to the park.
2. Visit a museum or art gallery and let the other patrons inspire you.
3. Get your wheels and rollerblade around town. You never know who you'll bump into; but whoever it is, try not to run them over.
4. Finish those pesky errands crowding your to-do list. You'll be well rewarded when you find yourself with more time than ever for after-work play. So go ahead and . . .

- Drop off those dirty clothes at the cleaners.
- Get that fabulous new coif you've been putting off.
- Get the drudgery of paying bills taken care of.
- Hunt for an apartment closer to work.
- Balance your budget.
- Do whatever it is you've been putting off.

the wealth of resources currently at our disposal. Technological innovations like the computer, microwave, voice mail, and cellular phone simplify our lives. Yet remember how reticent we all were to use them at first? Most of us tend to view personal ads, dating services, and setups through the same looking glass. Our first reaction to the mere idea of requiring outside help is shock: "God! Am I that undesirable?" or "When did I sink this low?" While these are common and natural responses, they must be overcome if any progress is to be made. There is no valid reason to feel ashamed and allow groundless prejudice to keep you from attaining your objective. Use these rationales to see you through any momentary lapses of reason:

- "What with work and all, I just don't have time to scout for dates."
- "My friends have better taste than I do."
- "I love surprises."
- "I want to meet a variety of people."
- "I hate the singles bar scene."

Dating in the '90s has been overcomplicated in almost every way imaginable. The rapid pace of modern life alone has forced many to re-evaluate their attitudes, redefine their terms, and accept setups, personal ads, and dating services as effective methods of adding spice to an already thriving social life.

The Fix Is In

With thousands of satisfied customers to back it (who, by the way, never had to shell out one thin dime), the setup date is one of the most popular methods employed by the lovelorn. This type of encounter always has the advantage of succeeding on the heels of low expectations coupled with an aroused curiosity. Often the result of this favorable combination is one of pleasant surprise. There are countless examples of people being fixed up only to find true love.

A setup can be concocted by anyone. While this may sound reassuring, we do not recommend diving in headfirst. You must take into consideration certain key guidelines before you accept or request a setup:

- Could problems ensue should the date be a failure? For example, is the proposed date your coworker's fave cousin? If so, trust us, you can't stay far enough away.
- Who is conducting this operation? If you're Joe Conservative, naked without your Chinos and Dockers, think twice about letting Sally Progressive set you up with her best friend and so-called partner in crime. Since the probability of sparks is so very low, just forgo.
- Does everything you've been told about the mystery person matter? This isn't a trial—information gained through hearsay is not only admissible but crucial. The vital stats come in two categories: appearance and personality. What you learn could save you a whole lot of time, trouble, and moolah.

Disclaimer: Taking these guidelines into account does not guarantee you a great date, but it does go a long way toward preventing a full-blown disaster.

If you decide you like this dating strategy, which would not surprise us in the least considering how many people do, it may become an actual hobby. Should this happen, you may want to do the following:

- Keep plenty of friends on hand to set you up.
- React to bad dates with grace (i.e., refrain from pummeling the person responsible).
- Get bolder, and organize setups yourself.

The Personal Approach

The personals are an effective way of meeting and connecting with other people. You will be surprised at how many have successfully navigated the personals course. Why else would newspapers be devoting more and more space to personals with each passing year? Personals get results; that is the bottom line. Perfecting your writing and responding technique is worth investing a little time in, considering the scores of great dates you may get in return.

Words have the power to influence, captivate, and entice. But they also have the ability to anger, disgust, and repel. The following adjectives could spice up your ad, without putting you on the FBI's most nauseating list:

Affluent	Irreverent
Alluring	Kind
Artistic	Mischievous
Cosmopolitan	Mysterious
Creative	Original
Daring	Petite
Delightful	Playful
Droll	Pretty
Elegant	Reliable
Enthusiastic	Romantic
Enticing	Saucy
Faithful	Sensual
Fanciful	Tailor-made
Gallant	Vibrant
Gracious	Vital
Honest	Zany
Idealistic	

Writing the Ad

Composing the right ad is not as trying as it appears, but neither is it a total breeze. Some key phrases, a few witty quips, and a grasp of what and whom you seek are all you need to come up with your own masterpiece. Just remember these three rules:

Rule #1—*Make them laugh.* Humor can distinguish your ad from the herd. Not taking yourself too seriously puts others at ease, and gets you a flurry of responses.

Rule #2—*Honesty is sometimes the best policy.* Some people want to ensure that their date is not fright at first sight, for either participant. If you are one of these and have a physical deformity of some form, reveal it in the ad. Others may want to paint a prettier picture, since bringing attention to a physical flaw might ward off prospective dates who, after meeting you, wouldn't give it a second thought. (By the way, if you are one who scares easily, always request a photo so as not to be frightened into premature old age.

Rule #3—*Target your audience.* This is the most basic rule of marketing and advertising. A personal ad advertises you, but to whom? Being the strapping buck of twenty-three that you are, do you want seventy-five-year-old ladies calling to get your number? Finding the proper home for your ad is crucial. Just as people come in all shapes and sizes, there are newspapers of all varieties to cater to them. Be specific about who you are and what you are looking to find; gender, marital status, religion, and race are only parts of the equation.

As a final precaution, read about two hundred ads before you begin creating your own. It's easy reading and shouldn't take you college grads more than a half hour. Here's a sampling to kick it off:

LOOKING FOR A FRIEND
SJF, 26, honest, attractive, dancing machine. Enjoys outdoors, travel, independent movies, Grateful Dead. ISO SJM, 25-30 with like interests for good times and possible LTR.

CHIVALRY LIVES!
SW Knight, 24, 6'3", 200 lbs., brown hair/eyes, seeks to rescue SW Maiden 21-28. Will wait patiently while you shop.

YOUNG AND VIBRANT
SBF, 26, bronze complexion, a lean knockout. ISO SBM 26-28, smart, dashing & cultured for jazz concerts, gallery browsing, stimulating conversation, and possible LTR.

The Sound of Your Voice

If the prospect of putting pen to paper daunts you, try turning the tables. Leaving a voice-mail message is currently the most popular personals response method. Each ad is assigned its own voice-mail phone number, through which interested parties can respond with just one simple call. Recording a fetching message can be hard work. People have a tendency to stammer, ramble, and forget their names. But all these mishaps can be prevented provided you follow a few simple rules.

Like the Pied Piper's flute, the voice is an instrument so potent that it can, literally, mesmerize the listener. While you may not be so gifted, do make sure that your voice reflects who you are and expresses those qualities you most wish to bring into the limelight. Take Donna, an intelligent young Ph.D. candidate, who had the voice of a flighty Betty Boop. Such unfortuitous vocal chords can be whipped into shape if you really put your mind to it. Try practicing with a tape recorder; just being aware of your voice can help you dramatically change its quality.

Keep It Short

A simple introduction followed by some bits of personal info (i.e., name, phone number, hobbies, unique gimmick) should help you avoid the dreaded, never-ending monologue.

Make a Cheat Sheet

Be prepared! Writing it all down will improve your overall performance. Under pressure, many of us have an annoying habit of forgetting

---

Newspaper Lingo

Get comfortable with the newspaper's abbreviations format. This section has a language all its own, and if you want to walk the walk, you've got to talk . . .

Gender
M: Male
F: Female

Marital Status
S: Single
D: Divorced
W: Widowed
M: Married

Race/Religion
W: White
B: Black
J: Jewish
A: Asian
Hisp: Hispanic
C: Christian/Catholic
NA: Native American

Sexual Orientation
G: Homosexual/Gay
Bi: Bisexual

Personal Habits
S: Smoker
NS: Nonsmoker
DF: Drug Free

Miscellaneous
ISO: In search of
LTR: Long-term relationship

the most obvious details. Your name, phone number, and any other information you would like to share should be on hand.

Practice, Practice, Practice

Rehearse your speech before delivery. When spoken, phrases that seem fine on paper may come out making you sound certifiable.

Matchmaker, Matchmaker, Make Me a Match!

In days of yore, it was common practice among the marriage-minded set to employ matchmakers. Today these small-time operators have been supplanted by grand-scale organizations. Much like in the past, dating services are not so much for the desperate (although to be honest, they do get their fair share) as for the efficient. If you're ready to settle down but have yet to find the right person, you may want to examine exactly where it is that you have been searching. Looking for commitment at singles bars is much like fishing for trout in the Dead Sea—not a good idea.

Dating services and singles clubs, on the other hand, feature people honest about their desire to meet a suitable partner. And no, they are not desperate. The ratio of desperate people in a bar is exactly the same as that in a dating service. You don't have to take anyone's word for it; go to a function and see for yourself how many attractive singles are sick of the old love 'em and leave 'em routine.

The bottom line on dating services can vary by thousands of dollars. The rates range from the super expensive—used mostly by the highly affluent and the wannamarry highly affluent—to the dirt cheap—used by the entry-level salaried. There's a great variety of formats to choose from as well. Some boast exact compatibility matches made with the help of computers. Others allow you to choose for yourself by screening videos a la Love Connection. Still others (and this wins hands down for personal favorite) set up lunch dates for their busy, single clients who work in the city. Hey, it's only three-quarters of an hour—you can't lose.

Less like a dating service, but still quite up front, is the singles organization. Every week or two, the members participate in some sort of social event. These clubs tend to run very specific—for example, Single Widows/Widowers with Young Children, Jewish College Graduates Under Thirty, or Singles with Advanced Degrees from the Ivy League. They meet at dance clubs, bars, coffee shops, or any and all places conducive to a good time. And there you have it—a party where everyone is receptive to a relationship.

HIGH-TECH ROMANCE

If you have America Online or a comparable on-line service, you can let your fingers do the talking as you chat your way into the heart of a soulmate, without the encumbrance of physical appearance obstructing your view. This is where personalities get their chance to shine. So if you've always felt a stronger bond with the "class clown" than with prom royalty, this venue is your ideal stomping ground. Newspapers and talk shows are abuzz with stories of the multitudes falling into cyber love. Who's to say you won't be next?

DATING . . . ON A SHOESTRING

Dating and filing for bankruptcy need not go hand in hand. Don't max out your credit card or squander that rent money to impress a love interest; they'll be impressed all right—with what a serious loser you are. Most entry-level positions pay barely enough to get you through the month. However, by showing a little ingenuity in cutting a corner or two, you can plan thrifty but nifty dates. After all, it is the thought that counts, and expensive dinners do not a great evening make (much less a great relationship).

The Budget Gourmet

Don't get taken in by take-out. Astound your dates with these money-saving recipes. You'll have them begging for seconds.

Cyber Love

The World Wide Web is a great place for twentysome-things to read and post personal ads. Surf your way over to these popular dating sites:

1. **Together Personal Introductions**— http://www.togetherdating.com/
2. **American Singles Dateline**— http://www.terminus.com/loveline/date.htm
3. **City Singles**— http://www.olg.com/citysingles/
4. **Heart-to-Heart**— http://www.hearttoheart.com/
5. **Bureau One Personals**— http://www.cupidnet.com/cupid/bureau1/

CAVIAR, SALMON, AND POTATO PANCAKES

Prep time: 10 minutes
Total cost: $8.95

1/2 jar Romanoff Black Caviar	$2.50
1 package Nova Scotia salmon	$3.50
6 ready-made potato pancakes	$2.00
1 avocado, sliced	$0.75
2 tablespoons sour cream	$0.20

Fry the pancakes, remove them from the skillet, smear sour cream on top of each, arrange slices of avocado and salmon, and then sprinkle with caviar. Voilà!

CHICKEN DIJON WITH PORTOBELLO MUSHROOMS

Prep time: 20 minutes
Total cost: $5.80

2 chicken breasts	$2.50
2 whole Portobello mushrooms	$2.25
1 cup mayo	$0.35
3 teaspoons Dijon mustard	$0.25
Juice of 1 lemon	$0.45

Grill or fry the chicken; saute the mushrooms. Remove from heat. Sauce: Mix mayonnaise, mustard, and lemon juice. Microwave 30 seconds. Arrange chicken, and place mushrooms on top and around. Pour sauce over the entire dish. It's a snap.

SUSHI
Prep time: 20 minutes
Total cost: $6.45

1 can salmon	$2.00
2 cups rice	$0.50
1 cucumber sliced	$0.60
1/2 avocado sliced	$0.40
1 teaspoon vinegar	$0.05
1 teaspoon sugar	$0.05
1 package seaweed	$2.25
1 cup soy sauce	$0.60

You don't need any fancy-schmancy sushi-rolling gizmos. Just cook the rice, and mix in vinegar and sugar. Let cool (fan for faster results). Place seaweed on cutting board, and dampen slightly. Put a layer of rice on seaweed, add salmon, cucumber and avocado, and roll it all up. You may need to practice a few times, so don't get discouraged. Serve soy sauce on the side.

AUTHENTIC GREEK PIZZA
Prep time: 20 minutes
Total cost: $7.90

1 ready-made pizza crust	$2.90
4 ounces black olives	$1.50
2 cups mozzarella	$2.00
2 tablespoons pesto sauce	$0.50
2 ounces feta cheese	$1.00

Microwave feta and pesto together for 20 seconds. Stir thoroughly. Spread mixture over entire pizza, add olives and cheese. Bake for 15 minutes. Experiment with different ingredients to create your own exotic flavor.

Cheap Dates

1. The zoo
2. A picnic
3. Thrift store browsing
4. Tennis
5. Play auditions—watch or partake in
6. Matinees
7. Karaoke
8. Free concert in the park
9. Bowling
10. Museums and art galleries
11. Poetry readings
12. The beach
13. Antique hunting
14. Off-Off-Off Broadway plays
15. A video—*Breakfast at Tiffany's* coupled with Cheerios

The Whirlwind Romance

Try these activities with your signifcant other:

- Send love notes via fax.
- Prepare a romantic candlelit dinner—serve mac and cheese.
- Instead of your usual workout, take a long walk together. Challenge him/her to a race while you're at it.
- Paint your apartment.
- Take your morning shower together.
- Engage in a heated game of Scrabble.
- Wake up early, make breakfast, and just talk.

BECAUSE WE CARE

Landing a date often requires throwing caution to the wind, acting a little reckless, and abandoning yourself to the thrill of it all. But after the elation subsides, you will hopefully begin to reflect and thereby realize that you are planning to meet a complete stranger who may possibly turn out to be a maniacal psycho, deranged stalker, serial rapist, or killer necrophiliac. Whoa! While you're on the right track, try not to get carried away, lest you become agoraphobic, hermetically sealed by a double-bolted door within the confines of your studio apartment. Films such as *Looking for Mr. Goodbar*, *Fatal Attraction*, and *The Crush* have made us a little paranoid about dating. But please don't whine about feeling unsafe and vulnerable; do something about it. During the "getting to know you stage," you should do the following:

- Meet in public places, preferably during daylight hours (lunch and breakfast dates).
- Arrive in your own car.
- Park your car close to an entrance or beneath a streetlight, or use valet service.
- Bring change for a telephone call and bigger bills for a taxi.
- Inform close friends or relatives of your evening plans—location, date's name, etc.
- Stay alert—avoid inebriation.
- Play What's wrong with this picture? Ask personal questions and try to spot inconsistencies.

EMPLOYED

Chapter Five

GETTING THE JOB
YOU SO DESPERATELY NEED

DAYTIME TV

Gone are the days of the leisure class, when the aristocrats filled their time with reading, conversation, and promenades through the park. You can lament the demise of this era, or you can rejoice, as the peasant life sank into oblivion right along with it. While you may have to go to work, at least you don't have to toil in the fields from dawn till dusk, only to come home to a trough of gruel. Welcome to life in the middle class. To support yourself, some of you will have to put aside the revolutionary principles you picked up in college. The bourgeois need for cash is what will keep you alive—survival rule number one, if you will. Once you come to this realization, the scramble for a decent-paying job is will be just around the corner.

Most of you would be wise to avoid contemplating how much easier you'd have had it in the '80s. But since you'll probably hit upon this bit of evidence for why "life is unfair" sooner or later, let's get it out of the way now. Yes, in the pre-Bush '80s, the United States really was a kinder and gentler nation when it came to college grads. Companies were recruiting at campuses as if preparing for a graduate shortage. In other words, a college education still carried some weight, clout, status, and opportunity for the good life. But that is no longer the case. In fact, you can easily find Ph.D.s waiting tables, competing for jobs, and engaging in the '80s melancholy right along with you. Okay, so we were born about ten years too late. Now that that's settled we may get on with the business of living, or scraping together a living, to be exact.

PREPARING FOR BATTLE

Before you can fully immerse yourself in the job scurry, you must undergo a series of trials and tests. You don't want to get in there lacking in either the equipment or strategy department. Many unprepared warriors have been chewed up and spit out by the system. The only way to avoid this common fate is to know what's in store for you. You need to decide on a career, hone your communication skills, and organize your search—all of which take time.

Choosing a Career

When thinking about which career to pursue, avoid the "What am I going to do for the rest of my life?" pitfall. You're not a sooth-sayer, and no novelty-shop crystal ball or trade-show palm reader can answer that question. Unless you received practical training for a particular vocation, such as engineering or medicine, you will be hard pressed to figure this one out.

When deciding on your next step, focus on what you've been good at and what you've enjoyed doing in the past. A liberal arts education may have transformed your rough-edged understanding into one of well-rounded symmetry, but it may not necessarily have given you a specific aim in life. Not to worry—you can use your broad sensibility and vast exposure to different fields to your advantage. Go back to a time when classes were the only "job" you had. Which classes were your favorites? Or in which ones did you find least cause for complaint? If biology rang your bell, how about working in a hospital lab? Maybe your natural proclivity for English could come in handy as an editor at a publishing company or as a copywriter at an ad agency. You may even decide that you loved a particular subject so much that you actually want to be a teacher and pass that love on to others. Since there are so many possibilities, you'll need to undergo a thorough self-assessment in order to narrow your search.

Know Thyself

Everyone is not cut out for the same vocation. While Debbie may love basking in the warm glow of her PC all day, Bill may be drawn to a more dynamic environment. Accountants devote lifetimes to the crunching of numbers, but many of us quiver before the task of tip calculation. No need to get down on yourself for the skills you don't have. Instead, focus on your strengths and accomplishments. Not only will such an assessment get you a job that fits, but it will give you an added boost of self-confidence, which is crucial to selling yourself. You can start this self-exam by writing down all of your best qualities. If you can't think of too many on your own, there's always Mom, Dad, or even Auntie Em. Once you've got a

long list of positive attributes going, get a Smoothie, look the list over at your leisure, and bathe in the inner glow.

Okay, you can stop beaming now; you've still got a lot of work ahead of you. It's time for another list. Enumerate your work/study habits. What atmospheres do you find most conducive to the conduct of business? Which are your peak work hours? Do you prefer supervision or slack beneath its oppressive weight? How about group thinks? Are they too distracting? If you head to the library in search of quiet study, you may find yourself thriving within a structured work setting. Those of you who like to watch a little TV, make a round of calls, possibly even play a couple of variations on the poker theme while hitting the books are probably better suited to a fast-paced and unconventional work setting. Initiative levels must also be examined. Are you a self-starter, or do you need to hear the crack of the old whip before you get your hide into gear? Answering these questions will require that you evaluate your past experiences. And please, for the sake of all that's holy, be honest; otherwise "you'll only be cheating yourself."

Delusions of Grandeur

You may have watched one *L.A. Law* episode too many and thus decided to pursue an "Esq." suffix at the ripe old age of sixteen. Or your family tree may be so ripe with bankers that no other option seems feasible. Sad but true, many of us are still following the same course carved out for us by our parents or by our childish whims. Take the popular M.D. vocation. It may pay well, but it is far from being the glamorous occupation portrayed by *ER, General Hospital, St. Elsewhere, Trapper John,* and *Quincy.* First, there's medical school to contend with; then, the grueling residency, and, finally, one emergency after another. Or what about the law enforcement business? Though we loved playing cops and robbers as young girls, through the years we realized that police work can be a dangerous business. While it may look exciting, the reality is that it can be dangerous and unrewarding. And you could end up as a meter maid!

The best way to demystify "glamorous professions" is to ask the pros. Get on the phone and call up a rep from every field that tickles your fancy. Ask your friends if they know anyone willing to talk to the new kid in town. A brief meeting should tell you everything you ever wanted to know.

Don't try to hit the pro up for a job at this meeting. The temptation may be great, what with the atmosphere ever so casual and the rapport approaching friendly fast; but if you ask for a job, you may find yourself brutally rebuffed. After all, if the person knew you were prowling for a job, (s)he may not have agreed to the interview.

One way to put new contacts to good use is to ask them to keep an eye out for any openings in the field. They probably have loads of connections in their profession and may have been sufficiently won over by your go-get-'em attitude to find it in their hearts and pocketbooks to extend you that offer themselves. Regardless of the outcome, make sure to send a letter thanking them for their counsel. You never know when your paths will cross again.

Career Profiles

Before deciding on an occupation, it would be a good idea to investigate several careers in terms of their potential income, responsibilities,

When meeting with each professional, here is a list of questions to keep in mind. Skip the shorthand courses, and invest in a small tape recorder. You'll probably be meeting with many people, so economize the time you allot to each subject.

1. What is your current position? How did you get your job?
2. Were you promoted by the company, and on what grounds?
3. Did anyone/anything help you to prepare for your profession (i.e., seminars, graduate school, a mentor)?
4. Is the salary good, average, or poor?
5. Are there any fringe benefits?
6. What are your main responsibilities?
7. What are the most frequently recurring problems?

and required skills. We've compiled a brief profile of some popular fields. But don't stop here; you need to know as much as possible before directing your efforts in any one direction.

- *Accounting*
  Entry-level salary: mid to high twenties
  Entry-level position: associate or analyst
  Main duties: reporting, validating, auditing, and analyzing financial data
  Requirements: degree in accounting, computers, or math
  Professional Association: American Institute of Certified Public Accountants

- *Advertising*
  Entry-level salary: high teens to low twenties
  Entry-level position: assistant, junior executive, account service trainee
  Main duties: account executives—dealing with clients, acting as liaison between clients and the creative department; media department—planning placement of print and broadcast ads, securing media time and space; copywriters and artists—writing or designing ads for clients
  Requirements: account executives—marketing and business background; media—degree in advertising; creative department—a portfolio of past projects
  Professional Association: American Advertising Federation

- *Banking*
  Entry-level salary: low twenties to thirties
  Entry-level position: auditor, analyst, or trainee
  Main duties: supervising work flow or analyzing financial conditions and overseeing database management
  Requirements: business degree
  Professional Association: American Bankers Association

- *Broadcasting*
  Entry-level salary: teens to low twenties
  Entry-level position: production assistant or researcher
  Main duties: write editorials, conduct interviews, make phone
    calls, attend shoots
  Requirements: experience and talent
  Professional Association: National Association of Broadcasters

- *Engineering*
  Entry-level salary: thirties to forties
  Entry-level position: junior or associate engineer
  Main duties: testing, producing, or designing machinery
    and systems
  Requirements: engineering degree, proficiency in math
    and computers
  Professional Association: different associations for various
    types of engineers

- *Merchandising*
  Entry-level salary: low to mid twenties
  Entry-level position: merchandising assistant or assistant
    buyer
  Main duties: purchasing merchandise, negotiating with whole-
    salers and manufacturers
  Requirements: retail experience, merchandising degree
  Fringe benefits: discounts on merchandise

- *Public Relations*
  Entry-level salary: mid to high teens
  Entry-level position: junior or assistant account executive
  Main duties: contacting clients, writing and editing press
    releases, creating press kits
  Requirements: degree in public relations, journalism, English,
    or communication; good communication skills
  Professional Association: Public Relations Society of America

The Informational Interview (continued)

8. Describe an average day on the job.
9. What is the most fascinating part of the job?
10. What kind of people do you work with?
11. What is the worst part of the job?
12. What can I expect to earn in an entry-level position?
13. Is there room for growth?
14. Would you choose the same line of work again, knowing what you know now?
15. Does the job require putting in a lot of overtime?
16. Is your schedule set or flexible?
17. How did you first become interested in this career?

- *Publishing*
  Entry-level salary: high teens to low twenties
  Entry-level position: editorial assistant
  Main duties: review manuscripts, coordinate layouts, assist
      with research and fact checking
  Requirements: degree in English, journalism, liberal arts

- *Sales*
  Entry-level salary: high teens to low thirties
  Entry-level position: account executive, sales associate
  Main duties: interact with clients, market research, customer
      service, traveling
  Requirements: good communication skills, sales experience

Go by the Map

While every town has its share of help-wanted ads, the one you're looking for may not be within a reasonable commute distance. To make your dream a reality, relocation may be in order. Unless you're into car manufacturing or factory work, Detroit may not be the bastion of opportunity your mechanical engineering friends have led you to believe. Of course there are smidgens of other offerings, but your search will reap a different sort of harvest depending on where you choose to conduct it. Most major metropolises offer a wide range of opportunities; but, make no mistake about it, even within this group some still come out ahead. If you want to get into publishing, New York City is the place to be. Aspiring actors should head to Los Angeles or New York; this is where the action is. Since your peers from every god-forsaken corner of the country and beyond are also looking for jobs, the competition may be on the steep side. So don't expect to make any easy conquests. You'll still have to go through the drudgery of job hunting, but at least you'll see a hint of light at the end of that tunnel, and plenty of role models to spruce up those flagging spirits. "If I can make it there, I'll make it anywhere . . . "—well, you know the rest.

Self-Improvement

Don't go running off to write your cover letter just yet. It may be wise to acquire some new skills or maybe hone the ones you already have. Get an edge over the competition by appropriating the experience and skills that will set you apart. This will not be a full-time job. Set aside some time, one or two hours per day, to work on improving yourself. Your vocabulary, speech habits, and computer know-how may all need some work. Or maybe you can use your spare time to volunteer at a job that will help fill in the gaping hole in the "related experience" section of your resume. With a dash of initiative, you can transform yourself in no time into the hot little property that companies will welcome aboard.

Speech Therapy

You know how, like, when you're talking to your friends, and you say "um" a bizillion times, and use that hip slang like cool, fat, fly, and maybe even dope? Well, that just won't cut Wonder Bread when you're talking to potential employers. Good communication skills are a must-have in every field. If you want to be taken seriously, you've got to talk the talk. We can't all sound like the characters from the latest Merchant and Ivory production, but you can x-nay on the slang and improve your grammar skills. Practice talking into a tape recorder, or request that your friends emit a loud BUZZ! whenever you're caught in the act of slanging it up. If you're still having trouble mastering your native tongue, invest in a speech therapy/elocution session or two—it'll be money well spent.

The Power of Words

You're chatting it up during an interview, and all of a sudden you're thrown a linguistic curve ball: "So, what are your views on the ubiquitous presence of obsequious employees and cronyism in today's corporate work force?" While "Duh, run that by me again" or "What you talking about mister" are perfectly appropriate responses, they won't win you any points with the inquisitor. Only the most pretentious of interviewers would stoop to such tactics, but expanding

Certain professionals will be in higher demand than others. Here are some of the top ten fastest-growing careers for the coming years:

1. Home health assistants
2. Human services professionals
3. Computer scientists
4. Systems analysts
5. Physical therapists
6. Special education instructors
7. Paralegals
8. Private detectives
9. Corrections officers
10. Travel agents

your vocabulary is still a great idea. Think of it as an investment in your future. Just pick up one of those word-a-day calendars and put it to good use. Stay up to date, and pretty soon you'll be the affected interviewer stumping the unsuspecting prey.

Computer Literacy

Still tapping away at that old electric typewriter? Fancying yourself at the forefront of technology with your calculator expertise? Well, get yourself together; this is the Information Age. If you're not computer friendly, consider yourself substantially handicapped. If you want to be adequately prepared for today's work force, take an introductory course. Computers were created to serve you, so don't freak out at the prospect of using one. Once you get over the initial fear, you'll wonder how you ever got by without your handy dandy PC. For a nominal fee, community colleges in your area can help you master the most commonly used programs such as WordPerfect and Microsoft Word. If you're low on funds, ask your friends for assistance. There's a hacker in every bunch, and you're bound to run into one who'll agree to take you on as his/her protégé.

Internships

You should have been busy completing internships during your summer vacations—yeah, should have, could have, would have, but made other plans anyway. Now that you're out of school, you may wonder how a person can live on an intern's salary (often amounting to a big goose egg). It will be tough, but there are ways. Most grads in your position intern on a part-time basis, taking on a second job at night or on their days off. It's manageable, and, if you're planning on getting into some of the more competitive fields, practically unavoidable. Advertising, public relations, entertainment, and publishing companies have a history of hiring former interns. Even if your temp job doesn't turn into a full-time situation, you'll be well on your way in the field. You'll have made contacts, learned important skills, and, oh yeah, put another notch on the old resume belt.

Organize, Strategize, Energize

You're nearly there. Only one thing stands between you and the full-force job search. Think about all of the phone calls you'll be making, the research you'll be conducting, the letters you'll be writing. How will you ever manage such a case load? The organized job seeker will have an advantage over the rest. Planning and keeping track of your job-hunting efforts will pay off in the long run. In the final analysis, a few hours of organizing can save you countless days of unnecessary footwork, and can make or break your quest for a rewarding position.

Clean Up Your Act

Now is the time to get your hands on a large-sized date book—to house all your appointments, names, and phone numbers while looking like something right out of *GQ* or *Modern Woman*. Just keep one thing in mind: This is a tool, not an accessory. This means you must put it to use if it is to be useful. Next to each entry write down all the pertinent information that space permits. For example, you're meeting Kay Marie for an interview at 1:00 P.M. at 10 S. Lipliner Way. You've got the who, where, and when—in a word, insufficient data. If you have ideas to discuss or background dirt on the company or the interviewer, by all means write it down. This precaution will not only ensure that you enter the meeting with a sense of purpose and familiarity but will also keep you from blanking on what's important once you begin the discourse.

> *When I arrived for my interview, I had just finished talking to a recruiter about another position. The guy had kept me on the phone, trying to sell me on this company, for at least an hour. As a result, I was so frazzled to get out of the house on time that I completely forgot my appointment book. Even though I had done thorough research and practiced my responses with anyone who'd listen, when I called the interviewer by the wrong name, the job I had been so keen on was lost to me forever.*
>
> —HOWARD, GEORGETOWN UNIVERSITY, '93

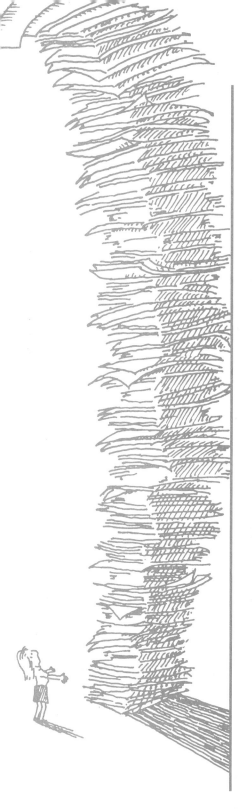

The Filing System

The information you collect along the way and any relevant documents, such as cover letters and articles, will have to be stored. You never can tell when the phone will ring. While you may have forgotten all about your application a month back, your credentials may very well have been making the rounds at the office all this time. Instead of incinerating old information, keep everything that is job-search related in an archive file. Also, keep a "record of activity" page in each corporate file. Notes detailing when you called, who you talked with, and what responses you received should be stashed on this one page. Thus, you'll know when a situation is ripe with employment opportunity or when a company has a zero turnover rate. Remember, waste not, want not; manage your time and information wisely, and you'll be on the fast track sooner than you think. Even if you've landed a prestigious position, don't get cocky. Don't purchase a paper shredder, and proceed to destroy all your painstakingly compiled research. You may not want to admit this so soon after your coup, but the future remains uncertain; another job hunt may be just around the bend.

Construct a Game Plan

In the sports world, a team without a game plan is a team without a prayer. You're no different. A plan of attack is crucial to your quest. The strategy need not be complicated or worked out in minute detail. But you should set goals, compose to-do lists, and carry through to the best of your abilities.

Right before college graduation, I got it into my head to become a copywriter for an ad agency. I hadn't majored in advertising, so I couldn't even interview when the big boys like Leo Burnett came to recruit on campus. Since I had no experience that could recommend me, I began watching for commercials and print ads that I felt could use some cosmetic touch-ups. I rewrote the copy, collaborated with a friend who was a graphic designer, and came up with a professional portfolio. My next step was to contact a career counselor back at school. She put me in contact with alumni in the business.

When nothing came of that, I began barging into corporate offices all over town. All the while, I was scouring the classi-fied ads. I was nearly at wits and funds end when one walk-in came through, and I finally got an entry-level position as an assistant copywriter.

—JACKIE, UNIVERSITY OF ILLINOIS, '94

Like so many other successful job seekers, Jackie devised a plan and stuck to it. You must be proactive and stay focused if you're to reach your goals. If you don't create and stick to a certain course, more strategic job hunters may beat you to the punch.

Jump-Start Your Drive

If you're still moping around the house, using old *Beavis and Butthead* episodes as the excuse for job-search avoidance, maybe you're not ready to work. Maybe what you need is a prolonged vaca-tion. How does following in Gauguin's Tahitian footsteps sound to you? Oh yeah! We forgot that your finances are null and void. So what the heck are you waiting for? We're not your camp counselors, you know; it's not our job to get you motivated. So rise and shine, up and at 'em, now! Need we remind you that the more time spent in slippers and soiled bathrobe, the less time left to invest your income, watch the savings grow, become a millionaire, retire, sail around the world, and lead that life of leisure for which we're all so nostalgic? Yes, all that American Dream hoopla can happen to you. But you must get hyped up. Yeah! Rah! Rah! Rah! Sis Boom Bah! No more bleeding Ma and Pa!

A good job will not come easy. Like all resume-toting grads, you will have times when you'll want to throw in the towel, curl up atop a brick oven, and dream of maiming your tormentors. Don't give in to such impulses, as those who have did not meet very pretty ends (straightjackets and Bellevue). Keep your head high and your eyes on the prize. You have no choice but to go out there and aggressively pursue your goal. Look at it this way: You have nothing to lose and an income to gain. Your next assign-ment is the resume and cover letter. Once those are complete, it's full steam ahead.

Employers favor certain skills. The following list is a sampling of the top contenders:

1. Speaking skills involve presenting your ideas in a coherent fashion to an audience.
2. Negotiating skills allow you to effect compromise and resolve differences.
3. Supervising/managing skills mean you can take responsibility for the work of others.
4. Customer service/public relations skills enable you to be a spokesperson for your organization.
5. Deadline-meeting skills enable you to work under pressure.

FOOLPROOF RESUMES AND COVER LETTERS

Look at a blank sheet of paper. Hopefully, you'll not find it nearly so ample as to be able to house your life story. So why fret over how your resume will relate the uniqueness and complexity of your being when, at this stage of the game, it should be no longer than this one page? As you're a relative newcomer to the world of work, this space should suffice to accommodate the fruits of your labor. We're talking tangible results achieved in the not-too-distant past. Unless you won the Pulitzer or the National Merit Scholarship, your high school days are water under the bridge. Too few employers will give extra credence to your cause based on your great ACT scores or your clinching the Most Likely to Succeed. Hey, we don't care if you were president of your senior class. What have you done lately? Don't pad your resume with archaic b.s. By wasting their time with the insignificant details of your childhood, you'll have become a liability.

The Righteous Resume Three Step

Resumes should speak loud and clear, focus on your past productivity, and delineate the means through which you were able to meet high standards. Considering your limited experience, the difficulty lies not in presenting the info on one page, but in getting your point across when the highlight of your career, thus far, has been a three-month tenure at McDonald's. How are you going to elicit the big "wow"? After all, employers want experience. You're sitting amidst a pile of want ads in your living room, and there is nothing, as far as the eye can see, that requires less than one year on the job. You may say, "But I just graduated! I HAVE NO EXPERIENCE!" Think again, pal. Have you been living in some kind of a vacuum? Trust us, you've got experience. It's the way you look at it that's causing you to circle the drain. You must re-evaluate your wealth of knowledge right here and now.

Step One: Identify Your Skills

A preliminary to any great resume is to gain a foothold on what the requirements are and why you are just the person for a particular job. Take a time-out to regroup and inventory your past. Get a sheet of notebook paper and jot down the following post-high-school activities in a single column on the left-hand side:

1. Jobs (no matter how hokey)
2. Volunteer experience
3. Internships
4. Campus activities
5. Relevant academic course work

All this *experience* has required the practice of skills. Now go on to elaborate your tally. Next to the activity, write down the abilities you implemented to succeed. Some of these may relate directly to the job you're now targeting; others may simply display the breadth of your resources. If you put your mind to it, you can relate any skill to the position for which you're aiming. What you now have is an idea of where you stand in the experience lineup. Keep this roster where your dog can't get at it, since you'll soon be using it to customize your resume.

_____
_____
_____
_____
_____
_____
_____
_____
_____
_____
_____
_____
_____
_____
_____
_____
_____
_____
_____

Give Them What They Want! (continued)

6. Budgeting skills involve concerning yourself with the employer's funds in such a way as to save your employer money.
7. Writing skills enable you to write your ideas in an organized manner in order to get results.
8. Training/instructing skills allow you to show newcomers the ropes.
9. Coordinating/organizing skills allow you to plan events or see projects through various stages to completion.
10. Interviewing skills enable you to ask tough questions, and then listen in order to get insight from the answers.

Step Two: Customize Your Pitch

After giving the matter some serious thought and being of a somewhat ambitious nature, suppose you've decided on a plan that will have you heading up the management of all eastern seaboard Taco Bells come year 2000. Since you've already put in time as a tacomaker, and have even garnered a couple of nominations for employee of the week, you probably figure you're on the right track. However, if you go into Taco Bell headquarters with this presentation, you'll be lucky to get your old job refrying beans back, much less a position in management.

What can you say on your resume to create the desired effect? Well, first figure out what the restaurant management job entails. Check out the occupational references listed earlier in this chapter, and then go to the want ads and see what duties are listed. Finally, pull out the list of experiences you racked your brain to compile. Attempt to connect some of those skills you picked up from your old jobs and classes to the sought-after position. If you find yourself a little hard up, remember there's no law against reaching. Ingenuity is always appreciated by employers. What's the worst that can happen? So you give someone a good laugh. You may just get a screening out of it. The point is "to build a bridge from the past to the future." For example, if your taco-making expertise catapulted you into employee of the week status, you might mention that your organizational skills increased the sales of the business by producing a higher output and cutting down the average customer waiting time. Then you may want to mention that customers who dealt with you at the cash register came back more often because of the rapport you had developed. Now you not only are well organized but also have interpersonal skills to back up your claim to a seat in management. Leadership is another biggie you may want to mention. While you may have worked under a supervisor in the past, did you ever suggest any new methods of restaurant operation that were implemented? If so, by all means, mention it! If you can't think of one instance in which you took charge, consider enrollment in a leadership seminar. You can show employers your initiative by so doing, and gain that confidence so clearly lacking in your past.

But what about action words? Select and use some combination of the following words on your resume and you're sure to be heard:

accelerated	conceptualized	effected	instituted	pinpointed	reviewed
accomplished	condensed	elected	instructed	planned	revised
achieved	conducted	eliminated	interpreted	prepared	scheduled
activated	consolidated	encouraged	interviewed	presented	selected
adapted	constricted	enlarged	introduced	preserved	served
adjusted	constructed	enlisted	invented	presided	serviced
administered	contacted	established	investigated	processed	simplified
allocated	contracted	estimated	issued	produced	sold
amended	contributed	evaluated	launched	programmed	solved
amplified	contrived	examined	lectured	promoted	stimulated
analyzed	controlled	executed	led	proposed	streamlined
applied	converted	exhibited	located	proved	strengthened
appointed	coordinated	expanded	maintained	provided	structured
approved	counseled	expedited	managed	published	studied
arbitrated	created	extended	marketed	purchased	suggested
arranged	cut	forecasted	mastered	recommended	summarized
attained	dealt	formulated	moderated	reconciled	superseded
audited	defined	formulized	modified	recorded	supervised
augmented	delegated	fortified	molded	recruited	supported
awarded	delivered	founded	monitored	rectified	systematized
broadened	demonstrated	gathered	motivated	reduced	taught
brought	designed	generated	negotiated	re-evaluated	terminated
budgeted	determined	governed	offered	regulated	traced
built	developed	guided	operated	reinforced	trained
calculated	devised	handled	organized	reinformed	transferred
chaired	devoted	helped	originated	renegotiated	translated
collected	directed	implemented	overhauled	reorganized	unified
communicated	distributed	improved	oversaw	repeated	updated
compared	documented	increased	participated	reported	utilized
compiled	drafted	initiated	perceived	researched	was promoted
completed	earned	inspected	performed	restored	worked
conceived	edited	installed	persuaded	revamped	wrote

Object Properly and You Won't Be Overruled

Career objectives are a tricky lot. Do you stick one in or let it slide? Do you get specific or remain ambiguous? Here's the skinny:

A general objective explains the direction that you want to take in the field. It also tells which personal strengths you think would be of service. The key word is SYMBIOTIC! You trade your skills for their job. Overly wordy objectives that say nothing will get you off on the wrong foot.

A narrow objective should be used only when applying for a specific job. If you exclude other possibilities, your resume will wither and brown with age in the dreaded "file." Fortunately, it's easy to alter the objective to match the position applied for.

Leave out the objective when you're looking to get into a particular company and are not sure which departments are hiring. You can always explain your interests in further detail in the cover letter.

Step Three: Put It on Paper

Now comes the hard part—making it look pretty. It's imperative that you look at some sample resumes to make this happen. A resume is a highly structured document, not a narrative where you ramble on and on about your experiences and how you can be of service to a company. The reason for this is simple: The resume hardly ever gets an attentive read the first time it appears. The eyes of the Big Cheese go directly from education to employment. The rest is left for topics of conversation should you be interviewed.

Your resume can fit into any number of formats. However, because recruiters appreciate it when you stick to what they know, you're probably better off using one of the two most popular structures: the *chronological* or the *functional*. You may decide to go all out and make one of each.

A *chronological resume* lists in a sequence the jobs you have previously held. This presentation works to your advantage when prior titles are relevant and likely to impress; when searching for a job in the same field as your prior jobs; when searching for a job in traditional fields, such as banking, government, and education; and when your job history shows a high level of progress.

Still in the dark? Check out the following example.

JOHN GRADUATE
85 Ivy Lane
Higher, ED 10011
411/555-1212

OBJECTIVE: To obtain a position counseling disturbed teens

EDUCATION: Big Ten University
B.S. Psychology, May 1997
3.8 GPA on 4.0 scale

WORK EXPERIENCE:

7/95–Present   Youth Counselor at Troubled Kids Network, Higher, ED
- Oversaw the academic progress of emotionally disturbed children
- Taught study skills to under-achieving teens
- Designed new program agendas, which received positive feedback from the participants
- Brought about a great improvement in the academic performance of students

10/94–6/95   Research Assistant for Big Ten University Psychology Department, Campus Town, ED
- Administered psychological evaluations to college students
- Coordinated group meetings for the compilation of research
- Modified test results to obtain desired statistical data
- Was promoted to first assistant after producing highly favorable results

ACTIVITIES AND HONORS:

Multiple Dean's List Appearances
Psychology Honor Society
Intramural Soccer Team
Fraternity Social Chairman
Phi Beta Kappa
Summa Cum Laude Graduate

SKILLS: Computer—WordPerfect 5.1 & 6.3, Microsoft Word, Windows, Lotus 1-2-3
Languages—Fluent Spanish; Competent French

REFERENCES: Available upon request

While John clearly pulls this baby off without a hitch, you should be careful when using the chronological structure. It could do more harm than good! Many a fresh-faced, wet-behind-the-ears grad may find that one or more of the following resume busters applies to them:

1. You haven't worked for over a year.
2. You are looking for that first job.
3. You've had to create mnemonic devices simply to keep track of the jobs you've held in the last year alone.
4. Your job history shows more variety than prestige.
5. Your careers goal take a dramatic turn.

Lucky for you there's more than one way to beg for a livelihood. You greenhorns out there take heart; the functional resume structure may be just the thing for your job-seeking woes.

A *functional resume* focuses not so much on what positions you've held and when but on what you've learned from your experience that would be of use in the future job. The functions you served in your old jobs are the crux of this format. The actual titles and dates don't come until the very end of the list. Do we hear a collective sigh of relief? Who can blame you? If you ask us, the chronological format is not at all democratic. If the field you're shooting for is not feudally orthodox, you can circumvent the titled class system by making proper use of a skills-centered resume. This way the employer gets a chance to see your substance as an employee, before being dissuaded by the lowly or wholly unrelated titles you've been given.

JANE JOBLESS
13 Unemployment Lane
Penniless, Iou 00001
123/456-7890

JOB OBJECTIVE   To pursue a career in the tourism industry that utilizes my organizational, communication, and interpersonal skills

EDUCATION

- Private University, College Town
  Bachelor of Business 1996
- College X Study Abroad in Tokyo, Japan

RELEVANT SKILLS

Organizational
- Planned and budgeted social events for two hundred residents of a university dormitory
- Updated and implemented a new filing system at a busy corporate office
- Developed a personal itinerary for a three-month tour of the Far East
- Expedited the delivery of as many as forty simultaneous dinner orders
- Computerized the accounts of a large restaurant and caterer with Quicken software

Communication
- Coordinated itineraries through effectively communicating with tourism businesses such as airlines, train companies, bus lines, travel agents, hotels, and hostels in various foreign countries
- Exhibited strong persuasion abilities to achieve highest sales in telemarketing division
- Presented explanations of meals to large parties of customers to help them select those best suited to their individual tastes and dietary needs
- Wrote promotional fliers for residence hall activities

Interpersonal
- Developed ability to interact with people from diverse cultures and backgrounds through extensive foreign travel and advising dormitory residents
- Established amiable rapports with restaurant patrons
- Mediated in multiple dormitory disputes to arrive at outcomes favorable to all parties involved

EMPLOYMENT HISTORY

8/95–Present	Resident Advisor: Freshman Dorm, Private U., College Town
5/95–8/95	Food Server: Smorgazborg, Suburb, Home State
5/94–8/94	Telemarketer: Unsuspecting Homes Co., Suburb, Home State
5/93–8/93	Secretary: The Tire Shop, Suburb, Home State

REFERENCES AVAILABLE UPON REQUEST

It All Boils Down to This

Keep the following basic rules in mind when pasting together your personal promo, and chances are you'll land on your feet:

1. *Neatness Counts.* To employers, a sloppy resume = a sloppy mind. So do it right, or don't do it at all.
2. *Grammar and Spelling.* Here's your chance to put all those junior high language arts courses to good use. Glaring typos, or even minor ones for that matter, have no place in the detail-oriented world of work.
3. *Made-to-order.* You're not going anywhere if your resume isn't geared to the job in question.
4. *Paper.* The wrong paper may very well end up in the trash before it so much as gets a scanning. Keep away from neons and other bright colors. Cream or off-white paper is always a safe bet. Using bond paper also adds a nice touch.

Do you think you can make the Ms. Jobless employment assortment look better? That's highly unlikely if you're using the chronological format. Put yourself in the Bigwig's vibrating armchair: In hot pursuit of a travel agent, event coordinator, or whatever tourist slot it is that you're so keen to fill, you look at a resume and see someone who's had less than a year total work experience, no prior positions in tourism, and a bevy of menial jobs. Paper shredder? You betcha! But toot the horn of your success before you deliver the no-industry-work-experience employment history, like Jane does, and your accomplishments may speak for themselves.

Would You Please Cover Yourself?!

A resume without a cover letter is as naked as Adam without the strategically placed fig leaf. The cover letter is one of the last vestiges of civility remaining in the modern world. A resume alone is just plain rude. What?! No introduction?! The nearest thing to a wham-bam-thank-you-ma'am in the corporate arena, a coverless resume screams, "I spit in the face of convention!"—a bad angle to take when asking for a job. Play it smart and cover your assets. A well thought-out cover letter will let an extra spark of your personality shine through, be that your confident manner, your conscientious attitude, or your strong motivation and drive. Besides, this letter is where all you well-connected milksops (don't mind us, we're just bitter) gain credibility by plugging your references. If you don't accept the cover letter as your personal savior, it will be nothing but the fire and brimstone of the soup kitchen for you.

The Cover Letter Trilogy: A Dramatization

Consisting of three crucial parts, the cover letter is also subject to format. This is a business letter, and as such you should keep it strictly business. Do not exchange pleasantries, or inquire as to the recipient's health. Why not? Two-part answer: (A) You'll not be getting anything in response but a form letter. (B) You are addressing yourself to the representative of an organization, and everything you need to know about the health of the organization (fiscally speaking) is in the stacks of a library. If you really care, you'll do the research and incorporate the relative comments in your letter.

The only thing to ask for is a meeting. This is where the interview comes into play. Notice that you never once referred to it in your resume. You know about the company through the media, or word of mouth. Now the company knows about you through your own version of a public relations mailing, your resume and cover letter. (Writing samples and portfolio clips are sometimes requested, in which case you should include anything that doesn't cause you to cringe with humiliation.) Now that both parties are informed as to what each has to offer the other, an actual rendezvous can take place . . . or not. The purpose of the letter is to open the door to such face-to-face negotiations. We've put together a sample that includes all the *necessary* parts of a cover letter, along with an explanation thereof (in italics). You are, of course, free to vary the tone and style to suit your own taste. Just make sure you don't leave out the content or wreak havoc on the format.

Rring! Rring! "Hello, this is Mr. Bakker from Jim and Tammy Fae, Inc. We received your resume and are calling to ask if you are interested in arranging a time to meet." Even before you can hang up, you're already jumping up and down, while visions of briefcases and expense accounts dance in your head.

Unfortunately, what you just read—a condensed version of the resume callback—occurs with no more frequency than the February 29th birthday bash. Yes, even a mass mailing will not necessarily obtain this oft-prayed-for response. You've got to get out there and put *all* your job-hunting skills to work. In this day and age, anyone with a high school diploma is eligible for a resume. It takes a fine-tuned, college-educated intellect such as your own to come up with new and innovative methods to get the job.

It All Boils Down to This (continued)

5. *Relevance.* Don't include anything that does not have to do with the job. If you're married, congratulations! But keep it to yourself. Don't include stuff about your religion, how much you love a good cigarette, or every class you've taken since day one. Jokes are also inappropriate. In other words, keep it focused, serious, and brief.

6. *"I."* This personal pronoun should never make an entrance.

7. *Lies.* "Oh, what a tangled web we weave, when first we practice to deceive!" Keep fibs off the resume, and in your personal life where they belong!

John Graduate
85 Ivy Lane
Higher, ED 10011

December 15, 1998

The opening paragraph should answer the following questions: Why are you writing? What position are you applying for? How did you become aware of the opening?

Ms. Holly Good
Educational Director
Up! Up! And Away! Company
3456 Smiling Child's Way
Samaritan, ED 10101

Dear Ms. Good:

It is with great interest that I am applying for the peer counselor position in the Educational Division of your organization. One of your teachers, Joan Humanitarian, informed me of the present opening, and I feel that my qualifications make me the ideal candidate for this position.

Since my graduation from Big Ten University, in May 1998, I have been pursuing my interest in psychology and education by working with troubled youths. My enthusiasm for this type of work grows with each passing day, as does my effectiveness as a motivational force in the lives of disturbed kids. As a result of my brainchild, the Raise Your Hand if You're Unsure! program, the group of adolescents that I tutored experienced unprecedented scholastic improvement.

The middle paragraph(s) explains why you feel you should be in the running for the position. By way of tooting the horn of your past success, this section should give the reader a clear idea of why you are interested in working for this company and what makes you a feasible candidate for the job.

As highlighted on my resume, I have also had extensive training in administering a wide array of psychological tests. Since Up! Up! And Away! is greatly advanced in such methods of assessment, I feel sure that my experience as a research assistant could be put to excellent use by your company.

I have no doubt that I could meet the challenge presented by this position and come through with flying colors. I hope you find that my experience, education, and strong sense of purpose merit further consideration. Should you wish to discuss my qualifications in further detail, please do not hesitate to contact me at (411)555-1212. Thank you.

Sincerely,

X marks the spot, you sign here

John Graduate
Enc.

The closing paragraph should do three things: ask for a one-on-one, thank the reader, and in a single sentence, give your final pitch. You could also specify a time when you will be following up—but more on follow-through later.

Enclosure denotes that other material is included with the letter, e.g., resume, work samples, whatnot.

BREAK ON THROUGH TO THE OTHER SIDE

So you think you've got it all under control? You've sent out about one thousand resumes (each with a cover letter!), and you're just waiting for the phone to start ringing. Envisioning the sheer volume of your outgoing mail, you're thinking you'll need a secretary to weather all those calls and incoming letters. However, after about two weeks, your bubble may burst. For some of you, it will be more like a month. But after the tenth letter stating that your resume has been reviewed and put on file, burst it will. You'll wonder how your goof-proof scheme ever failed, and will rue the day you spent $200 on stamps alone. You're now ready to learn about how to become a master of follow-through—without this knowledge, all of your bubbles are doomed to end in a loud "Pop!"

Phone Calls

Follow-up phone calls are critical factors of the successful job hunt. Timing these babies properly is of the highest importance. Once you send out your resume, writing samples, and dental X rays, make sure to call the employer to confirm receipt of the treasures. This move will demonstrate that your work is important to you, you are conscientious, and you have a great phone voice and phone-side manner. Politely ask whether your application has had a chance to be reviewed. Do not badger the employer about setting up an inter-view; you'll only meet with, "We're still looking over the resume, and we'll be setting up appointments next week." You may want to slip in something to the following effect: "I was working on it all last night, and wanted to make sure that the sleep deprivation did not affect my spelling. Is Patty spelled with a *Y* or an *I*?" Patty will be tickled pink by your concern (most people hate their name being mis-spelled). She'll also be reminded of the human element behind your credentials. This may be all it takes to ignite her interest in meeting with you face to face.

E-Mail

Most of your important contacts probably have e-mail addresses, and your job is to sniff these out. Why? People love getting e-mail. It may be the novelty, but phone calls won't excite someone half as much as an e-mail. With the touch of a button, this fairly new phenomenon can transport you right into the top exec's office. It almost beats time travel, doesn't it? The only catch is in the difficulty of finding your contacts' electronic mailbox numbers. There are no E-Mail Directories in the works just yet, but you can phone the company operators for assistance. Sound official and throw out a big corporate name. "Jim Denver here. I'm calling from the National Bank Alliance" should get them scurrying for the info. Once you've compiled a lengthy list of addresses, you can write a general letter and import it to any number of employers with one fell swoop. You can send as many as five hundred e-mail letters with one solitary jerk of the old index finger. And when you're ready to follow up, you can e-mail them again. That's the beauty of e-mail; you can send as many letters as you want directly to the person you want (bypass the Personnel Resume Graveyard). No postage stamps to buy, no envelopes to lick. There is, however, such a thing as e-mail etiquette. Sending more than one message per day is not recommended. You want to stand out for your perseverance, not for your obsessive-compulsive e-mailing disorder.

Other Impediments

Secretaries and personal assistants are trained to keep your kind at a safe distance. The defense weapon of choice is the click of a disconnected phone line. When the precious concentration of the boss is at stake, these people will spare no effort at keeping the peace. They can spot a phony trying to wrangle his/her way through the door from a mile away. But they will be no match for you. Pretending to be an old friend from college is an easily detected approach. If you're sure that a three-minute conversation with you will arouse your contact's curiosity and may even secure you a position, try the grandparent route. Assume your most decrepit, shaky voice and then invent a pet name for your target. David could easily be transfigured into Davie, Susan into Susie, Elizabeth into Lizzy, and so forth. Even though Becky may be the wrong nickname, you won't be questioned since you clearly knew Ms. Rebecca Howe way back when, and who knows how many permutations her name has gone through since then. If you're pressed for identification, say you're an old friend of the family (just in case the grandparents turn out to be long-standing members of the dearly departed). Once you've got the person on the line, deliver your message in a loud and clear tone of voice. Some people may fault you for your lying ways, but others will recognize a go-getter when they hear one and give you a chance to audition for the team.

There are other ways to duck the St. Peters of the pearly company gates: for example, the brisk "this is x, returning his call" line. Quite simply, when asked who is calling, state your name (first or full—it's completely up to you), and then behave as if you're doing someone a great favor by calling back. Say, "I hardly had a chance to finish lunch when I got his urgent message requesting that I call him back immediately." This should trigger a secretary's fear of upsetting the boss (thereby disturbing that all-important peace and concentration). The mental scales and balances will quickly figure in your favor after the option of not helping in an emergency gets weighed. You'll be given the benefit of the doubt; the rest is up to you.

The southern charm/sob story combination can do the trick as well. Practice your southern accent beforehand. Try it out on some friends. If the reviews are raves, you'll know you're ready to tackle the pros. When the administrative assistant answers the phone, launch into a long, convoluted tale about the hardships and difficulties you've experienced since you moved away from Sticksville. (S)he'll either feel sorry for you ("Gee, the kid deserves a break") or try to shut you up ("I've got ten lines ringing and this kid's not winding down. Aha! I'll let the boss tell him where to go"). Either way, you'll most likely get transferred to your desired destination.

Through the Stomach

There are people in this world who still believe in a free lunch and will never pass up a meal when it's on you. Trust us when we

Beat the Secretary

Whether these strategies work for or against you depends on how suave and clever you can be. Disclaimer: Each technique has really landed someone a job; but we stress that there are no guarantees—you might find yourself in an embarrassing situation.

1. Dress up as either a food- or flower-delivery person.
2. Ask the security guard what time it is, and run for the door when he/she looks at his/her watch.
3. Wear your most expensive, outfit and walk in like you own the joint. Say, "I'm meeting Bob for lunch." Then, walk in before (s)he even has a chance to announce you.
4. Wait until the regular receptionist goes to lunch, and then try to trick the substitute.
5. Find out which car belongs to the guy/gal on guard, and then call with the news that its lights are on or it is being towed.
6. Get your friends to call and tie up every line just as you're heading in. In all the confusion, slip in undetected.

tell you that bribing someone with filet mignon (or even a burger) may get you a screening. It's all in how you handle it. Once you get past the support network, offer to take the boss out to lunch, breakfast, or an afternoon snack. It is important that you come off sounding interested in the person, and not in getting your name on the payroll. Say that you're an ingenue looking to get the lowdown on the industry. If (s)he broaches the subject of the recently vacated position, play dumb. But don't leave your resume back at the homestead. After all, you never can tell what may transpire. Try a little flattery to break the icy reserve. For example, say, "I was interested in learning about the business from a real pro." If being plastic just isn't your style, think of it this way: It's no more than you'd do for any date.

Gate Crashing

Desperate times call for desperate measures. If you plan on storming in—brazenly breezing past the horror-struck secretary, straight into Mr. Big Shot's office—take precautionary measures. If you happen to make it through but are at a loss for adequate backup (i.e., a good introduction, a solid presentation, charts, graphs, a prospectus, etc.), you'll end appearing totally incompetent. You'll be laughed right out the door, if you're lucky. Strong warning: Unannounced intrusions won't get you arrested, but your dignity may suffer the blows delivered by the resident security guard. On the other hand, if properly executed, this method may get you on your way to the corner office.

Being a cartoonist, your body of work has to speak for you. But after applying to several news publications in my area, mine was met with stone-cold silence. I had to act. All I wanted was for someone to evaluate my work. I was positive that once they saw my ability up close, they would extend an offer. I packed up my best work, found the names of my victims, and proceeded to dress up as my lead cartoon character. I told the assistants that I was a singing telegram and would need to deliver my message in person and in private. Some employers were less than enthused with my approach. I guess they didn't get excited over the singing telegram. But most took the time to look at my work anyway. They gave me plenty of advice as to how I could improve it to better suit their markets. One guy, however, gave me a job as a part-time layout assistant. So far, I have had two cartoons approved for publication, and I hope to be working as a full-time cartoonist by the end of the year.

—MATT, UNIVERSITY OF CALIFORNIA, SANTA BARBARA, '96

WORKING THE JOB RUNWAY

Finally! You're all set to go, and probably bursting at the seams with nervous energy. If you followed the foregoing guidelines, you have laid good groundwork for success. Nevertheless, don't take this to mean that the bulk of your effort is behind you, because it isn't—not by a long shot. Having geared up with a life preserver, you're ready to jump the sinking ship of unemployment, but you'll have to deal with some serious turbulence before you can get to shore. But don't worry. There are plenty of guardian angels out there. You need only identify them to receive a helping hand.

Friends in Need

Resources for the unemployed are in abundance, and we're not talking about welfare checks. The assistance you're after will help get you into a career, not on public aid. Some of these resources are more effective than others; once you settle on a profession, so draw upon as many resources as possible to get yourself advantageously situated.

The Classified Approach

Actually, there is nothing classified about looking for a job through the newspapers. Sure, a few job seekers may strike it rich, but the odds are against you. Large city papers have a vast circulation, so you can count on some heavy competition. The company you're applying to probably will be bombarded with enough applications to fill up a dozen post office boxes. Therefore, your offering may or may not get the attention it deserves. Since 80 percent of all vacancies are filled before they're advertised, the classified pickings are slim. But people have been known to get lucky, so it's worth a try.

I was big on the classifieds for a while. I loved to mark up the paper with bright red slashes and circles. It was more fun than the crossword puzzle. Unfortunately, this pastime was nowhere near as rewarding as it was entertaining. I wrote what seemed to be hundreds of cover letters, and altered my resume to suit the criteria in the ads on a daily basis. I would get a nibble here and there, but nothing ever panned out. Someone later told me that many of the jobs advertised aren't even legitimate positions. And then I got a call and was invited to interview at a small catering company looking for a general assistant. I did get the job, but I wouldn't count on the classifieds to get a job in the future.

—STEVE, MICHIGAN STATE UNIVERSITY, '95

Your Own Personal Job Hunters

If you're just starting out fresh from academia, don't expect headhunters to help you out. The executive search firms are paid by employers, and your lack of professional experience puts you straight into the unprofitable bin. Consider this resource later on down the line, once you've added some kick to your resume. These busy beavers are an invaluable resource if you're established and looking to make a savvy career move. They save execs the trouble of looking for a job—execs being the key word—so if you're not top-drawer material just yet, read on.

Employment agencies are probably more your speed at this career juncture. Double, triple, or quadruple your chances of success by signing up with more than one. The reputable agencies are usually compensated by the employers, so if you're asked to pay up front, make for the door. This method has allowed many a job seeker to banish the old interview suit to the rear of the closet, and isn't that what it's all about?

Temporary agencies are often dismissed by the college-grad crew as being beneath contempt. Such snobbery will get you nowhere. In fact, temporary agencies are a great way to get in on the corporate ground floor; just make sure you request placement with a company specializing in your area of interest. Once so installed, you can make all the right contacts while watching for a more upscale position to become available. A temp job need not be synonymous with a dead-end job. If you can bide your time and schmooze like a pro, bigger and better things will come your way.

Career Counseling/Vocational Centers

This resource is richest if you're looking for a calling or hoping to find a job prior to graduation, but it can also come in handy for the alums. Such centers can help polish your resume, put you in touch with other alumni in your chosen field, and provide helpful hunting tips and listings of available positions. If you're light years away from your college town, try to bamboozle your way into a center at a local college. They may let you pillage their stock of valuable resources—in any case, it can't hurt to ask.

The Internet

Surfing for jobs on the Net has grown in popularity, and with good reason. The Internet lists thousands of jobs just waiting for your perusal, and all from the privacy of your own home. Many sites offer the additional bonus of listing your resume in their databases at no extra charge. Employers from all fields will have the chance to scan your credentials. Also available is the option to apply for specific positions via e-mail. You'll be saving a lot of time by taking advantage of this feature and will be able to apply for twice as many positions, if not more. Here's a rundown of the World Wide Web's leading job sites:

http://www.careermosaic.com
http://www.tripod.com/work/safari
http://www.jobtrak.com
http://www.monster.com/home.html

The Who's Who Networking Directory

Your network is wider than you think. Provided you put them to good use, the following people may all contribute to the making of your stellar career:

- College professors
- Relatives
- Friends of the family
- Sorority sisters/fraternity brothers
- High school teachers/ guidance counselors
- Friends and neighbors
- College alumni
- Friends' parents

http://www.adamsonline.com
http://www.careershop.com
http://www.collegegrad.com
http://www.jobboard.com
http://www.jobweb.com

Networking

The "hidden" job market does exist. Do you know why? Because most employers prefer hiring someone they know or someone who's been recommended by a colleague. Depending on your talent for networking, or lack thereof, this could either work for or against you. If you're not the connection collector you want to be, keep in mind that great networkers aren't born, they're made. A few critical moves can have you skillfully weaving your web of associates in no time.

People Inventory

This ploy may seem silly—maybe downright inane—but who cares? It's not dignity you're after. What you need is a job. So make out a list of everyone you've known, right down to distant cousins and friends you haven't talked to in years. Then get on the phone and call every single last one of them. Make sure you left things on a good note before ringing; you'd hate to call someone only to be brutally rebuffed. Chat up a storm, and ask if they want to get together for lunch or a drink. In the course of normal conversation, present your predicament and ask if they know anyone in your field. If you unearth enough people from your past, you're bound to wind up with several valuable career leads.

Come Prepared

When contacting random people from your past, think about how each one can contribute to your pursuit of employment. Your friends may not have any close relations with professionals, but their parents might. Asking close pals to contact their relatives on your behalf is a most effective way of building a network—as long as you have no problem reciprocating the favor. Teachers come into contact with experts from various fields on a daily basis. Asking these icons of scholasticism about their associates may secure you several informational interviews with leaders in each industry.

If you're serious about networking, you can't afford to bypass the business card. Buy yourself a set, and give one to anyone who'll have it. Have plenty on you at all times, because the more you get into circulation, the greater your chance of pinning down another connection. You may think you've got the best-looking card on the circuit, but should someone seem less than enthused to accept your well-adorned voucher, do not force it on them. Remember, it's not only no that means no; a vigorous shake of the head or a backing away and a frown all mean the same thing—keep your card in your pocket. If you're really bent on scoring the reluctant connection, you could always request his/her card, and call when (s)he's in better cheer.

A good self-introduction is a tremendous asset to your networking agenda. Aim for a perfect balance of brevity and completeness. Don't simply call someone and say, "Hi, Mr. Pitt. This is George. Elaine told me you do quite a business in the stock market. Do you mind telling me about it?" No, no no! A thousand times no! Write out a short statement, including not only what you want but also who you are and how you are qualified. If you waste people's time, their opinion of you will take a nosedive. So practice your delivery before giving the pitch, and make sure to tailor each one to the situation at hand.

Whenever and Wherever

Networking is a commitment. You must always be on the lookout for new opportunities. You never know when or where you'll meet your new employer or an industry expert. Being prepared to network in even the oddest settings will have you interviewing for more positions than you ever thought possible. As a matter of fact, the more unorthodox the place, the more likely you are to get a job out of the situation. The sneak-attack strategy hasn't become the number-one battle cry for nothing.

Hot Networking Zones

Some places are optimally suited for carrying out your networking schemes. Here are some you may want to check out:

- Business seminars
- Industry trade shows
- Fund-raisers
- Professional organizations
- Religious institutions
- Conferences
- Community events
- Health clubs

We were at my friend's bachelor party and sitting next to these middle-aged men in suits. One of my buddies struck up a conversation, and the next thing you know, we're one big party. I'm talking to one of the guys, telling him about how hard it is to get a break in television production in Chicago. I couldn't believe it when the guy told me he worked for NBC. I asked him a ton of questions, completely ignoring the exotic dancers and the guest of honor. By the end of our talk, he said he might be able to help me. We exchanged cards, and a couple of days later I was being interviewed for the position of production assistant on a popular daytime talk show. I was given an offer the next day.

—PERRY, OBERLIN COLLEGE, '94

OPEN WIDE: THE ORAL EXAM

You've done the work, pestered the employers, outmaneuvered the support staff, and obtained a hearing. Yippee! But once on your agenda, the interview may begin to seem more like a trip to the dentist than a visit to Disneyland. All that work and expectation hangs in the balance, just waiting to be uprooted like an extraneous wisdom tooth.

Stop right there. You'll not get a job by showing up a nervous wreck. If an interviewer sees you're desperate—the sweat-stained shirt, unkempt hair, and stammer are all dead giveaways—the job that rightfully should be yours will go to your competitor, who was obviously too dim-witted to understand how much really was at stake.

While there are interviewing rules to adhere to, they're hardly the material sleepless nights are made of. We won't hold you in suspense a moment longer. There's no secret to doing your best at an interview. Here's the comprehensive dope on handling the job interview dilemma.

Market Analysis

Knowing how to approach each company and what skills to emphasize will require that you know something about the company.

If all that emanates from your interview is ME, ME, ME, employers will question your willingness to play ball with the team. Show them you're willing to go the distance by conducting your own investigation before hitting them up for an offer.

Hit the Books

Corporate directories can tell you anything and everything there is to know about a company, or just enough to get you through the interview. *Don's Million Dollar Directory* and the *Corporate Yellow Book* will get you up to speed and won't strain your brain. These books list a company's name, annual sales, main officers, address, and phone number. If you're in a bind and need a crash course, look no further than these volumes. One good way to impress the brass is to pick a name from the tally of executives, telephone the V.I.P. masquerading as a journalism student looking for a quote about the industry, and then barrage him/her with questions about the company. Don't be shy about reiterating your newfound knowledge along with its source to interviewers; they'll never look at you the same way again. You'll have gotten on the inside track and left your "chance applicant" status in the dust—along with the rest of the losers.

In the News

Time to wave good-bye to *MAD Magazine* and *Cosmo*. If you're hoping to join the white-collar ranks, you had better begin reading the proper literature. Business newspapers and magazines can provide you with updated and timely data. But if rifling through a mile-high stack of business periodicals unnerves you, head over to your library and conduct a magazine database search. *Forbes* and *Business Week* are the leaders, but there's more where these came from. The computerized scan won't steer you wrong, and you'll be able to print out articles directly from microfiche.

The Wall Street Journal is the official selection of executives nationwide. This paper gives most industries good play and is more informational than overwhelming. If you're interviewing with large corporations, always peruse this newspaper beforehand. But don't

When Silence Is Golden

At an interview, you are encouraged to talk about yourself; but do not mistake this curiosity for general acceptance. Certain things are better left unsaid. If the following phrases, or any variation on their themes, should ever pass your interviewing lips, don't come crying to us when you're given the old "we're going to be interviewing many candidates" dismissal.

- My old boss was an overbearing and manipulative liar.
- Your office is really small.
- I am an incorrigible procrastinator, a bad speller, and so on.
- I prefer to work alone.
- So how much funding do you have to back this position?
- I was fired.
- I am such a %#@*ing hard worker!
- Hey, you got a light?
- How about you and me discuss this over dinner, baby?
- Did you ever hear the one about the lesbian, the priest, and the little boy? Well . . .

count on this corporate news maverick to provide you with scoops on the smaller companies in your area; scan your city papers for the late-breaking stories in this arena. Heaven forbid that you lack an answer to the perennially favored question, "Why do you want to work for *this* company?" Employers want to feel as if they're special, and not just money in your bank. Paraphrase some of their positive news clippings, and you'll be going places soon.

Self-Analysis

While the environment is an important consideration, don't forget about the flip side—self-awareness. We don't mean the kind that you reach through long colloquies with your shrink, but the kind that allows you to see how you look in other people's eyes. And whatever conventional wisdom may have to say on the subject of judging a book by its cover, we believe it's safe to say that most people are not conventionally wise. Like any best-seller, you must pander to your public, through appearance as well as through content.

Groomsville

Your professional image can plummet if your look is not up to par. A common mistake college graduates make is skimping on the effort to maintain a polished personal appearance. Before an employer sees your work, they see you; and if you look messy, they will assume that your work is messy too. Aside from your performance, the company's image is at stake. As an employee, you are a representative of your company. And who wants a disheveled-looking representative? Even if you are considered a hot number by all MTV standards, you may strike out in the corporate world. Wild hair, nose rings, and flashy clothes will spell P-U-N-K to prospective employers, and these people are from the generation that still uses this word as an insult. So leave the night look for the clubs, and get ready for your corporate makeover.

1. *Hair.* Men should keep their locks trimmed and shave off any hint of goatee and sideburns. Parting with that precious stubble is a difficult thing for any young man; so make sure you have a couple of supportive friends around when you're

finally ready to take it all off. And don't be ashamed to cry. Getting it all out now will keep you from breaking up at the sight of any man sporting a five o'clock shadow.

Women need to tame their tresses before being seen in any work environment. The long hair you've been growing since birth need not automatically be brought under the knife, provided you come up with some creative ways to keep it out of your face.

2. *Makeup and cologne.* The question of fragrance is answered with a simple no. That goes for men and women. Don't take the chance of being turned down for a job just because someone doesn't agree with your scent. Obviously, body odor is never a welcome smell; so keep it clean folks. And tread lightly on the deodorant, since too much can be worse than the most unappetizing perfume.

Makeup is strictly off limits for men. While the CK's of the world are busy catering to men's newfound vanities, the employers are usually of a more traditional lot. If they spot eyeliner on you, it'll be as if you showed up at the meeting sporting a teddy.

Women are entitled to wear makeup, and are even encouraged to do so. All that PC stuff aside, a well-made-up face gives a woman polish and adds to her professional persona. But since anything resembling excess is ill-advised, keep it to a thin crepe instead of a thick pancake. This isn't a beauty pageant, nor is it a bordello; so bear in mind that heavy maquillage will definitely detract from your appeal.

3. *Clothes.* Gentlemen prefer suits; so don't start getting creative. You may feel stymied by the standard corporate getup, but don't try to bend the rules too much. If you want to distinguish yourself, wear a bold or patterned tie. It may even become a handy conversation piece when it comes time to break the ice.

Women have many options when it comes to professional apparel. Some choose pantsuits; others stick to the more widely accepted skirt. If you're of the latter persuasion, make sure the skirt isn't too short, too tight, or too flowy.

Also, keep close watch for runs in the hosiery. For you slacks gals, try not to mix pieces from different suits. You're already running the risk of being criticized as a nonconformist; so keep the look as traditional as possible.

Accessory guidelines parallel those for makeup. Men should not wear any. That's right; it's time to remove the earrings. Even the tiny diamond studs have to hit the jewelry box. The same goes for pinky rings, gold chains, and bracelets. Women are given more leeway in this department. A sparse exhibit of jewelry will not raise any eyebrows. But chunky bracelets, dangling earrings, and numerous rings can cost you the job.

Practice Your Presentation

You've doubtlessly heard of Darwin's theory of adaptive traits and the "use it or lose it" maxim. Take this rule into the interviewing realm. The more you use your interview muscle, the stronger it will become. So recruit as many people as possible to run through test interviews with you before you go in for the kill. Your friends and relatives are just part of the subject pool. Since all interviews follow some variation of the question-and-answer format, apply for even those jobs in which you have no interest. Through this repeated exposure, you'll adapt to the interview atmosphere and gain the confidence needed to succeed at the more high-stakes interview.

The Big Day

It's nine A.M. and your alarm has been ringing for the past twenty minutes. You realize that today's the day. The dream job is on the line. Are you nervous? Not a whit, if you followed the instructions. You know about the company's recent merger, and have considered a few of its implications. Your ensemble has been dry-cleaned and is ready to wear. Your hair is in tip-top condition, and—a big sigh of relief on your part—those three tattoos are all in discreetly hidden areas. Actually, you've been on so many of these test runs already that you're feeling a bit blasé about the whole thing. Perfect! Now go make everybody proud and give it your best shot!

The First Impression

Do you know that funny feeling you get when you're being watched? Well, you'll probably experience it tenfold as soon as you pass the company threshold. Go ahead and conjure up the spirit of the Outgoing Interview Person. Don't get all philosophical about it; you'll just have to be a fake and a phony . . . yes, all those things you've been brought up to deplore with self-righteous zeal. If you can get over your identification with Holden Caulfield (of *Catcher in the Rye* fame) long enough to make nice-nice with the receptionist and anyone else who passes you while you're stuck reading *U.S. News and World Report* in the holding cell—we mean the waiting room— you're halfway there.

While you're waiting, be sure to look poised and at ease. Don't give free reign to your nervous or just plain disgusting habits. Do not bite your nails, pick your nose, pace up and down the room, move your lips as you read, realign any private anatomy parts, and so forth. As you are probably well aware, cameras have been turning many department-store dressing rooms into human fishbowls—now what makes you think that the reception area is all that different. Make no mistake about it; someone is spying on you. So watch yourself.

Behind Closed Doors

You'll be either ushered in by the receptionist or greeted by Mr. Big himself. Here's your chance to exhibit that handshake. However, don't make this a power play. Too firm a grip makes you a threat. Ignorance is no excuse; know your own strength and temper it. For all you who dismiss the old handshake as an outmoded formality and don't even bother to grip, change your ways when meeting the potential boss. A simpering handshake sends out warning signals. While the hand may be weak, the message is strong: IMMATURE, LACKS CONFIDENCE, INDECISIVE, APATHETIC, NOT COMPANY MATERIAL! REJECT!

While a good grip is important, getting the job is not quite all in the wrist. The ability to maintain good eye contact with your inter- viewer says that you are unafraid and ready to cooperate. People who cannot maintain a fair amount of eye contact look as if they have something to hide, or are disinterested in what the other

Interview Formats

There's something you should know. Interviews, like people, come in all shapes and sizes, and each requires a different approach. Now all you have to do is look like you're enjoying it.

1. *The directed interview.* This interview is fairly straightforward and to the point. The interviewer goes through a list of standard questions. Your responses should be short but creative. Just because your interviewer is reading off a list doesn't mean you should forgo the ingenuity.

2. *The exam.* Whether the test is for typing, spelling, geography, or math, you'll be glad when it's over. And you thought your days of test taking were long gone! Employers often want to

person is saying. Look straight into your interrogator's eye, but don't try to stare down your interviewer in some misguided quest to prove how genuine and uninhibited you are. Aside from your old high school chums, it's rare that you'll find someone willing to engage in an all-out staring contest with you. Train yourself beforehand to give meaningful looks at the right time, and look away (with furrowed brow) whenever you get lost in thought. Averting your gaze at key moments can give the impression of serious concentration, and hide the "I wonder what's for lunch?" reality.

Another aspect of your image that you can monitor is body language. Your mouth isn't the only thing that's doing the talking. Your posture, hand gestures, and walk can all wreck an otherwise flawless interview. To avoid this, envision your idea of a professional and copy it as best you can. Your paragon of competence is probably not sitting slumped over in a chair, gesticulating wildly with his/her hands, and shuffling along like Ronald McDonald's friend Grimace. You already know what a professional would do. This is your chance to impersonate one without being charged with fraud.

Relax and Speak Easy

You're bound to get nervous at some point during the interview. Learning to stay calm will keep you from slipping into your Stuttering John mode. It's a fact that once the adrenaline starts flowing, speech patterns become somewhat distorted. One surefire way to stave off panic attacks is to enlist the aid of breathing exercises. There isn't an aerobics instructor alive who hasn't ordered his/her followers, "Don't forget to breathe!" While an interview is no step class, it does take endurance. So keep that oxygen circulating. Once the inhale and exhale are down pat, you too can sound broadcast are perfect.

The leading way to stay composed during the inquest is, of course, to see the process in perspective. You can do this through the philosophical approach: If you don't get the job, worse things have been known to happen. You cannot control how the recruiter feels and acts toward you; all you can control is how you react. Or you can take the approach known as the rationalization: If the interviewer is acting aloof, he or she is probably just intimidated by your self-confidence. If you don't get a position, the interviewer was probably too jealous of your fabulousness. If a joke fails, the interviewer has no sense of humor and is ugly to boot. Although this latter approach is not very constructive, it is a definite ego booster. And we all need a good shot of ego when we're on the interview circuit!

The Aftermath

When you interview smart, you never leave the office without finding out when you can expect to hear word of the decision. If you're having trouble obtaining a firm response, inform the screen that you'll be calling within such and such a time frame. Ignore any and all don't-call-us-we'll-call-you replies; you deserve to know as soon as the decision is made. Recall that your interview time, transportation costs, and pain and suffering were not compensated for, so this is the least they can give you for your trouble. In any case, if you don't show stick-to-itiveness—a word that businesses can't seem to get enough of these days—you'll never end up on top.

Follow Through

Thanks-for-letting-me-sweat-in-your-office-while-you-watched-callously letters are a critical factor in any successful job search. These should be mailed immediately after the interview. Here's your last chance to ingratiate yourself into the job. Write a brief synopsis of how interesting and informative the experience was and how excited you are to be considered for a position on their "team." Flattery followed by an overt display of confidence is always a good angle to take. One would have to a be regular Gargamel to burst your bubble—especially after you tried so hard to inflate theirs.

Here's another tip to get you right up there with the millennium's greatest masterminds: Send your professionally word-processed thank-you letter in a decorative envelope and address it in a big, flowery scrawl. Most employers discard notes of bogus thanks before you can say "but I slaved over it all day." Yours will appear like a card from an old friend or relative, and they're bound to give it the look-see it deserves. Never forget that all's fair in jobs and money.

Interview Formats (continued)

know if you cheated your way through college or concocted your high GPA. They think that by giving these moronic tests, they'll have a better grasp of the applicants' abilities. Our advice: Grin and bear it.

3. *The group interview.* This type of interview can be a real pressure cooker, especially if you're not comfortable speaking in front of groups. You will be asked questions by all those participating, so be prepared to concentrate. This type of interview makes it all too easy to get flustered, but by responding to one question at a time and taking pauses between answers, you will show them how capable you are of working under pressure.

Going, Going, Gone

Well hip, hip, hooray for you. The job is yours! Save the victory dance for later, and get down to brass tacks tout de suite. Negotiating a salary can be a tricky business. You stand the chance of having your bluff called, and then you're right back where you started. But that doesn't mean you're supposed to accept an indecent proposal. Some employers will want to take advantage of poor, starving college grads, and will get you all excited about working at their company, only to extend a salary offer that would make a high school student laugh. You'll have to fight for what's rightfully yours. That means knowing your cost of living and sticking up for yourself.

Avoid talking finances until you receive the offer. Then you will be informed of your starting salary and benefits plan. After you hear the first bid, tell the employer that you are grateful for the offer but will need a few days to consider the proposal. Even if the offer is more than generous, avoid accepting right off the bat and, come what may, stifle that cheer of triumph. Wait a few days, and then go in for the kill. Always add on five thousand to the starting price. If the employer takes the bait, you're in; but if he/she won't budge, you'll have to decide once and for all. Don't base your decision on what you think you should be making. Entry-level salaries are often very low, starting anywhere from high teens to low twenties.

If you're somewhat content with the distribution of funds and are ready to merge forces, make sure you have the offer in writing. If you haven't discussed health insurance and other benefits, like a 401(K) plan and vacation time, do so immediately. Then request that everything be outlined in your contract; otherwise don't sign on the dotted line. You have rights, and if something looks amiss (like the addendum stating Tuesdays will be the day you clean out the office fridge), then it's time to go back to the bargaining table—that is, if you're still interested.

Perseverance

It's all too easy to get discouraged during the purgatorial task of finding a job. You may feel like you're climbing a ladder with no end in sight. Forget about the corporate ladder—you should be so lucky! You can only dream of climbing those steps. For now, you're probably more interested in just getting hired—anywhere. What happened to all that brash self-confidence? Is it old age or is it unemployment that's finally getting to you? Everyone feels victimized by the system at one point or another during their job hunt, but that's part of the deal. If you mean to prevail, you must persist and never lose sight of your goal. Going to countless interviews, sending out hundreds of resumes, and winding up with bags of rejection letters would try even Gandhi's patience. Rejection can be looked at in one of two ways: (1) You are a retarded fool who can't make it in the real world. (2) Someone had more experience or more important connections in his/her family tree. You're better off subscribing to the second explanation. It will keep you from assuming the popular victim mentality that has brought such a financial windfall to the American Psychiatric Association. And since you don't even have the health insurance to cover a residence on the shrink's couch, we recommend you view each disappointment as a lesson. As long as you learn from each failure, you'll be one success after another.

> *I was exasperated with looking for work. I was perfectly qualified for a position at a record company. I had completed two internships and worked at a record store practically since birth. But it seemed that everybody knew somebody in the business, and I was definitely out of the loop. The industry was so tightly saturated that I couldn't even score a seat by the phones. All the while, I'm thinking that I went to college, phi beta kappa, and he wonders if I can answer a phone?! How humiliating. The future seemed really grim, and I was tired of waiting tables just to support myself. So I decided to focus on finding another job. One day this guy sits down in my section and starts to chat me up. He's asking me whether I'm an actress, and I'm thinking he's another tool trying to be cute. I wanted a tip, so I asked him what he did. Lo and behold, he worked at Electra Records, and knew of some entry-level positions. With his recommendation, I finally broke into the industry.*
> —AMY, COLUMBIA UNIVERSITY, '96

Finding a job can take anywhere from a few days to a couple of years. What happens in the meantime, however, can teach you a lot about who you are and what you want to accomplish.

The Boomerang Effect

There may come a time when the interviewer will turn the tables. Don't freak out if you don't have your pen and paper ready. Just look at this situation as an opportunity to find out if the company is right for you. Figure out what you're looking for and fire when ready. Here are some ideas to get you started:

- How long has this position been open?
- What is this company's/department's employee turnover rate?
- Who would be my supervisor?
- What is the advancement potential?
- Does the company provide any training programs?
- How do you like working here?
- How long have you worked here?
- In which position did you start out?

CORNER OFFICE

Chapter Six

YOUR PROFESSIONAL IDENTITY

RECEPTION DESK

Now that you're finally employed and contributing to the GNP like a responsible citizen, you've some decisions to make. You could slide by like many did in college or you could turn yourself around and become an overachiever. Imagine your workplace as Dante's *Inferno*. As a beginner, you are in the ninth circle, the hottest and least comfortable place. Unlike hell, of course, the work world gives you an opportunity to climb your way out of the broiler and into a sunshine-filled room called the corner office.

Your professional identity will determine whether you'll remain stuck in a thankless and often boring job or whether you'll move on to greener pastures fraught with the opportunity to wield some real power and make serious decisions. You have very little time to decide how you will tackle your job, as the impression made in the first few months is a lasting one. So once you get in there, don't expect anything to be handed to you on a silver platter. Your initial assignments will elicit thoughts such as, "A trained monkey could do this!" and "I didn't realize I had applied for a custodial position!" But if you grin and bear it, you'll eventually move on. When the next new kid arrives on the block, you'll either be in a position of seniority or acting the part of the rookie at some other locale. It's up to you whether your career moves are vertical or lateral, but as things stand, you have no place to go but up.

GETTING A FOOTHOLD

Your first day on the job may be a disappointment. You probably expected an office but received something called a cubicle, which, frankly, looks more like a cubbyhole to you. Then, you thought you'd be given an assignment and the opportunity to display your abilities right off the bat, but instead you were presented with a stack of books or made to follow some numbskull around all day. Well, you can't do much about your workstation just yet, but if you hit those books and learn from watching how others perform, you'll be displaying your acumen and garnering applause soon enough. Just worry about learning the ropes and impressing the bigwigs upstairs, and the workstation situation will take care of itself.

You've Got a Lot to Learn

Don't be insulted if you're not trusted with responsibility upon arrival. Look at the first three weeks on the job as a training period. You're just learning your way around. How are you supposed to handle any serious business if you don't know where the bathrooms are, much less who's who in the corporate hierarchy? So now that you're officially "in," use all the learn-the-ropes time you're granted to your advantage. The day when you are given your chance to shine will come sooner than you think. If you're caught off guard, you could be back on the outside looking in.

Training Programs

Companies of the Fortune 500 variety often offer training seminars. These may be on-site or in an altogether different city. Many government agencies also follow this style of training. What happens, in a nutshell, is that all of the new recruits are given a time and place to begin the learning process. If you're forced to relocate for this crash course, chances are you'll be getting dumped in with new employees from across the nation. Once you show up, it's company business from dawn to dusk. Going back to school may not be what you bargained for, but this is a love-it-or-leave-it proposition. If you can't at least pretend to be psyched about every aspect of the company, you'll be served walking papers.

Watch and Learn

Smaller companies do not usually have the kind of funds that can set you up with a month-long intensive-training period. Such courses usually involve hotels, conference rooms, and money spent paying you for producing absolutely nothing; thus, the smaller corporations have you train on the job. Such a method will either give you carte blanche to ask questions or will have you writing notes as you shadow some none-too-thrilled employee about the office. No matter what strategy your company uses, the point is to get you on your feet as soon as possible. Even if you're not feeling pressured, use this time to get on the ball. You may not hit a homer your first time at bat, but if you observe carefully, at least you won't strike out and embarrass yourself.

The Corporate Subtext

By now you're old enough to know that what you see is not always what you get, and that there's more to life than meets the eye. This conventional wisdom goes double for the world of work, where survival of the fittest has been perfected into an art form. Your office is all about subtlety. Smooth operations and cold calculations are what lurk beneath deceptively open faces. Everyone's working an angle. We do not recommend asking anyone about theirs directly. First law of the land: Thou shalt keep your advancement agenda and all correlating strategies strictly confidential.

Because you're still the novice and haven't worked out a scheme, you're above reproach. Nevertheless, you will be watched carefully, because an innocent person is also a dangerous one. If you're Mr. Clean, who's to say you won't soon be tidying up the office? This doesn't mean that you should go out and rob the postage meter just to get accepted. What you should do is watch your back, even if you are the office goody-goody.

You'll also be tested. When the corporate atmosphere gets stale, it's always fun to get a beginner and play How much will the neophyte bend? If you don't want to end up as the human pretzel, you'd better set some basic ground rules. Again, you can't just breeze in and refuse to perform the grunt work thrown your way. After you see how things are done, you'll know when and how to say, "NO! ASK ME AGAIN AND YOU'RE ROADKILL, BUSTER!"

The Buddy System

Use all of your charm to land a seasoned company veteran for a pal. No matter how high your fear of intimacy, this is one mutually advantageous relationship to which you need not be afraid to commit. Since you'll be judged by the company you keep, the only complicated aspect of this union is picking your mentor. Stick with a few basic guidelines, and you won't wind up with a loser. First of all, your corporate guru should be someone well respected by the firm. This individual should also be established, since competition is the last thing you need from a mentor. You should also feel comfortable in his or her presence. Finally, whoever you decide on should be willing to play coach to your rookie.

Once you've chosen your guide, you need only approach him/her with your plan. You're a wide-eyed tenderfoot in search of good advice. What kind of a person could turn down such a flattering request? If you are shot down, never fear. There are others who would love to help you out. Just proceed to your alternative. Even if an older and wiser colleague doesn't come to your rescue, there are plenty of people who would join forces with you on a more equal footing. Sometimes all you really need is an ally to make work easier. Just remember that whether it be a mentor or a peer, make sure (s)he's in good standing with the higher-ups.

THE POLITICAL CLIME

The workplace is a regular hotbed of gossip and intrigue. The more people you've got on your crew, the steamier the temperature. With all those eyes watching, those mouths talking, and those ears listening, it could get so that a person is afraid to venture two feet from his/her desk. Paranoia is not uncommon. Where do you think the phrase "the walls have ears" comes from? But don't worry; if you learn to play the game, office politics is by no means a no-win situation. And, just to clue you in, if you're not playing, chances are you're being played. So, if you want to set the company on its ear, keep yours to the ground.

Office Political Success Story

It's not as complex as you may imagine. While everyone has a career path all laid out in their minds, you as rookie will not often be involved. Staying up nights concocting ornate scenarios of how Bill wants to get you out of the way, or how Heather is probably snooping through your desk while you're at lunch is highly discouraged. This all-too-prevalent first-job suspicion will sooner land you in the cuckoo's nest than the higher-income tax bracket. "Trust no one" may be a popular line of movie dialogue, but, as real-life advice, it simply doesn't hold water. Let people earn your trust and don't start swapping recipe secrets until you know your words will go no further.

Pick a Winner

You know the mentor is a bust when . . .

- (S)he hits you up for a loan.
- (S)he verbally abuses you.
- (S)he gets caught red-handed with the petty cash.
- (S)he tells you to get lost.
- (S)he tries to play footsie with you under the conference table.

Whether you like your job or are just in it for the money, never, ever use the following set of sorry excuses. Even if you are doing a first-rate job, giving this type of lip service will ensure that no one remembers the first thing about your accomplishments:

- "I ran out of time."
- "It's all her fault."
- "I forgot."
- "My nails were wet."
- "The janitor must have taken it."
- "I'm just on edge."

Correct Yourself

What with the bad press and all, you may have learned to laugh at political correctness by now. But when it comes to work, this is no laughing matter. Look around. People are defensive and probably with good reason. There's Ruth, a strong proponent of affirmative action. Then again, there's Peter, complaining about the reverse discrimination his kids are suffering. And who can forget Alice with the glass-ceiling-sized chip on her shoulder? These are just the kind of observations that should never pass your lips. Of course, they should be kept in mind, as these are the thoughts that will dictate the taboo joke subjects. No matter how well a Paglia or a Limbaugh may argue against it, PC is alive and kicking in the corporate office building.

Friend or Foe?

Figure out which coworker will rat you out the second you leave your desk a minute too soon before quitting time and which one will cover for you when you decide to take that hush-hush day off. You can imagine what a boon such omniscience would be to your working life, but may wonder how to attain it. Look no further than the employees themselves. If you watch their actions and listen to their words, you'll soon spot the weasels. Go out to lunch with the staff, share experiences, get to know them. Okay, so your office mates aren't necessarily going to become lifelong buds, but they can help you to pass the time. And how else are you ever going to figure out who's got the evil eye for whom? Do not do anything stupid like break into the personnel files. Such files are strictly confidential and kept under lock and key. And should you get caught diddling the keyhole with a paper clip, you'll be fired forthwith. That means no severance pay.

If a friend is what you want, a friend is what you must be. Help someone out with a rush report, and they could be the first in line to assist you in your hour of need. Just as we can all be sure to get our fifteen minutes of fame, we can all bank on that sixty minutes of need. So get over yourself. If you're not planning shelter from a whole day's worth of rain, at least plan for a rainy lunch.

HANDLING THE BOSS

You probably think your boss exists for the sole purpose of making your life miserable. The media often paints these authority figures as vulgar, demanding, and unjust. Consider the flicks *9 to 5, A Christmas Tale,* and *Working Girl*, or cartoons like "The Flintstones," "The Jetsons," and "The Simpsons." From childhood through adulthood we're told that bosses have control over our lives. In real life, however, you'll encounter bosses who spring for office pizza parties every Wednesday as well as those who force you to have their coffee ready and waiting at nine o'clock sharp. The sadistic boss stereotype does have some exemplars in reality, but most employers don't make a practice of cracking the whip. If they did, employees would be striking around the clock. In fact, supervisors are just human beings whose main goals in life are something other than kicking you around. So give the chief some slack, and leave preconceived notions at home. You and your boss are in the same boat, and must find a way to work together effectively. If both parties cooperate, you may have very little to complain about.

A Team Effort

Once you substitute the "boss as ruler of the underworld" mentality with the "boss as fearless leader," you can begin to build a relationship based on mutual respect. Think of your boss as the captain of a team; and without you, the starting lineup, the team would have very little chance of scoring. Remember, the boss needs you as much as you need him/her. Neither of you can make it on your own. On-the-job success depends entirely on your ability to work together.

Voice Concerns

Unity can only be established when both you and the boss have a clear understanding of each other's expectations. You may think that arriving a fashionable five minutes late here and there is no big deal, but your boss may be inclined to disagree. (S)he may forgo mentioning the problem, but the resentment will build up all the same. How is that your problem? Well, the fifth Friday evening spent toiling over a pile of "last-minute" assignments should show you that as tension mounts, so does your workload.

If both you and your boss keep silent about your grievances, there's very little chance of their going away. Sooner or later, you'll both get fed up and begin to act out of spite—maybe even going so far as to sabotage one another. This is not teamwork. This is anarchy. So if you want to come out of the office building whistling a happy tune, be ready to ask the boss what (s)he expects of you, as well as to disclose how you, in turn, expect to be treated. Just so there's no confusion, sticking up for your rights will not get you fired if done with tact and finesse. And once you and the boss have a mutual understanding, working in sync will be a breeze.

Study the Boss

Your superior has his/her own share of responsibilities and duties to perform. Make your boss's life easier by figuring out what his/her work priorities are and then helping to manage them. Anticipating your supervisor's needs will make you the top promotion contender, or will get you a top-notch review when the time rolls around. "I already took care of that" is music to any boss's ears. Say that phrase enough times and everyone will know that you're not the kind who needs constant supervision; you care enough to go the extra mile. If you're fielding calls while the manager is out of town, for example, don't simply jot down the messages or page him every chance you get. Try to handle matters yourself. If you know what must be done, and do it before being asked, your boss will soon realize what a great asset you are.

Responsibility Is Not a Four-Letter Word

The "not me" mindset is a liability in the corporate world. Whether the superiors need someone to put on the Kit Cat account or to lay the blame on for a big business boo-boo, praying that you're not the patsy is the wrong approach. Whenever a new project comes up and all hands stay down, go ahead and raise yours—even if only to make a suggestion. Stepping out of the line of fire when the executives are on the warpath is just another way of shirking responsibility. You have to give the impression that you can handle anything, and that includes owning up to your mistakes. If the boss demands an explanation, don't ever pass the buck if you were somehow at fault. Instead, say, "It will never happen again," and make sure it doesn't.

Extra work won't kill you. But if you already have more work than you can handle, the thought of taking charge of new projects is about as appealing as a hole in the head. On the other hand, if your job gives you a great deal of thumb-twiddling time, then taking on extra work is exactly the route you should be following. Take control and be a leader. Once you accept responsibility for completing a project, you can recruit assistance. This will be easier to obtain once the accountability is placed squarely on your shoulders. After all, it's only your reputation at stake if something goes wrong, and should everything work out splendidly, everyone who contributed gets a pat on the back.

It's Not Personal

Professional criticism from your boss must be taken in stride. That's what (s)he's there for and you'll not learn any other way. Wait a second . . . you didn't actually think you were perfect, did you? If your boss decides to give you some feedback, resist the urge to cry, yell, or defend yourself. It will only make you look like a college kid begging for extra credit. This is what is called tough love. Your boss probably hates this part of the job and feels terrible each time (s)he excoriates your performance.

With this in mind, you must take all reprimands very seriously. Talk to your manager when you feel you've improved, and find out whether the feeling is mutual. If you blow off your boss, (s)he'll soon tire of making the effort to clue you in to how much your work sucks. You'll be passed over for promotions, stiffed in the salary-increase department, and the first to fall prey to the axe of corporate downsizing.

The Terrorist Exception

If your boss is truly a bully and blames you for things that are really not your fault, you must alter your strategy. Ignore the first few accusations altogether. Instead of letting this unceremonious treatment affect your performance, just shake it off. Tell yourself that your boss is clearly a moron who doesn't know diddly-squat about management. Remind yourself that if you keep up the good work, you'll soon have his/her job.

If the obnoxious behavior persists and you are repeatedly accused unjustly, take matters into your own hands. Explain that you are not to blame, along with a play-by-play of what actually happened. If this tactic proves ineffectual, consider the otherwise unthinkable—going over the boss's head. With the situation quickly heating up, what can you possibly stand to lose? Keep a log of all your activities so that when you're pushed to the brink of termination, you'll have something to back up your claims.

Social Hour

There is no law stating that you and your boss should not be on friendly terms. Some people are actually quite close with their bosses and vice-versa. They may take each other out to lunch, bake each other pies, and provide each other support in times of crisis. It all depends on the personalities involved. You are more likely to get along with your boss if he/she is slightly older and doesn't constantly pull rank. If you find that you and your boss have a lot in common, personally as well as professionally, don't stress about taking the alliance to the next level. It is not uncommon to invite your boss over for dinner, do lunch, and even go on trips. Just make sure you don't use the friendship to slack off on the job. It's easy to forget that even though you had a wild night on the town with your friend, the boss still expects you to be sharp and ready for action come Monday morning. If your work begins to suffer, the chief may finally pass on the buddy thing altogether. (S)he may think that you were being nice to get out of having to work for a living. If that's the case, you'll be exposed soon enough.

I began working as a legal assistant right after college. My boss, Larry, was only eight years older than me, and we loved to shoot the breeze at work. We would head out to the local deli for lunch almost every day. Larry was a real loon and always asked if he could go out and meet some of the younger chicks with me and my friends. We hit the casinos together, and he even invited me to meet his family. I was thrilled to have stumbled upon such a cool and laid-back boss. Since he and I talked for hours about nothing in particular, I naturally assumed that if Larry wasn't around, I could talk on the phone all I wanted. Although my productivity levels plummeted, I thought Larry wouldn't mind. I was wrong. When he realized that I was not getting anything accomplished and was talking on the phone with pals besides, he had no qualms about giving me the boot. I realized, albeit too late, that no matter how solid the employer/employee relationship, certain behaviors are never acceptable.

—PAUL, UNIVERSITY OF NEVADA,'94

Stand Up and Applaud!

Give yourself a big round of applause whenever possible. Go ahead, you deserve it. Pat on the back are rare in the corporate world, even when you are doing more than your fair share. People are either too busy or too envious to notice your handiwork. Your boss may or may not be aware of your progress, and it will be up to you to spread the word. Each time you do something above and beyond the call of duty or find a better and faster way of accomplishing a task, notify your boss about it. Say that (s)he may also need to know how to expedite this task or use this program in the near future and that you have found a way to save precious time. Instead of coming off like a braggart, you'll appear to have your manager's best interests at heart. One such crafty maneuver may find you a permanent place on the boss's good side.

Another way to make your supervisor notice you is to encourage all satisfied clients to call in and voice their appreciation of your talents directly to your boss. Subtly inform them that you're having a hard time with your boss, but that such a call can make a huge difference in your office image. If you get enough calls, the company may create an Employee of the Month Award just for you.

Time Will Tell

Playing nice with the boss can be a difficult proposition. After many spurned efforts to get along, you may just decide that what you two have are irreconcilable differences. You'll find that time and patience are on your side when it comes to buttering up the boss. (S)he may just be a big softy with a gruff manner. If his/her habits are strange and his/her moods volatile, study them carefully to figure out how to deal.with them. After you're duly informed about your boss's quirks, getting along will be much easier. Learning what your boss is all about is just a part of adapting to your new environment. If (s)he's cranky Mondays, you'll know to steer clear. You'll also know not to ask for time off when you can see that the boss is frazzled. Think about it. Isn't that the least you would do for a friend? So why not for a paycheck?

BUSINESS ETIQUETTE

Doing the right thing should come naturally to us, but for some reason most people are at a loss when it comes to the simplest matters. Just think of all the commotion that would be avoided if people had the sense to do the following: dress casual on Fridays, conduct themselves properly at company picnics and office parties, and keep their opinions to themselves. Be consoled. If you're unsure of how to handle a situation at work, others are probably as confused as you are. You will have to appropriate a whole new set of traits once you set foot into the work world. But it's not as complicated as it seems. There will be a few rules to adhere to, and some pitfalls to avoid, so listen up and never again be accused of gross impropriety—at least not on the job.

Personal Habits

You'd be surprised at how many people still have the audacity, the raw nerve, and the outright gall to chew with their mouths open, swear, chomp gum, and adjust their various private parts right in the office. Your professional image should not be lost as soon as the job is landed. You should keep up appearances as long as you're in uniform.

Bubble Gum Politics

Imagine that you're busy working away, scrambling at breakneck speed to finish the proposal you were supposed to have on your boss's desk yesterday, when the big Kahuna himself/herself sidles by and asks you how you're doing. Just as your eyes meet, you obliviously emit a large bubble the likes of which even the *Guinness Book* has yet to record. She looks at you with terror as you make a pathetic attempt to appear dignified while scraping the gum residue off your face. But the damage is done. It's too late. So, how do you avoid this horrific scenario? Leave the Bazooka at home, kids. Even if you can resist the urge to blow bubbles, who's to say that your incessant jaw work won't incense the higher-ups? They're probably much older, and if they could, they would probably force you to sit through an entire day with that gum affixed firmly to the tip of your nose. So bypass the gum, and reach for a breath mint instead.

One Drink Too Many

You'll be coaxed and cajoled to drink alcohol during many office outings,s at which alcohol consumption is not only condoned but encouraged. If you venture out with a superior or an important client, and he/she suggests you throw back a few, by all means partake. There's no sense in being antisocial, and you just may insult the big shot by refusing. But stick to one drink and one drink only. Make it last by nursing it throughout the meeting. If you're egged on to drink more, explain that your tolerance is rock-bottom low. Exceeding your limit could mean losing your edge and getting sloppy. In an uninhibited moment, you might say and do what you otherwise wouldn't. Clients and supervisors are the last people with whom you should take such a risk.

Happy hour with coworkers should also be monitored in terms of alcohol consumption. Even though they seem like your friends and act like the best of chums, how do you know they're not out to get you talking about inappropriate subjects with which to later feed the rumor mill? Even if they're on the level, suppose you lose control and go off with Benny from accounting for an evening of fun and games. The next morning he's at your desk with bagels and coffee:

Topics to Avoid

Being on good terms with your boss is great, as long as you maintain some semblance of distance. There's no reason why your boss should know anything about your:

- Sex life
- Psychoanalytic therapy
- Drug and alcohol use
- Violent outbursts on the home front
- Bizarre recurrent nightmare
- Honest opinion about coworkers

"Hi honey bunny!" Aargh! Maybe we're a bit paranoid, but isn't it better to err on the side of caution and decline that second drink?

Feeding Frenzy

Eating gracefully may take practice. Whether you're out with the boss or some other bigwigs, chew with your mouth closed; that means no talking mid-bite. Another food no-no is the messy dish—that is, buffalo wings, sloppy joes, spare ribs, or spaghetti. Limit yourself to those foods that call for a knife and fork. Silverware is the only civilized way to go. Also, contrary to popular belief, the salad is not easy to eat daintily. You'll end by having gigantic lettuce leaves hanging out of your mouth, and dressing on your lip, which is not the most professional demeanor. So unless you're a seasoned salad eater, look no further than the steak or fish entrees. Let the others order what they will. Once you obtain more clout, you too can be as messy as you please.

You should also remember that the desk is no substitute for the cafeteria. Imagine your department head's dismay when (s)he brings over some clients to meet you, and your handshake leaves grease stains on every right cuff. There's also the pungent odor of your nuked gyros to consider. If lunch is looming distant on your horizon, but you've got the snack attacks, go for a candy bar. They really do satisfy.

Smoking in the Boys' Room

By now most towns have very strict public building smoking ordinances. Most offices have even stricter office policies and would rather have you freeze in subzero temperatures than set up a smokers' lounge. Those of you working at such offices will have to resist the temptation to light up in the bathroom, the stairwell, or the broom closet. Imagine the alternative: getting busted for smoking! Come wintertime, bundle up and think of your Siberian exile as a much-needed escape from the confines of the office building. You'll also get a chance to bond with other smokers. Higher levels of the hierarchy are also prone to nic fits on occasion, so you may just get a chance to do some power networking.

Hygiene

Brushing your teeth on a daily basis and taking showers and washing your hair regularly can all contribute to your job success. Imagine working with someone whose idea of good hygiene amounts to changing their clothes every day and showering once a week. Such a lack of self-preservation, if you will, can get very distracting, and people will tend to gravitate away from such a person. Remember that you have a responsibility to maintain a clean lifestyle. You're the fresh new face in the office, so make sure you live up to that description.

Tidy Up

Folklore has it that a cluttered desk denotes a scattered mind. While your enlightened brain may balk at this old wives' tale, your boss could very well still be in the dark age. Don't hang up a sign that reads "If you think this is bad, you should have seen Einstein's office." Instead of trying to debunk the myth, simply keep your desk clean. All work-related materials can be neatly organized into binder bins and filing cabinets. Don't let the papers pile up. Once you're done with a particular assignment, collect all of the paperwork and place it in the corresponding file. Just five minutes per day will keep you from misplacing vital data and wasting precious time in useless searches— that's what we call five minutes well spent.

Also, your desk is not a display case for your party photos, stuffed animal collection, or moldy coffee mugs. Keeping your desk free of such personal items will give you that professional demeanor. If you're looking to jazz up the space, a plant is always a nice touch. A large, brightly colored calendar can show that you're schedule oriented. The idea is to keep out anything that has "I'm still an immature young'un" written all over it.

Interpersonal Skills

Communicating with your coworkers can turn into one set of crossed wires after another. But as always, there's the polite way to behave and the crude way. If you were an undisciplined and willful child, hopefully, somewhere along the line, you learned the fine art of civility. The work environment will demand that you refrain from hitting, biting, and scratching your colleagues, as well as adhere to a few other guidelines.

Watch Your Mouth

However tempting it may be to swear and use foul language of any kind, don't do it. It may put your image as a pro in grave danger. You are not at a truck rally and your friends are not around to second your motions. If you feel the urge to spew expletives, inhale deeply and count to ten. One method that works for us is to sit quietly at our desks and, in muted tones, mumble in a foreign language every conceivable @%$*&#! that we've ever been taught. Ahhh! You can feel the sinuses clearing already. If you want to get across how cross you really are, use only those substitutes that three out of four grand-mothers recommend. You can be just as emphatic with "fudge," "oh gosh," "darn it all," "what the heck," and "shoot." That will show them!

Controlling Your Emotions

Billy had no excuse for taking credit for your ad idea, and Amanda could have shown more consideration when your cat died. But is storming in like a disgruntled postal worker going to ameliorate your situation? Even though this fascist crew may be bad, the prison populace is probably only marginally better. And then there's that awful prison fare to put up with. Artillery being out of the question, what is left for you to do? Even in the face of the meanest and most diabolical, you must swallow your anger and smile. This way, even if some schmo gets under your skin like a thick splinter, (s)he'll at least lack the satisfaction of knowing it. Playing tough will show fellow workers that you're not one to be pushed around. Emotional people are the scapegoats of any office, so wise up and bite your lip if necessary. Unless you're ready with a convincing, rational, and succinct argu-ment, the fury of your indignation will not win you any points.

Dangerous Liaisons

You can have a love affair with your work, just don't have one at your work. Some of you lucky ones won't have to wrestle with your urges, as no one in the office has what it takes to ring that bell. But if your department is a regular den of the bold and beautiful, crushes may develop. Spending forty-plus hours with the same people each week may make it difficult to keep your distance. With the pull of animal magnetism going strong for eight hours each day, is it any wonder that so many people save that midnight oil for late night, desktop massages? At first, the affair may be more fun than a box of brownies. There's the copy machine, the sexy e-mail, and the sharing of a secret. And who can forget the meaningful glances and stolen elevator moments? NEVERTHELESS—and by the way, we're sorry to be dropping a bucket of cold water on you—STEER CLEAR OF OFFICE ROMANCES! All professional relationships should be kept strictly on the up-and-up. It only takes one person and the news is spread all over, up, and down the hierarchy. If you think breaking up is hard to do, imagine the aftermath of an office romance breakup. Day in and day out, the person who dumped you is before your very eyes, talking on the phone, laughing it up—probably with her new and more attractive boyfriend, for all you know. Learn the mantra and spare yourself the torment: Business is business and pleasure is pleasure, and ne'er the two shall meet.

The Office Etiquette Hodgepodge

When it comes to privacy, don't count on getting any at the office. After-hours desk inspections are the boss's way of saying (s)he cares. Don't start in on that "oh no, not my boss" nonsense. Any boss who's of sound mind will check your workstation drawers for crossword puzzles, stolen office supplies, and dead bodies in the blink of an eye.

E-Mail

In these advanced times, your e-mail folders speak volumes about your lost time from work and low productivity level. Don't use

Top Five Reasons Not to Have Workplace Affairs

1. Paula Jones
2. Anita Hill
3. Demi Moore in *Disclosure*
4. Demi Moore in *St. Elmo's Fire*
5. Bob Packwood

e-mail to vent nasty thoughts about anyone at the office, because, as things stand, someone will most likely read your mail.

Another rule to keep in mind is that you shouldn't send more than two personal e-mails per day. If your boss, while putting in another late night at the office, just happens upon your mail and notices that within the span of one hour you managed to send ten electronic missives—detailing your designer drug habit—to your best friend, prepare to clean out your desk come morning. Any personal or risqué mail should either be trashed upon receipt, or copied onto your own private disk (and never leave your disk at work). Look at the supervisor as the Orwellian Big Brother; to him/her, nothing is sacred.

Phones

Again, the term *use sparingly* comes to mind. If you absolutely must check in with the gang at least twice a day, wait until your superior is out of the office to start tying up the lines. Should your boss catch you with your pals, don't sweat it. As far as (s)he's concerned, it's your first personal call of the day, and an honest-to-goodness emergency to boot.

Dress for Success

Your wardrobe may have to undergo major reconstruction if you want to measure up to the office policies. Of course, all workplaces set their own rules, which can often differ dramatically. Comparing the dress code of an investment banking firm with that of a city newspaper, for example, is more like comparing bananas with grapes than apples with oranges. If your company's policy is so conservative that it has you longing for the freedom of the Victorian era, you'd better invest in a subscription to *Modern Maturity*. This magazine offers plenty of tips on how to dress conservatively. Get ready to maintain that look for the long haul. Don't try to mix it up as soon as you've swapped jokes with the other suits. You may be more comfortable, but the rules will not have changed and neither should your appearance.

The casual workplace can seem a breeze in relation to its uptight brother. A no-holds-barred policy can mean whoopee! or it can mean trouble. If there's a distinct lack of guidelines to keep you from going overboard, the responsibility to arrive at the job in appropriate gear is all on your shoulders. A "casual" dress code does not imply an anything goes free-for-all. You're still expected to appear somewhat employee-like. Look around you. Are the other workers wearing sweats, baring their midriffs, and paying homage to Bart Simpson with their shirts? If not, chances are you can forget the dress code as long as you don't break it.

TGIF

The fact that such an acronym exists is sad in itself. But what's even more pathetic is that many companies are giving the axe to their Casual-Fridays policy because many people, of whom you may very well be one, abuse their casual-dress privileges. As we just explained, *casual* is not synonymous with *sloppy*. What then is it? In the interest of Casual Fridays nationwide, we have decided to clue in some of you less-coordinated individuals.

This special day is all about the proper mixture of apparel—a nightmare for those who cannot see past the two-piece suit. This weekly gift from senior management need not turn into a punishment for you. Take your comfy new jeans or chinos and combine them with a blouse/shirt or sweater. Throw a blazer over the ensemble, and you're laid back in full effect. The look you're going for is *Great Gatsby* meets *Annie Hall*. If you're still having trouble, it's straight to the fashion mags for you. Find a look you like and emulate it as closely as possible. Look for items resembling your ideal in style rather than in price. Imitation should remain the highest form of flattery, not the leading cause of bankruptcy. If you've mixed and matched every item that your closet and Banana Republic have to offer, all to no avail, don't despair. Help is just a toll-free phone call away. Dial 1-800-DOCKERS. A casual counselor is standing by to lend you an ear along with some solid advice.

The Dreaded Barbecue

This event is a favorite with the executives. They get to meet the little people and feel good about providing the masses with jobs. These outings can really do a number on any self-respecting person.

Here—on your day off—you are expected to eat processed meats and pretend to be having fun as you pucker up to the boss. More chips anyone? A game of volleyball? How about another brewski, sir? And the more the environment changes, the more your stature in the hierarchy remains the same. Even though the Head Honcho doesn't have an athletic bone in his entire body, you're still expected to behave as though you like the wretch. Beating your boss in anything even remotely resembling a sporting event is strictly out of bounds. Letting the bully have his way may not give you any immediate satisfaction—especially if he starts in with that "So what do you say? Pretty good for an old man" business—but you'll be glad you did once you're back in the office.

Ho! Ho! Ho!

The holiday season can take a toll on employees. Office parties are none too fun when keeping to the two-drink cocktails-with-the-enemy limit. Neither is the whirlwind of cookie baking, presents shopping, and feigning of gift-induced pleasure as full of Yuletide cheer as you may have remembered.

So why are the work-related festivities such a killjoy? Well, it all starts with the parties. Considering that the boss is plowed, the executive assistant, Rob, is hanging all over you, and you're dying for a drag in a smoke-free room, is it any wonder you're having a hard time keeping that frown upside down? If you've a hankering for some real merry-making, go home and have fun with your friends or family. Make an appearance at each office party, sample the wares, and then get the dickens out of there. Leave little suspicion about your loyalty to the company by bringing "homemade" goodies. There's no need to slave over a hot stove. Simply buy some bakery fare, place it in an ornate tin/plastic container, and present it at the party as your own handiwork. If it looks like you slaved all night, no one will think twice about your hasty exit.

Gifts impose yet another conundrum upon the fatigued minds of employees. All offerings should be thought out well in advance. For your own sake, purchase these gifts before the department stores get mobbed by last-minute shoppers. Your boss makes more money than you, so don't break your bank to get her/him something (s)he already has, in multiple colors. And you don't want your boss to think that you're trying to buy her/his good opinion; (s)he may go out of his/her way to show you the error of your ways. Besides, your raise won't come any time soon if your expenditures say that you're raking in more than you know what to do with.

A considerate gift is one that's based on the person's need and personality. Simplify the gift-giving ordeal by asking your coworkers about their weekend activities. Sports fans love anything with their favorite team's logo, and the rugged outdoorsmen/women appreciate your concern when you present them with a first-aid kit. And those who read during their lunch break will not object to your adding yet another book to their collection. If you're confronted by a real enigma, there's always the bookstore gift certificate.

SELF-PROMOTION

Publicists work day and night to bring positive attention to their clients. You'll have to work even harder to give your name its due recognition. Every task you complete, project you put together, and deal you close should be announced and run through the office grapevine. Most companies have a network of unrecorded information circulating at all times. That accomplishments aren't given top billing in print doesn't mean they cannot feature prominently in the collective office subconscious. Nothing is more aggravating than having to listen to a coworker's success story when you know full well that you're getting twice as much done in half the time. If you're not motivated enough to blow your own horn, be prepared to sit on the sidelines watching the careers of others take off. There are two parts to every job: the part you give to the advancement of the company and the part you give to your own advancement. You bear the burden of advertising your progress to anyone who'll listen. You cannot afford to forgo the self-promotion. Food for deep thought: If you work yourself ragged and no one's around to see it, did it really happen?

Leader of the Pack

One sure way to get your name in corporate lights is to be different. You can go with the tried-and-true methods taught at training sessions or you can add a dash of your own creative genius to the recipe. If there's one means to an end, there's bound to be another faster and more efficient way. Here's your chance to stand out and challenge the status quo. But don't inform others of your plans until they've proved fruitful; you don't need an audience when your blueprint for success is debunked. Once the results are in the bag, you can talk yourself hoarse about the triumph.

Challenge Yourself

Coasting, slipping past, and getting by are relics of the academic years. While taking on the easiest projects may seem appealing the first few months on the job, you should never be afraid to accept the tougher assignments for fear of failure. Challenging yourself and learning as you go will benefit your flagging motivation and earn you kudos from the brass. Fear of failure is only beneficial when it spurs you on to work harder. Your courage will be applauded, and even if you can't meet the deadline on your own, you can always recruit a more experienced colleague to come to your rescue. If you continue to test your strengths and go out on the limb, people will notice and value your contributions.

Newswire

Sending statements of success can help you rise above the muck of your entry-level career station. If you worry about sounding like a brazen braggart, send your announcement as an aside to a special occasion greeting card, either on the recipient's birthday or during the holidays. You can wish them joy in the coming year, and then identify yourself as the leader of the "American Cookie" account. For example, say, "Wishing nothing but the greatest success to an executive who does the title justice. Your standard of excellence helped me enormously with the 'American Cookie' project. Thank you and many happy returns. Jenny Fields." That should get your name on the promotable list. Just make sure to route your notices to the right contacts (those with decision-making power). They'll have you on their minds when a position opens up in their department, or they may recommend you when something juicy opens up elsewhere in the company.

To save time, you can set up an e-mail address book for all executives in your office. When you have something to shout about, it will be easy to send everyone a complete, albeit less personalized, report of your progress. That way, the office power brokers can stay updated on all the late-breaking headlines of your career life. The more they know, the better your chances are of getting promoted.

ONWARD AND UPWARD

Eventually you'll be juggling tasks with the skill of an expert. Along with this newfound competence comes a strong desire for either a raise or promotion. If you feel you deserve it, never be afraid to ask for more compensation. The speed at which you traverse the career path is all up to you, and the next step on your professional road is to make sure your accomplishments and hard work do not go unrewarded.

Performance Reviews

On your semiannual report card from your manager, you'll be rated on everything from promptness and attitude to productivity, complete with notes in the margin. Unless you're an incorrigible slacker, your interests are served best by such reviews. They are usually scheduled every six months and can lead to bigger and better things, such as raises and promotions. If your boss should forget to evaluate you, by all means remind him/her. The last thing you want is to get lost in the corporate shuffle, and that's just what can happen if you don't demand to be reviewed on a consistent basis. Remember that a recent evaluation is your best exhibit when making a case for a salary increase.

You should always know when you are scheduled to be reviewed. This knowledge will give you the foresight to clean up your act before it's too late. Don't be tardy, make sure to look extra busy, and try to be ever so much nicer to your boss before the results come in. If the little act falls flat and the supervisor reminds you of all those times you were caught sleeping at your desk, make a concerted effort to improve your performance in time for the next review. There's always room for improvement.

Promotions

No question about it, you stand a better chance of being promoted at some companies than at others. Those with a high turnover rate usually have a promotion rate to match. The more turnover, the more likely you are to be considered for new positions. Good performance reviews come in handy at such times. Promotions and raises usually go hand in hand, but if your boss "rewards" you with a fancy new title, but no extra funds, that's just your tough luck. While not quite grounds for a bona fide labor dispute, you still have the option to quit. But remember that patience is a virtue. Good things come to those who wait, so enjoy your new title and responsibilities. If you can cut the mustard, the money will come later. In the meantime, have fun showing off your new batch of business cards and impressing your friends with your new role as Junior Executive Vice-President of Primary Accounts.

Look on the bright side; at least you're the one with the promotion. If you should be passed over in favor of a less-deserving specimen, feign happiness and wish him/her luck in the new slot. Don't be a sore loser, and maybe one day this same colleague will give you the promotion you were initially denied.

Raises

Look at it as a pat on the back, a bribe, a bigger piece of the pie, or a first prize trophy, but a pay increase by any other name still means extra money in your pocket. Forget for a moment that you should have been making twice as much to begin with, or that a miserable 3 percent hike hardly qualifies as a pittance. Yours is not to bargain; just take the money and run before they change their minds. While you should be grateful for the gesture, you don't have to profusely thank your supervisor for giving you a cost-of-living raise. When inflation rises, so does per capita income. Basically, you barely break even.

If your contract specified a raise after a probationary period, don't be surprised when your check reflects this new salary. This is just a formality. However, there are the substantial increases that signal you are truly valued by your employer. Throwing cash your way is the only means by which the company can keep you happy and on board. The bigger bucks can also come after threatening to quit. However, before you go the blackmail route, make sure you'll be missed. Otherwise, prepare for early retirement. If your employers honestly appreciate your contribution, they will more often than not shell out the extra bucks to keep you.

THROWING IN THE TOWEL

People don't like to think of themselves as quitters, but sometimes there's very little choice in the matter. If your work is stressing you out, and nothing short of your family's or roomies' combined efforts can pull you out of bed in the morning, maybe it's time to re-evaluate your career development. Set up a two-month trial period; if things don't improve, be ready kiss your workplace good-bye.

Use these two months to search for another job. There's nothing that takes the edge off quitting like a ready and waiting income. Sneak out on job interviews during your lunch hour or use vacation and sick days to conduct your pursuit. However you do it, remember that it's always best to look for work while employed. If you're clearly looking to leave on your own, your employer is obviously willing to keep you on. Ergo, you're more in demand and a hotter property.

Security Is a Sound Mind

Unless your paychecks are one windfall after another, don't be afraid to leave for financial reasons. While unemployment compensation is reserved for laid-off employees, this job has already taught you

---

Quitting Time!

In case you were wondering, you're not being a total baby if you decide to bolt from your job for the following reasons:

- You're earning minimum wage.
- You're asked to add toilet cleaning to your repertoire.
- Your boss asks you to postpone your vacation, and then says, "Ha! Ha! I tricked you. Don't you know vacation days don't carry over?!"
- You're forced to contribute fifty bucks toward the president's birthday gift.
- No one's talked to you since you forgot to bring something for the Christmas party grab bag two years ago.
- Every time something turns up missing, people look at you.
- When you call in sick, your boss calls you back at home with a "just checking."

The last two weeks at a job can take a toll on anyone. The supervisor and peers may feel betrayed if they think that all your declarations of loyalty and demonstrations of good cheer have been a ruse. There's nothing you can do, so just go about your business. Try to maintain a good attitude and . . .

- Never brag about your new job.
- Never disparage your old one.
- Never shirk your present responsibilities.
- Never break office policies (e.g., come in late or smoke in the rest room).
- Never be rude to your supervisor.
- Never leave before time runs out.
- Never steal office supplies.

that money and happiness don't always go together. No one's saying you should run off to a chicken ranch in Utah; just find a non-ulcer-inducing job in your own field. Finding a greener pasture shouldn't be quite so difficult when you have some solid experience under your belt.

Bidding Adieu

Throughout the span of an average lifetime, Americans will change jobs seven to twelve times. Gone are the days when you'd let one company bleed you dry. Enhanced mobility and a general restlessness have contributed to the job-hopping phenomenon. If you're less than content at your position, there's simply no reason to turn down another offer. Whether it be for a salary increase or a change of career direction, no one's standing in your way. Let the exit signs—the beacons of liberty—serve as a constant reminder that you are always free to leave.

There's only one hitch: You must give two weeks' notice. Even though the thrill has been gone for months and you'd rather eat cicadas than mechanically engineer another gadget, burning a bridge with a clumsy exit is never a good idea. Resist the temptation to run for the nearest elevator screaming, "Free at last! Free at last! Thank God Almighty, I'm free at last!" You'll more than likely need that manager's reference down the line. Giving two weeks' notice and showing up each and every day of that fortnight to either train or prepare some guidelines for your replacement will get you rave reviews and help you feel better about yourself. If coworkers are bitter and give you the cold shoulder, remember that come Friday evening these people will be nothing but a memory, and whistle a happy tune.

Ph.D.

Chapter Seven

MASTERING GRAD SCHOOL

M.B.A.

The rigors of the real world have hundreds upon thousands of college grads asking, "Should I go to graduate school?" Some feel that their choice of specialization is no longer satisfactory and decide that now is the time to pursue that long-burgeoning interest in art history. Others feel that they've been rounded to obtuseness and decide to sharpen a particular skill, such as podiatry. Who'd a thunk it?! It's all good—just as long as your decision isn't based on some misguided attempt to relive the good old coed days. Completing a master's or a doctorate is grueling work, leaving little time for navigating the party circuit with the youngsters. On the bright side, you will at long last be allowed to concentrate purely on your chosen field, get the opportunity to hobnob with world-renowned professors, and, last but not least, have the chance to mold (torment) a sea of undergrads who had the good luck to get you as their teacher's assistant.

Money plays a significant role in many people's calculations. Sure, you'll be deeper in the hole come graduation, but your prospects for clawing your way out in the end will be that much better. F.Y.I.: Job applicants with "hot" advanced degrees can easily bring in as much as double and triple the earnings of their undergraduate counterparts. Many companies know the value of employing the highly trained; so don't be surprised if you should find yourself being wooed by competing recruiters even prior to graduation.

What's that about "hot" degrees? Well, certain specializations attract employers like heat-seeking missiles; others could have you sitting on the sidelines for years to come. You can bet your entire year's entry-level salary that not all grad school grads are set for life. If, for instance, you're going to go the Latin or philosophy route, make sure you're either loaded or prodigious. Otherwise, you'll have plenty of federal henchmen on your tail for student loan money, but not a single job offer to accommodate your overeducated gluteus maximus.

SO MANY PROGRAMS, SO LITTLE TIME!

To make an educated choice, you'll need to ascertain all of your options before setting your sights on a particular program or institution. If your sign reads Med School or Bust, you have a wide array of schools to pick from, but little choice in terms of curriculum. All doctors have to know that the knee bone is connected to the . . . well, we don't know, but that's what physicians are for. If the world of high finance is where you'd rather be, your options are nearly infinite. You can choose the degree you want, the curriculum you'll pursue, and the school where this will all go down. Draw out your plans with care, because be it an M.D., J.D., or M.B.A., you'll have to succeed if you ever hope to get that B.M.W.

To What Degree?

If you don't know the difference between a professional and an academic degree, rest assured that you're in good company. Nonetheless, once grad school is firm on your agenda, you'll need to unravel all the subtle distinctions to decide which one suits your interests best.

Academic Degrees

These are great for you theoretical types who hate to get your hands dirty. Your classes will skew sharply toward analysis and research; be prepared to do your fair share of hypothesizing. Biology, English, and history degrees all fall under the abstractions of this category.

Professional Degrees

A professional degree will give you plenty of opportunity for practice. All lawyers, surgeons, and ophthalmologists have to earn these babies before they can begin charging their exorbitant fees. Comforting, isn't it? Theory has its place, but when you're on the operating table, you want a doctor who knows her way around a scalpel. If you're going to dive headlong into any such field, keep your eyes open to the real-life scenarios with which you'll eventually have to contend.

If you're hard pressed to figure out what to study, consider the following options. An advanced degree can tell you all you've ever wanted to know about the following:

1. Agriculture
2. American Studies
3. Archaeology
4. Architecture
5. Art History
6. Biological Sciences
7. Business
8. Chemistry
9. Communications
10. Comparative Literature
11. Computer Science
12. Criminal Justice
13. Dentistry
14. Economics
15. Education
16. Engineering
17. English
18. Environmental Sciences
19. Film/Television/ Broadcasting
20. Foods and Nutrition
21. Forestry

Master's Degrees

Depending on your course load, such a degree can take you anywhere from one to three years to complete. Beware all ye scribe phobics; the program involves one lengthy work known as the master's thesis. You'll have to pen it and then detail it to experts in the field if you want to get your qualification. When forced to face the job-hunting challenge, the Master of Art/Master of Science (M.A./M.S.) degrees can come in quite handy. With an extra reserve of knowledge, you'll be considered a more viable risk. These degrees are available at nearly every school, for nearly every field, and are perfect for anyone who wants an edge in the work force.

Doctoral Degrees

Doctoral degrees are ideal for anyone who is dying to conduct research and be referred to as "doctor." Acceptance to such programs is competitive to the nth power. And let's not get started on the commitment quotient. Most programs, clocking in at four to seven years, outlast many of today's marriages.

And don't expect the corporate red carpet to roll your way once the deed is done. Ph.D. usually equates to highly paid, and a lot of companies just don't have sufficient need to justify expending so much capital. With this degree, you may find yourself cornered into one of two categories: research or university teaching. If you opt for the latter, you'll have to do a lot of both. So, if these pastimes float your boat, go ahead and start filling out your applications. Just do yourself a favor and make sure you're in love with your area of potential expertise. Getting out of a doctoral program could wind up to be nearly as difficult as getting in.

Picking a Field

It's as easy as one, two, three. Ideally, it shouldn't take more time than figuring out which was your favorite subject in college, and then applying to the appropriate school. Unfortunately, many of you will make the gargantuan mistake of studying something just for the money, regardless of whether you like it or get a rash just considering it. Since we do not approve of such behavior, we'll only say that should you persist, you will rue the day. Those dollar signs in your eyes will not end up in your money clip; people cannot make a killing when their work gives them suicidal tendencies.

Some graduate programs, for example, in psychology and medicine, will expect you to have followed a pertinent undergrad program. If this dawns on you a bit late in the day, don't worry. Unless you've made yourself the alma mater's persona non grata, you are always welcome to come back and sign up for the necessary courses.

If you just can't commit to one field of study, consider advancing your degree in a field that won't narrow your options. Business and law school graduates, for example, don't often end up pigeonholed into set career paths. But don't limit yourself to these old standbys. People with advanced degrees in English also get to pick and choose, as do those who study communications, the social sciences, and so on. Use your head, check the want ads, and ask around. You'll soon get an inkling of what types of degrees are preferred by the fields that most pique your interest.

Where to Study

After you have your program all figured out, you can begin thinking about applying to schools. There are countless colleges and universities in the United States. You couldn't possibly apply to all of them. Graduate school applications are not as breezy as the ones you may recall filling out your senior year in high school. These are application supernovas. The first rung of the "getting in" process will be to narrow your prospects. What follows is a smattering of the factors you should consider when choosing a school.

The Faculty

Before getting your heart set on a program, take a good look at who your mentors will be. Top-notch professors not only give great seminars but also increase the prestige factor of the school as well as your chances of finding a job. Find out who the instructors in your program are, what they have published, and how recently. Much of your curriculum will depend on the professors' interests,

Graduate Fields of Study (continued)

22. Geography
23. Government/Public Administration
24. History
25. Humanities
26. International Affairs
27. Journalism
28. Languages
29. Law
30. Library Science
31. Mathematics
32. Medicine
33. Music
34. Non-Western Cultures
35. Nursing
36. Oceanography
37. Optometry
38. Pharmaceutical Sciences
39. Philosophy
40. Physical Sciences
41. Podiatry
42. Psychology
43. Religious Studies
44. Sociology
45. Social Work
46. Speech
47. Theater/Drama
48. Veterinary Medicine

paradigms, and past research. If you find that the teachers have a penchant for aspects of the subject you happen to find particularly unappetizing, keep looking.

The faculty/student ratio is also a vital indicator of the program's quality. This will inform you as to how much attention will be lavished on you. Grad school is no time to slouch in your seat in fervent prayer of not being called upon. You want your last penny's worth. This includes being motivated to do your gosh darnedest.

Course Requirements

It's important to find out if the university offers courses of interest to you. If you commit to a program in which every class sounds like an awful lot of hooey, you're in for a long two years. You should also find out about course-selection freedom. Some schools set up rigid guidelines in an effort to maintain consistency of thought among the student body. With such programs, the motto is "woe to he or she who strays." Others will allow you some class-selection leeway. It could mean the difference between a tailor-made suit and ready-to-wear. If the school's program fits, great! But if it restricts your breathing or some such other vital function (like independent thought, for one), you may want to keep searching. If workload is important, give the credit requirements a look-see. Too high a number may mean trouble. With all the graduate programs out there, you can afford to be selective.

Geography

Maybe the idea of moving away from friends and family is just too much for you to bear. Or could it be that the northern climes are what have you up in arms? Geographical concerns should be considered before you waste time filling out applications to universities situated in undesirable locales. Some grad wanna-bes prefer completing their degrees closer to home or may have part-time jobs lined up in their city. But what if that wanderlust has you drooling for a school in New York City, the place that never sleeps, or Los Angeles, the city of angels and great sushi? Attending graduate school in your dream town can make the entire experience that much more rewarding.

Educated Decisions

To make a solid choice, research is a must. You should figure out what you're getting into before you begin the lengthy application process. You have to do your homework in order to get a peek at the program's strengths and weaknesses—no short-cuts here.

Delve deep into the academic histories of your profs-to-be. This intelligence will boost the odds of your being selected. Knowing the ins and outs of the program will come in especially handy during the grueling essay/personal statement portion of your application. You'll have the inside track, while the ignora-muses will be racking their brains and asking, "What do they want to hear?"

Directory Assistance

Directories are a great source of information. But depending on the course of study you will be embarking upon, some may be a challenge to find. Candidates for law, business, and medical schools (the big three) will have no trouble getting their sweaty paw prints all over the bevy of comprehensive directories available. Everything from admission requirements to faculty to cost will be neatly outlined therein. All graduate school hopefuls can benefit from *Peterson's Annual Guide to Graduate Study*. The *Directory of Graduate Programs* should also prove an invaluable source for most aspiring scholars. These gold mines of statistics can be obtained at book-stores, libraries, career counseling centers, and various professional organizations.

Directories can dramatically reduce the time you spend on research. But if your graduate school plans are too far off the beaten path to get a directory listing, you may have to do some extra dig-ging. Hey, no one said being unconventional would be easy.

Internet Graduate Program Directories

These days finding out about graduate schools and programs is as easy as logging on to the Net. Most schools even have their own web site. Do not proceed with any steps until you've checked out what the Internet has to offer.

- http://www.wwcareers.com
- http://www.taponline.com
- http://www.schoolguides.com
- http://www.usnews.com/ usnews/fair/ccadvise.htm
- http://edap.bgsu.edu/ACPA
- http://www.Kaplan.com
- http://www.review.com/ index.html

Applying Yourself

Petitioning for admission to graduate school is not for the weak of heart. If you thought looking for a job was a challenge, just wait until you get a load of this! The many tasks that go into the application process have droves of applicants enlisting the costly aid of professional guidance counselors. And the pressure! Grad schools admit only a wee fraction of the total candidates into their programs. Evaluators are missionaries paid to weed out the losers. The competition for admission is stiff, the stakes are high, and the overall experience is strenuous. But that's the bad news. The good news is that what does not kill you makes you stronger.

Forms

Application forms are used by every school in the league. Why ask why? Just fill them out or it's no school for you! Obtain a couple of copies from each school one year in advance of your planned starting date. A submission deadline looms over each application. Mark the date on the calendar or program your computer to remind you—anything to make sure your application does not arrive tardy. The deadline will not be moved up because you were irresponsible.

Keep revisionist history out of the application. You will be asked about everything from job experience to extracurricular activities in college. Unlike most companies, the admissions committees go the extra fact-checking mile. Chronic embellishers beware.

Spelling counts; this is graduate school we're talking about. Grammar counts too. Make sure your sentences are phrased properly. Could it be time to refresh your sentence diagrams? You be the judge. Your handwriting should be calligraphy neat. Electronic application submissions are becoming increasingly popular with each passing cyberyear. The good old electric typewriter is the best way to go for the computer illiterati. Just make sure you employ a machine with a working correction ribbon, as Wite-Out will surely be a zit on the face of your petition.

Transcripts

Did you actually think you could get by without corroborative evidence? Your word, simply put, is not good enough. Official copies of your college course work and grades will be required for the evaluation of your application. Your class load, degree of difficulty, and G.P.A. will all be analyzed by the admissions committee. It is up to you to get these make-it-or-break-it forms into the judges' possession. This is the easiest maneuver of the application obstacle course. Simply call the school registrar, and say, "Hi. I would like a copy of my official college transcript to be sent to the universities of _____, _____, and _____ ." These copies will be mailed directly to the programs you designate. You may very well have to sustain a small service fee. But what's a buck or two when your future hangs in the balance? Because these requests take time to process, contact your old college(s) right away. You've got a date with a deadline.

Personal Statement

Many people look at the "talk about yourself" question with dread. "Who am I? Who am *I*? Who *am* I? *Who* am I?" A few sing this tune right up to the snap, crackle, and pop of the unnecessary breakdown. You don't have to get caught up in this broken record if you look at the question with a bit of perspective. First of all, who are you, who are we, yada, yada, who knows? No one can answer such an open-ended question. So stop your crisis right here.

This is your chance to speak out about how great you and your reasons for going to grad school are. You won't get many such opportunities in your lifetime. Go ahead and tell them about how you scored so well on all those exams and still found plenty of time to be dorm backgammon champion. Feel free to share with them how it was the enthusiasm with which you approached the subject matter that made you the darling of all the professors! Take your boasting to new heights and explore the final frontier in self-promotion. Modesty be hanged; have a great old time of it! Just be eloquent as you do so.

The Essay

The wagon of hopes, dreams, and goals that rides on your ability to articulate the thoughts about the proposed topic could make this the most difficult paper you've ever had to write. Expect

Graduate school applications need to be filed well in advance of the specified deadlines. Since you'll probably be applying to many schools, follow the general timeline we've provided. But different schools will have different deadlines; so keep them in mind when applying.

Summer

- Begin looking through college brochures and researching schools. Make a tentative list of those you will be applying to.
- Set up meetings with faculty members and alumni to discuss various programs.
- Register for standardized tests. Begin the preparation.

the questions to be specific. Your opinions on a political or social issue, your favorite writer, what you would discuss with Abraham Lincoln, and scads of other such ditties will be presented to you as dissertation topics. If you think one sentence says it all, think again. Colleges want to see the ostentatious display of an insightful and analytic mind. This is no time to be laconic.

Considering the importance of your essay, second and third opinions should be actively sought out. If the work loses focus, strays into incoherency, lacks organization, or is in any other way objectionable, fix it. Only after you polish it until it shines can you finally get it off your hands and into the postal carrier's.

Letters of Reference

Professors' recommendations are another way of letting the selection committee recognize your talents. While you should have been compiling an endorsement reserve throughout your college career, there are still ways to jog the former mentors into near total recall. Calling them by phone with pleas to "think back" is a bad idea. The ideal means of groveling for support is the appointment. You need only come in with samples of your past course work, proof that you had aced their class, and a readiness to discuss the reasons for continuing your education to provide a basis for their recommendation. An A+ term paper should jar the old memory bank in your favor.

Those of you who attended college out of easy commute distance will have to employ the phone system. When you call your professor, spend a minute on pleasantries. Then get straight to business. Explain your goals and how the prof fits in. If you're not well remembered, offer to send them your research papers or anything else they will need to make their decisions.

Be selective when choosing your references. Graduate schools expect professors to comment on your leadership, maturity, and commitment. Yikes! If you enlist the services of only those instructors who had time to see you in action, you may still come out ahead.

Don't be afraid to ask former employers for recommendations. As long as two of your recs come from academia, one from an employer is acceptable. Pick a boss or supervisor with whom you were on the best of terms. An employer's recommendation should include praise of your efficiency and dedication, as well as emphasize your outstanding work record.

> *When I realized that I needed to obtain recommendations from professors to get into law school, my heart sank. It's not that I was a bad student or in any way offensive to the teachers. I was simply not in the habit of chumming it up with strange men and women. I always considered all those kids who surrounded the lecturer after class as either the neophytes, the learning impaired, or both. But now, I was the one with the problem. Who would remember me? There was only one small class in which I really bonded with the prof; all the others were impersonal at best. I procrastinated for a long time. Then I took action. I called the one professor whom I was sure would remember me. His understanding response gave me the courage to tackle the other professors. I tried to remember the names of those teachers who gave me the highest grades. I sent each one the papers I had written (especially the ones with the most generous comments) and was promised another three references. The process was not as difficult as I had imagined it to be. Needless to say, I am now in law school.*
>
> —ANDREA, SUNY, '93

The Interview

A small percentage of schools will not accept you sight unseen. Most elite programs want to see you in the flesh for a formal screening. If you look better in person than on paper, consider scheduling an interview even if it's not required. Read over the program descriptions and each faculty member's curriculum vitae before going in. Once you have become familiar with the institution, you'll have no problem explaining why you chose that particular school as your stomping ground.

At the interview, make sure to display impeccable manners, wear your most collegiate ensemble, and know what you're going to say.

Application Timeline (continued)

September/October

- Outline and write a personal statement.
- Complete standardized tests.
- Start preparing financial-aid strategy.
- Obtain recommendations.

November/December

- Request that your registrar's office forward your official transcripts.
- Submit applications.
- Begin applying for fellowships or grants.

January-March

- Make campus visits.
- Wait patiently.

April

- Receive admission status.

You can't just walk into a testing room, plop down your knapsack, and proceed to fill out the test forms impromptu style. You must schedule your test in advance and pay the standard processing fee, which can range from $25 to $70 per exam. If you need to retake a test, you'll have to pay the fee and register all over again. You can write these offices for deadline, fee, and registration information:

Graduates Record Examinations
Educational Testing Service (GRE)
P.O. Box 6000
Princeton, NJ 08541

The Psychological Corporation
(MAT, PCAT, VCAT)
555 Academic Court
San Antonio, TX 78204

Remind yourself of all those righteous deeds and accomplishments you forgot to mention in the personal statement. If you included them all, go ahead and rehash them. Very often it's not what you say, but how you say it.

Entrance Exams

You can travel to the farthest reaches of the universe without finding a single thing further from fun than standardized tests. Just thinking about scantrons, no. 2 pencils, and distracting coughing fits in crowded testing areas can be a nightmare for anyone who has ever taken the SAT. Nonetheless, you will have to go another round. Prepare yourself well in advance for what lies ahead. Graduate schools are sticklers for these scores; a cutoff score is often involved. These tests are designed to measure how much you've learned and your potential for learning more.

The admissions committees do not judge you solely on the basis of your test scores. It is the combination of G.P.A. and test scores that determines their decision. If you were an A student all the way through college, but performed poorly on the test, you may be given the benefit of the doubt. And poor grades in college can be overridden by great test scores. But if both grades and test scores are low, consider your chances of being accepted into a graduate program slim to none. Here are some of the various tests that graduate school applicants may be required to take:

1. *Graduate Record Examination (GRE).* Most schools require that you take only the general test. However, some require that you take a subject exam as an added bonus. The subject exam tests your knowledge of a particular subject. The general test measures your verbal, quantitative, and analytical skills. Both tests can be taken in rapid-fire succession, or they can be scheduled on separate days.

   The subject test comes in sixteen different varieties: biology, biochemistry, chemistry, computer science, economics, education, engineering, geology, history, English literature, mathematics, music, physics, political science, psychology, and sociology.

2. *Graduate Management Admissions Test (GMAT)*. This four-hour test is required of all students pursuing an M.B.A. degree. The GMAT tests general verbal and mathematical skills.

3. *Law School Admissions Test (LSAT)*. The LSAT measures the skills needed to complete law school. Three types of tasks round out the test: logic games, reading comprehension, and deductive reasoning. Since this is considered a reliable way of quickly assessing law school applicants, law schools tend to base their decisions more on test scores then G.P.A.

4. *Medical College Admissions Test (MCAT)*. The MCAT is offered in the fall and in the spring, and tests knowledge of chemistry, physics, and biology. It also assesses the applicant's reading, quantitative, and analytical skills. The MCAT should be taken at least eighteen months prior to entering medical school.

5. *Miller Analogy Test (MAT)*. The MAT examines reasoning ability by way of verbal analogies. Many schools accept this test as a substitute for the GRE.

Other tests that must be taken when seeking admission to certain professional programs include the Dental Admission Test (DAT), the Optometry Admission Test (OAT), the Pharmacy College Admission Test (PCAT), and the Veterinary College Admission Test (VCAT).

Preparation

The key to making the grade is to study till you can study no more. The library and bookstore reference shelves are lined with hundreds of manuals bearing titles like *Beat the MCAT* and *Ace the LSAT*. Always check to make sure that these study manuals include sample tests. Practice tests are your most effective tool in the standardized test game. Drilling yourself on the testing procedure will ensure that there won't be any surprises come test time.

Say what? You fear you lack the motivation to supervise your own study program? Well, good for you. As we always say, it's a

Graduate Management Admission Test (GMAT)
P.O. Box 6101
Princeton, NJ 08541

Department of Testing Services
American Dental Association (DAT)
211 East Chicago Avenue, Suite 1840
Chicago, IL 60611

Law School Admission Services (LSAT)
P.O. Box 2000
Newtown, PA 18940

MCAT Program Office
P.O. Box 24720
Oakland, CA 94623

Optometry Admission Testing Program (OAT)
221 East Chicago Avenue, Suite 1840
Chicago, IL 60611

Registration and Fees (continued)

wise man or woman who is aware of his/her own limitations. There is no shortage of programs that will gladly relieve you of several hundred bucks to help you out. The monetary investment will provide an incentive to put forth the effort, and the valuable test-taking tricks and strategies to which you'll be privy will help inch your score a few crucial points higher. You never know; it may make the difference.

FINANCING

Everybody knows that a graduate school's stamp of approval can bring you bigger bucks in the world of work. But in the meantime, it can take a substantial toll on your financial well-being. Funding education has always been a major consideration for students seeking advanced degrees. It may mean sacrificing certain things, cutting your expenses, and doing without the items you used to take for granted. While times may be hard, you will have options and assistance available to you. So don't give up on graduate school just yet. You may have to choose a school with a lower tuition and cut down living expenses by shacking up with your folks. But think about the nobility of making sacrifices in the name of higher learning and knowledge. Once all is said and done, you'll be glad you made the commitment.

Before you start whining about the astronomical cost of graduate school, take some time to appraise exactly what you will be spending. Once you come up with a figure, you'll know whether you need to take a year off to work for extra cash or whether a loan or a work-study program can cover the expenses. Either way, you'll have a better idea of what your finances will allow; and you may even choose a school based on that decision.

Helping Hands

Once you have a better idea of what your costs will be, you can start tapping into your resources. Family, the university, and the government can all help to keep your head above the murky financial waters during your graduate school years. Cover all your bases and leave no avenue unexplored by researching all the sources of assistance for which you are eligible. You'll have to engage in yet another bout with a battery of forms. But there's no time to lose. Applying for financial assistance has to be done immediately. Funds are distributed on a first-come, first-served basis; so have your forms filled out and ready to be mailed way ahead of time.

Parents

The last thing you may want to do is ask your parents for yet another loan. But that is exactly what many grad-school-bound students opt to do. Parents can be an invaluable source of assistance, if they can afford to help. They may grant you the funds as a gift or choose to lend you a certain amount each year. Since parents are unlikely to charge you interest, this may be a better solution to your problems than borrowing from a bank.

If you are uncomfortable with being dependent, independent student status is always an option. Independent students are eligible for government and school funds that are doled out on the basis of need.

Getting Your School to Pitch In

The university you choose to attend might give you some help in financing your education. For example, you could become a teaching assistant (TA)., This gig would reward your efforts handsomely. Much of the tuition is waived and you learn more about your field by having close contact with a faculty member. You may have to clean a petri dish or two or sacrifice a few precious hours to the proctoring of an exam. But in return, you have the opportunity to run your own classroom. Students interested in becoming professors benefit most highly from this teaching experience.

Another way to finance graduate school is to become a research assistant (RA). As an RA you might, for example, help a professor conduct research that could count as part of your thesis/dissertation. You acquire solid research experience and are reimbursed for your trouble. Research assistants are much-sought-after positions; so announce your interest as soon as the opportunity arises.

The Graduate School Expense Report

By filling out this work sheet, you will get a better understanding of the costs of graduate school. If you're at a loss for a figure, do your best to estimate the amount.

Estimated Expenses Per Year

Tuition: $_____
Fees: $_____
Room: $_____
Food: $_____
Books and Supplies: $_____
Entertainment: $_____
Transportation: $_____
Other:
_____ $_____
_____ $_____
_____ $_____

Total: $_____

Income Per Year

Your contribution:
$_____
Parental contribution:
$_____
Loans, Grants, Fellowships:
$_____
Other:
_____ $_____
_____ $_____

Total: $_____

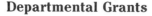

Departmental Grants

The departmental chair assigns grants only to the Brandon Walshes of the student body. Extremely promising applicants can expect their grants to range anywhere from $10,000 to $15,000 per year. You'll have to produce consistently good work, since grants are assigned on a yearly basis and can be withdrawn during your studies.

Minority or extremely needy students are often eligible for a tuition waiver or tuition-reduction program. Some schools decrease or eliminate the tuition costs for students who, for financial reasons, would not be able to attend the university otherwise. Find out whether the school to which you're applying has a history of waiving or reducing tuition for minority or needy students.

Your State to the Rescue

State schools can alleviate the money worries of many grad students. They are subsidized by the government and that means less for you to pay. Here's the catch: You have to be a resident before you can capitalize on the benefits of a state-sponsored education. But many graduate school applicants choose a school and then move to that state and work there for a year to qualify for in-state tuition. Although you have to post-pone your education, it's worth the money saved.

States also offer financial-aid programs to residents. Each state has different requirements and forms to fill out; so go to the library and find out which programs can benefit you.

The Feds

The government offers low-interest loans, grants, and fellowships to grad students. If you've been a taxpayer and don't have anything shady lurking in your past, you will be eligible to receive some type of support. Here is a list of the possibilities available. Since you can receive assistance from more than one program at a time, explore them all.

1. *Work-Study*. This program is federally subsidized and provides funds that you earn through the university. You must

register to be a part of the program and to be eligible to work on campus. Your university is responsible for finding you a job. The pay is often low, but it is a convenient way to finance your education.

2. *Cooperative Education.* This is a needs-based program; it combines academic study with off-campus, field-related employment. The government employs over 19,000 students in this program. As one of them, you would benefit from direct contact with professionals in your field.

3. *Federal Perkins Loans.* These loans are awarded on a need basis and allow students to borrow up to $40,000. The interest rates are a very low 5 percent, and it is to your benefit to apply as early as possible.

4. *Federal Stafford Loans.* Depending on your financial status, you may be able to benefit from this loan program. Eligible students can borrow $8,500 per year and up to $65,000. Repayment begins six months after graduation.

5. *Javits Fellowships.* The government awards fifty-six fellowships of up to $14,000 per year to students pursuing advanced degrees in the humanities, arts, and social sciences.

6. *Patricia Roberts Harris Graduate Study Fellowships.* These fellowships were created to assist women and minorities in the pursuit of advanced degrees.

A Solid Foundation

Fellowships can be obtained from other sources as well. The competition is steep, but it is in your best interest to apply. You will have to fill out many forms and meet the specific deadline set by each foundation. But in the final analysis, a fellowship can considerably ease your financial burden during graduate school. These awards were designed to get students focused on their studies and leave the part-time work for summers and school vacations.

1. *National Research Council.* This foundation provides 750 students with fellowships of up to $14,000 per year. Eligible students must be pursuing advanced degrees in the sciences, the social sciences, mathematics, or engineering. To obtain

more information, contact the National Research Council, 2101 Constitution Avenue NW, Washington, DC 20418.

2. *Mellon Fellowships.* The Woodrow Wilson National Fellowship Foundation grants eighty fellowships of one year's tuition and a $12,750 stipend. Graduate students in the humanities are eligible. To obtain more information, contact the Mellon Fellowships, Woodrow Wilson National Fellowship Foundation, P.O. Box 288, Princeton, NJ 08542.

3. *Spencer Dissertation Fellowships.* To be eligible, students must be pursuing a doctoral degree (in any field of study). Dissertation topics must concern education. Each recipient is awarded $17,000. To obtain more information, contact the Spencer Foundation, 900 North Michigan Avenue, Suite 2800, Chicago, IL 60611.

There are various sources that provide a comprehensive list of fellowships. The pickings are vast, but most fellowships have their own set of criteria. Depending on their course of study, students are eligible for some fellowships and not others. The library has a solid collection of financial-aid data; all you need to do is ask. If you can log on, make sure to visit www.finaid.org and www.studentservices.com; both have extensive lists of fellowships available to graduate students.

MAX IT OUT!

Chapter Eight

MONEY MATTERS

WATCH THE
PENNIES

Credit Wars!

Never leave home without it. It pays to discover. Master the possibilities. These are just a sampling of the slogans credit companies are concocting in their mad dash to beat the competition. Choosing the right card is tricky, considering the gallery of options. Ask your parents and ask your friends; but when all else fails, refer to the following rundown:

American Express. This card demands that you pay your monthly balance in one lump sum. While it exacts a hefty annual fee of $50 for the privilege of membership, those who have a habit of paying only the minimum will end up saving a bundle on interest.

Visa and MasterCard. These people are bank affiliated and, therefore, more like lenders. You get to stock up on stuff and then pay in installments. Of course, there is the little matter of interest, otherwise known as the annual percentage rate (APR). Because different cards are backed by different banks, you end up with a choice of interest rates and annual fees. Shop around for

Even if it can't buy love, the good life money can offer is nothing to snigger at. If you've renounced all of your material possessions in favor of the spiritual life, we salute you. But for those of us mired in the cesspool of never-ending ambitions and desires, finances can make or break our state of mind.

However, learning to manage your money early in the season will keep you from making grave mistakes that can impair your future. Staying out of debt and maintaining a good credit rating will come in handy down the line. Suppose that you get married and decide to buy a house or a condo. But to your dismay, your loan application is rejected! "Why me?" you ask yourself, as the memory of the custom-made armchair you just couldn't live without comes back to haunt you. No self-respecting bank will issue a loan to someone who bounces checks as if they were basketballs. Since the spending habits you acquire now will follow you like a faithful pup, you'd better start taking financial responsibility before your budget is a sick, old dog that can't learn new tricks.

Most college grads know very little about personal money management. Some major in finance and could balance the federal budget if they had to, but when it comes to their own money, they're lost. Universities all over the world should teach students about personal finances. Until that happens, if you want to learn everything you need to know to make the most of your money, you'd better read this chapter.

ADDICTED TO CREDIT

Let's face it, we, the people of the United States, are addicted to credit. "Charge it" has become a most popular phrase, beating "I'll be paying with cash" or even "personal check" hands down. It's hard to compete with credit card incentives—pay as you go, no money down, layaways for the strays and losers. Who could resist the allure of instant gratification? Obviously only a select few, since records show that Americans have amassed a staggering $200-billion credit card debt during the '80s alone. That amounts to $2,000 of credit card debt per taxpayer. TSK, TSK, TSK. Wait a minute! You have nothing to be ashamed of. Back in the '80s, you were still trying to make the most out of your allowance. So with your tabula rasa credit history, you wouldn't dream of endangering your spotless record by abusing your credit card privileges. Right?

Most credit card companies will be vying for your business even before you become financially independent. One college senior claimed that she received at least three credit card promos per week. While it's a good idea to start work on a solid credit history early on, it's not wise to stockpile the plastic by accepting every offer that comes your way. You will have to be very selective and shop around. Keep focus on the key aspects of each credit card, and don't fall for all that glitters. Credit card companies know that new graduates aren't exactly card-carrying connoisseurs of credit. Expect them to try and dazzle you with flashy trinkets, and keep in mind that their hard sell may just bring about your hard luck.

One Per Customer

You simply don't need more than one card. While the average American carries eight to ten, this is one time it's best to fall below average. You may opt for two cards, one to act as an emergency backup, but that should be the absolute limit. Don't worry about your credit line being too low; the card companies usually gear the credit limit toward your income. Spending more than your allotted figure could be a signal of financial woes to come. It's plain and simple: More cards mean more expenses and more checks to make out every month. Talk about a hassle!

Comparison Shop

We implore you to do some detective work before signing up for your first card. The annual fee is a case in point. Some banks will take you for a ride even before you sign for your first purchase. The annual fee can differ dramatically from card to card. Some banks waive this levy all together; others expect you to cough up as much as $50.

Credit Wars! (continued)

the best deal before you commit yourself.

Discover. Recently celebrating its tenth birthday, the Discover card is one of the newer contenders. It functions like a Visa or MasterCard but without the wide commercial acceptance. In other words, any place that takes this card will also take the others, but not vice-versa. It will, however, refund up to 1 percent of your purchase total at the end of the year. A few Visa and MasterCard lenders have also adopted this payback feature.

Department Store Cards. Store credit cards are utterly useless. The APR is sky-high, so why even bother? You might feel there's a certain cachet to carrying around Saks Fifth Avenue-inscribed plastic, but who really cares if you buy your socks there?

Gas cards. Gas cards must be paid off monthly, and can be easily substituted with any major credit card. You may want to take a pass on this type of card just to avoid writing out an extra check each month.

Don't let the offerings extended by the banks wrangle you into an unwise investment. Some will try to entice you with free long-distance phone minutes; others will throw frequent-flyer miles your way. But don't be swayed. The annual fee may be that much steeper. The credit card companies are counting on your laziness and reluctance to delve into details. Prove them wrong by flipping over the page with the big, bold offers to uncover the fine print. That's where the real story unfolds. Read it carefully, and don't subscribe to any deal unless it's the absolute best your money can buy.

Your Best Interest in Mind

How do you think credit card companies stay afloat? The balance that accrues every time you pay only the monthly minimum carries a heavy load of interest. Suppose that you're at a store and spot the sweetest pair of Birkenstocks, just begging to follow you home. "Just this once," you say as you sign on the dotted line, figuring you can pay the minimum this month at 5.9 percent and in three months you'll have it all paid off. However, your introductory annual percentage rate of 5.9 percent may have expired. Low intro APR's have a tendency to climb by as much as 15 percent after the introductory period expires. The average rate is somewhere in the mid-teens, but a few companies charge as much as 20 percent. These high APR's have been the downfall of many a well-meaning card holder. So, either find a company whose interest rates won't leave you in the poorhouse, or force yourself to pay the full fare each month. Frankly, if you can't afford to pay, you can't afford to buy.

Saving Grace

A grace period is the span of time a card company gives you to scrape up and fork over the cash without being charged either interest or late fees. Most companies will give twenty-five interest-free days. While this is standard, there are certain less scrupulous creditors who charge interest the minute you walk out of the store. You can negotiate extensions if your credit history is in good standing, but the easiest solution is to find a company with a gracious grace policy.

Credit Debt

Being in debt is not the end of the world, provided you're paying off sound investments. If you're $10K in the hole and have nothing except an outdated wardrobe to show for it, cut up your credit cards until you mature into a responsible consumer. Don't stress out if your money has been spent on necessities such as furniture or a stereo system. These will be with you long after you've paid them off.

A certain type of debt is inevitable (for example, student loans, mortgage, and car payments), but credit debt should be avoided like an erupting volcano. Late payments take center stage on credit reports and most always get in the way of obtaining new loans. Credit card companies take debt very seriously. It's the cornerstone of their business; so don't be surprised when your credit activity is recorded with the precision of a Los Angeles seismographic report. In other words, you get a strike for every time you're overdue. Many lending institutions only need to see one X on your record to consider you a bad credit risk.

Credit Reports and Bureaus

Careful . . . someone's always watching. Credit bureaucrats are the people who keep track of your every credit move. Every credit card purchase, every late payment, every carried-over balance, and every consolidated loan is registered in their computer system. So if you're looking to a career in politics, take care where you put your Visa. Even if it's discreetly delivered to your home in a brown paper wrapper, someone out there knows you've been to the fetishist. You'll have a hard time pulling the wool over the credit intelligence agency's prying eyes. These vigilant bloodhounds are divided into three camps: TRW, Trans Union, and Equifax.

You may access all the proper channels, cut through miles of bureaucratic red tape, talk to management until blue in the face, and even consult a lawyer about repairing your credit rating, and still not receive satisfaction. However, don't lose hope. There are agencies that can help. If you air your complaints to these people you may just find yourself shouting "Hallelujah!":

1. **Consumer Credit Counseling Services (800-388-2227)**
2. **The Bank Card Holders of America (540-389-5445)**
3. **Office of Consumer Affairs (Check your local directory for the number.)**

To ensure a strong credit history, keep track of your annual credit reports. These can be obtained from any of the three credit reporting services and should cost no more than $3. To get a look at your report, all you need is your social security number, date of birth, current address, home and work numbers, and a copy of your driver's license. Since computers are run by people, human error often factors into credit reports. Check yours annually to make sure all is copacetic when applying for that all-important loan.

Credit Disputes

Credit bureaus are notorious for wreaking havoc upon lives of the most exemplary of consumers. Go over your credit card bills with a fine-toothed comb. If you find an error on your bill, call the credit card company pronto! If you don't catch the mistake until looking over the credit report, which is, by the way, made available to banks, phone companies, universities, airlines, and so on, fill out the dispute form and send it in immediately. The bureau will check into the matter and report their decision. If they still find you responsible, you can take the next step. A statement of no more than 100 words should explain the problem as concisely as possible. Then sit back and wait to hear the verdict.

Talking to the bureau phone operators can cause the type of headache associated with banging your head against a wall. You will probably be transferred from one operator to another; so don't waste your sob story on each and every one of them. If you ask to speak to a manager or supervisor, your story might not fall on deaf ears. The company probably won't change your record unless you have some solid evidence to back you, but an affordable payment plan can always be worked out.

Remember that once a mark is made against you, you can consider yourself a target for all manner of legalized persecution—including collectors calling at 6:00 A.M. And the stigma will not be removed from your record for seven years.

Words to Spend By

Document each and every time you plop down the plastic in a credit diary, even if the amount incurred is only a meager couple of dollars. Once the results are in, you can analyze your pattern of consumption. Knowing the days on which you're most likely to impulse shop, the friends that bring out the spendthrift in you and the purchases you could have lived without will catapult your credit awareness to an all-time high. And that's exactly what can keep you from repeating the same mistakes time and again.

When all is said and done, there is only one surefire way to avoid bequeathing a million dollars in credit card debt to your heirs, and that is by using cash. The green stuff is still an acceptable form of currency. Take a good look around. Chances are, an automated teller is in sight. Nearly every 7-Eleven in the nation comes so equipped. If you're short on silver, don't head straight for the credit card. Use the machine! Credit cards make spending too easy. "Relax and enjoy yourself," they tell you. "Buy now and pay later" . . . and for the rest of your life! This is diabolical stuff, especially considering the hefty fine of repossession that comes with refusing to make good on your end of the bargain. With cash, everything is on the up-and-up. You pay, you play, and NOT the other way around. The score is settled immediately, and you make fewer frivolous purchases as a result. There's a reason why casinos use chips instead of cold, hard cash!

INSURING YOUR PEACE OF MIND

"You'll live forever and no harm shall ever come your way." Are you still whistling this old tune? You'd roll your eyes if this was a fortune-cookie prophecy, but not even a Chinese restaurant would insult your intelligence with this brand of inanity. If you have zero discretionary income or are still struggling to escape the comforts of your parents' home, insurance may be dead last on your list of priorities. But this is not smart. Forget that balderdash about a high-fiber diet; insurance is the most important thing you can do for yourself. Shuffle your priorities so that insuring yourself and your possessions tops out the list. Then get an insurance agent on the phone and

There are many health plans out there. Although different companies use different health insurance providers, most stick to one of the three listed here. Check with your human resources rep to find out which one is included in your benefits package.

1. *Preferred Provider Organizations (PPO).* PPO coverage is a stellar plan. Unlike other plans, you are given more freedom to choose your physicians and specialists. For all this luxury, you may have to pay a higher copayment (the portion of the bill that is not covered by the insurance company), but at least you can make an appointment with a specialist whenever hypochondria sets in.

2. *Health Maintenance Organization (HMO).* Some say it's a good standby plan; others claim it's a curse. Your employer garnishes your wages to collect the premiums, in return for which you are allowed to visit a designated medical center chock-full of general practitioners. While HMOs are notoriously reticent to refer patients to unaffiliated doctors, the cost certainly is low. Is it a pox or a blessing? You decide.

3. *Blue Cross and Blue Shield.* This insurance institution is regulated by the government and offers a wide array of plan options. As a young and vital person, your best bet is to request a high deductible (the total amount you have to pay before the insurance monies kick in) so that you need not pay a high monthly premium. Hopefully, you won't rack up enough medical bills to meet your deductible (up to $3,000 per year). But should push come to shove and you're under the surgical glove, at least you'll know your tonsillectomy won't cost you the house.

Word to the unemployed: If you are "let go" or quit for reasons of your own, you may be able to extend your coverage for up to eighteen months. The COBRA plan allows you to keep your old company's insurance plan alive. We suspect it's called cobra because the cost stings like one. But check into the matter. You never know when you'll be in need of coverage. The day you're between plans may be the day you break a leg.

start filling out the required forms. Peace of mind costs, but believe us when we tell you that there is no substitute.

Health Conscious

The most hassle-free way to manage your physical health expenses is to get coverage from an employer or through your parents' policy. Some insurance providers allow parents to include their progeny on their policies until the ripe old age of twenty-three. So check with your parents before applying for a new plan; you may still be in the clear.

Companies have a way of telling you they care and keeping you glued to your desk: It's by providing employees with a health insurance plan. To get the goods on what is covered versus what is not, you have to study the terms of your policy. Most plans cover or defray the costs of hospitalization, medication, ambulance expenses, and visits to the doctor. Optometrists, dentists, and immunizations may not be covered. Many plans outfit you with a list of preferred medical professionals that you will have to choose from if you don't want to get stuck footing the bills yourself.

Rules of the Road

You should have your head examined if you so much as think of driving uninsured. Car insurance is so important that most states have actually made driving without it illegal. It can cost you a bundle or a mere pittance. The rates are based on factors such as the driver's age and gender, the make and model of the car, and your location. A red car will run your costs up a significant percentage. And if your driving record is spotty, your rates may go through the roof.

The type of company providing you with insurance is also important. Some charge you next to nothing, but when it's time to pay the piper, years of litigation will not succeed in getting a dime out of them. Other companies charge exorbitant fees, but at least they'll back you up in time of need. Comparison shop—talk to insurance agents and

personal injury lawyers alike. Anyone in a position to know should be able to offer a valuable opinion.

The type of coverage you take out will have you wrangling with the horns of yet another dilemma. There's the standard liability insurance, which will pay for the property and bodily damage of the unsuspecting driver who's had to suffer the consequences of your freewheeling ways. If that's not enough, there's collision insurance. It will pay for damages no matter who was at fault. Though that may sound pretty nifty, insurance is not your ticket to the demolition derby. Every fender bender is not meant to be reported. The driving record you stack up can and will be used against you when calculating your rates; so be careful out there.

Yes, it's true what you've heard. Even with all the laws, many people still drive without car insurance. They'll total your car and then tell you to sue them. If you think you would do just that, the joke's on you. Not only does such a person not have insurance, but neither does (s)he have a house, a bank account, or a job. Unless you want the soiled shirt off his/her back, your insurance must fork over the moolah to cover all your damages.

Behind the wheel of your car, though, sits an altogether different type of driver. You probably have some worldly possessions that you'd like to keep in the family, maybe even pass down to your grandchildren. If you're sued, all your bounty is fair game for the liquidator. Your Barbie collection and grandma's antique jewelry should all fetch a nice sum. So if you want to keep your goods from the auction block, you'd best stop dallying and sign up for some coverage A.S.A.P.

When the Roof Is on Fire

Only one thing is better than water when the roof is on fire, and that's renter's insurance. Calamity Jane knows no justice; so be prepared when she strikes. Whether it's a fire, a tornado, hurricane Bertha, or a cat burglar named Ralph, paying $100 to $200 per year on renter's insurance can protect your valuables from all sorts of disasters. Should anything go terribly wrong, forget about your black leather sofa with matching lacquer coffee table, and run for your life. Once you're safe and sound, your renter's policy should help to replace the lost treasures.

UNCLE SAM'S SHARE?

Zzzz . . . zzz . . . zzz . . . oops! Sorry we dozed, but come on! Taxes?! Talk about an abysmal bore! Here's the way it all works. The IRS expects a wad of hard-earned money from your pocket, but do they take the trouble to fill out the forms themselves? Oh no! You better make all the arrangements to make taking your money easy on them, or else you go to jail!

The What and the Why

Considering that no less than 20 percent of your paycheck goes to the powers that be, you have every right to know who these vultures are and why they need your money. If you thought that the United States was the world's leading superpower based on some kind of United Nations lottery drawing, you have a big surprise coming your way. Whoever said the best things in life are free clearly wasn't talking about running water, national defense, and the space program.

The Breakdown

Your net (posttax) wages come in the form of a check. Attached to this bounty is a stub listing all the taxes being lifted automatically out of your pocket. Your gross (pretax) salary is designated at the top, and then the minuses begin to do their dirty work. If you have questions regarding the deductions, don't bother taking them to your boss. You would be the running joke of the office until someone did something even sillier, and who knows when that would happen. So before you do anything foolish, here's where your money goes:

1. *Federal withholding.* The U.S. government takes a bite out of your living allowance. This is what pays the government employees, keeps up the emergency relief fund, and pays for the huge defense budget and the even larger slew of

federally funded social services. You could knock it, but just think where you'd be without it.

2. *State withholding.* Your state has its own government, but you already knew that. Remember that field trip to the state capital with your grammar school class? Yeah, those were the days. This amount is a fraction of the federal government's asking price. However, the state doesn't give money to the grand puba, whereas the federal government is constantly throwing money your state's way.

3. *FICA.* FICA is either listed as such or under two headings: social security and medicare. The former packs a wallop and we're still not sure as to why—something about funding our retirements, although most people in their twenties don't believe they're ever going to see a social security check bearing their name. This, of course, is not a valid excuse to quit paying. Besides, there's nothing legal you can do about it. Medicare pays for the medical expenses of senior citizens, and if you want to know more about it, just tune into the news. You're bound to hear all manner of horror stories about the Medicare crisis approaching as the baby boomers get set to retire.

Paper Pushing

Only three kinds of people need scurry for an accountant before the dreaded April 15th due date rolls around: those who bring in more than $50K, those who are self-employed, and those who have mucho dinero tied up in investments. Not only can those of you who fit into these categories afford a CPA, but with the dough an accountant can save your overprivileged behinds, you can't afford not to have one. For the rest of you who fit smack dab in the middle of the "none of the above" category, breathe easy. Filing your taxes is a cinch.

W-2 and W-4 Forms

Initially, the names of these numbered forms can be harder to remember than those of the *Star Wars* androids. However, after repeated exposure you'll be an old hand.

You fill out the W-4 form your first day on the job. Declare any and all withholdings. There's nothing to it. Read the form carefully and follow the instructions. Don't claim allowances for dependents or spouses you don't have. And you definitely should not claim an exemption unless you fit the bill. If you're wondering how these withholdings affect your take-home pay, here's the formula: More allowances = more on the bimonthly deposit. There is one catch: If your allowance cup runneth over, you may very well have to make out a hefty check to the IRS at the fiscal year's end. This can be a budget buster for many. On the other hand, if the only allowance you claim is yourself, whoopee for you come tax season; there's a bonanza coming your way! The income tax refund may not bankroll a cruise around the world, but for once you'll feel as if money really does grow on trees.

The W-2 form is your employer's responsibility. You receive one from each company you worked for during that year. W-2s show the taxable income you obtained throughout the past year. You cannot file your taxes without this form because the IRS requires that you include a W-2 stub with your tax return. Save the rest of the W-2 form for future reference; you never know whose name will come up for an audit. Be prepared just in case it turns out to be yours.

The Tax Form

What was that about filing being a cinch? Well, as we mentioned before, if your salary is under $50,000 per year, you have no dependents (i.e., children), and you have earned less than $400 in interest from investments, consider yourself one of the lucky people who get to fill out the 1040-EZ. This form is the bewildered taxpayer's lifesaver. It comes with easy-to-follow instructions; and best of all, it requires almost no thought! With the most basic of calculations to perform and no riddles to solve, an untrained monkey would have little trouble completing this form. With a 1040-EZ, the IRS is on your side. They have even had the heart to set up a hotline so that you can file your taxes by phone, even online. This is reminiscent of those happy days in college when course registration was first introduced to the telephone. Should you decide to mail in your form, make sure all your responses are legible, and double-check your calculations. If everything is clear and no careless errors are found, you'll have your hot little hand around that refund in no time.

The tax business can get a bit overwhelming for young entrepreneurs, savvy investors, and high-income earners. The forms are

Extra Help

There are resource guides available to anyone whose tax filing just "don't come easy."

- **By phone**—Use the Tele-Tax numbers in your tax booklet. Call to find every conceivable question answered via recordings.
- **In person**—Voluntary Income Tax Assistance (VITA) provides free help from retired accountants. The guide can be found at your local public library or community center.
- **The Net**— http://www.irs.ustreas.gov

stacked against you, if only because of their sheer volume. While you can't go the EZ route, you still have options. We strongly recommend enlisting the aid of an accountant. You never know how much you can skim with impunity until you've seen these tax jockeys. For all the staunch do-it-yourselfers out there, we've got your number. Call 1-800-TAX-1040, and ask away.

The Home Office

You may think home is where the heart is, or where you hang your hat, but most surely not where you keep the filing cabinet. That's okay; it's never too late to learn. Huge stacks of paper are a terrible nuisance. They are fertile breeding grounds for roaches, and you can trip on them. Papers here, papers there, and no end to the paper trail in sight. If in one sense our lives are just so many streams of documents, then how do we curb the mess and declutter? The most popular approach, the discard, is also the most foolhardy. Sure it will keep your place clean, but only until you tear it apart in your mad search to contest a bill or stick it to the auditors. Good organization keeps tax-related paperwork out of your hair and at your fingertips. Keep all of your tax records for six to eight years. Then, if your unwavering integrity is ever questioned, you can proudly take the moral high ground with a triumphant "I told you so, nah-nah nah-nah nah!"

While you're building your at-home tax document shelter, make sure to set up sections for old bank statements, receipts, and paid bills. Automatically tearing up your credit carbons is a nice safety precaution, but as certain purchases may figure prominently in the tax deduction column, such a habit can cost you dearly in the long run.

Meeting the Deadline

Waiting till the last minute to file your returns could land you in hot water. Make sure you obtain all tax forms well in advance of the April 15th deadline. If you wind up owing the government money that you don't have, you can arrange to pay it off in installments. All unpaid taxes carry a 5 percent interest, so financial responsibility dictates that you pay up front and in full. Ironically, the refund you get from the IRS does not come bearing interest for time spent in the government's employ.

BALANCING THE BUDGET

While certainly not the most exciting of evening prospects, keeping track of your expenses should not be shirked for a night of carousing and throwing dollars to the wind. Granted, it's a major pain to scribble down every purchase, right down to your underwear, and you may get frustrated when rationing the amount of movies you see, dinners you eat out, and articles of clothing you buy. But ponder the alternative—whining about never having enough cash, staying home weekends because the ATM has blacklisted you from its premises, and to top it all off, not knowing where all that money went. This is one of those times when a dash of personal responsibility is in order. You can't blame the tax collector for the rest of your life.

First of all, relax. Sound budgeting will not take away from your joie de vivre. More likely, the near constant worry about being declared a financial disaster area will be replaced by a sense of entitlement and heightened appreciation of those pleasures in which you can actually afford to indulge.

Get It on Paper

Any setback is temporary once you learn the treasurer's art. What if you did pay too much for that Slinky or take a bath on those donkey earmuffs? You can live it down, provided those expenses don't join an anonymous mass, but are acknowledged in writing. The Slinky can easily squeeze into entertainment, and the earmuffs are obviously clothing. After you start recording all of your expenditures in your trusty budget notebook, you'll never be caught spending more than you can afford or buying items you don't need. By planning for upcoming expenses, you'll also ensure that you never feel like a deprived child again..

My friends and I planned to spend our two-week vacations together. We decided to make a pilgrimage to Memphis, home to Graceland, and then head to New Orleans for the Mardi Gras. My job wasn't what you'd call a thrill a minute, so during those down times, I'd think about the upcoming trip and feel better. I had never thought of money as a problem, until we started dis-

cussing the price of hotels, gas, and food. The other guys had been cutting back to fund the trip, but I just figured that expenses shouldn't amount to more than what I would otherwise spend. Ha! Aside from having to pay my usual bills, I had to come up with my share of the money for gas, hotels, and food. Gordon, the anal accountant that he is, had it all figured out. He hadn't counted on my dire straits. Even though I promised to pay everyone back after the trip, their attitude was so negative I decided not to go.

—LANCE, CARNEGIE MELLON UNIVERSITY, '93

A working budget requires a serious commitment. Set aside a half hour each day, just before you turn in for the night, to calculate all the day's expenses. Trace your wallet and don't forget to tally even the smallest of purchases (i.e., a pack of gum, the morning paper, coffee). Be they small or moderate, regular purchases add up. One pack of gum per day amounts to $201 a year, the daily newspaper amounts to $128, a small cup of coffee amounts to $347, and a daily Starbucks can ruin you altogether. Still wondering what mystical force removed all that money from your wallet? Once you eliminate such "trifles" from your list of expenses, you can invest your savings, make a down payment on a car, or maybe even take a vacation. Yes, all this can be yours if you just stop chewing that gum, brew your own coffee, and read someone else's paper or listen to the news. That's the beauty of budgeting. After you figure out where your money goes, you can keep it right where you want it—in your savings account.

Your Personal Budget Planner

We've created a plan that will make budgeting your money simple and fast. You can make copies of this page, and fill it out on a monthly basis. After calculating your expenses, make notes on a separate piece of paper about what you could have saved on, what were your most frivolous purchases, and what you will do to improve your spending behavior in the month to come. Is everyone ready? Then let's budget.

Monthly Income (take-home pay) $ _____

Debt   List all organizations or persons you are in debt to and the amount paid each month.

         1. _____ $ _____
         2. _____ $ _____
         3. _____ $ _____
         Total $ _____

Rent and Utilities Monthly rent or mortgage $ _____
         Electricity bill $ _____
         Water bill $ _____
         Average monthly phone bill $ _____
         Cable bill $ _____
         Total $ _____

Food   Average monthly grocery bill $ _____
         Average monthly eating out bill $ _____
         Total $ _____

Transportation   Monthly car payment $ _____
         Monthly insurance payment (divide yearly sum by 12) $ _____
         Average amount spent on gas $ _____
         Car maintenance $ _____
         Average amount spent on subway, bus, or taxi $ _____
         Total $ _____

Entertainment   Movies (rented or in theater) $ _____
         Bar-related expenses (cover charge, drinks) $ _____
         Concert tickets $ _____
         Total $ _____

Miscellaneous   Health and renter's insurance $ _____
         Clothing $ _____
         Furniture $ _____
         Laundry $ _____
         Magazines and newspapers $ _____
         CDs and books $ _____
         Other:
         1. _____ $ _____
         2. _____ $ _____
         3. _____ $ _____
         Total $ _____

The Final Analysis
         (Monthly income) $ _____ - (total expenses) $ _____ = (savings) $ _____

Personal Budget Planner

Allocation of Funds

Extreme deprivation is a common money management error made by first-time "budgeteers." The trick is to live as you save; so here's a new lesson called proper distribution of funds. Without it, you may as well kiss your budget resolutions *arrivederci*. Lesson number one: If you're a film critic, don't forget to make special allowances for movie going. Let's go one step further; if you're a chef, don't forget to make allowances for cooking publications. Everyone has different hobbies, jobs, and pursuits, and there's no reason to skimp on items you know you'll end up paying for anyway. You'll just skew the delicate budget balance with a shopping binge. And then you'll be overdrawn and without a penny to your name.

Try to be realistic about your needs. If you can't live without new clothes or are a video game addict, figure in these expenses in your monthly budget. Do not omit these categories from the list simply because society labels them as extravagant or frivolous. To you they may be therapeutic. Some people will have a small fortune allotted to dining out; others may have more money going toward concerts. Since you are a unique, special person, expect that your budget plan will be unique and special as well. There's no better way of sticking to the plan than by keeping your lifestyle and preferences in mind. Otherwise, all attempts at budgeting will be doomed to end in failure.

The Penny Pinchathon

Managing personal finance is all well and good, but what if your carefully outlined plan leaves your savings account with an ostrich-sized goose egg for a balance? Now is the time to get acquainted with the dormant Ebenezer in all of us. Make cheapskating your pastime. Figuring out creative ways to live well on the cheap can be a fun and lucrative activity. Too many people have what we call the blockbuster attitude. They think that in order to live in splendor they have to bring in a chart-topping paycheck. Well, we beg to differ. With so many cost-cutting strategies at your disposal, you don't need the budget of *Waterworld* to make your life one interesting scene after another. Everything from clothing, transportation, gifts, and entertainment can be reduced in price. If you're one of those people who isn't happy unless you're paying full fare, you either have money to burn or belong to that sucker class that they say proliferates at the rate of one per minute.

Cuisine Economy

One of the all-time largest expenses to ever find its way into a budget is grocery shopping. Aside from a few fasting waifs, we all have to eat, right? A large percentage of college grads refuse to indulge in store-bought goodies. The self-denial of these well-meaning but ultimately self-sabotaging individuals is evidenced by the stark contents of their fridges. Yes, they try to scrimp and save; but one look at their pizza-box-laden garbage cans, and you know the hunger pangs were stronger than the willpower.

So, if abstinence is not the answer when it comes to groceries, what is? Does salvation lie in diurnal macaroni and cheese/Captain Crunch casseroles? If you were still in college, with bars and beer uppermost in your mind, this would pass for creative cuisine. But out in the real world, you need your strength. Keeping the stomach growling at bay on a small budget is no mean feat. You must implement serious grocery shopping strategies if you don't want your savings to be swallowed up by the bottomless supermarket pit. First and foremost on your agenda is to drive to the store on a satisfied stomach. If you go hungry, there's no telling what you'll find in your cart at the checkout. Make a list of staple food items, and stick to it as you cruise the aisles. The Entemann's shelf will look fetching, but with the aid of a list, you'll be sure to resist. If you know how to shop parsimoniously, clipping coupons will not have to become your hobby. Buying generic labels or in bulk can cut your costs down to size. If mass quantities of oft-consumed favorites is what you're after, make sure that the products are not perishable and that your alcove of a kitchen will house that ten-pound box of Oreos.

Dining out presents another dilemma altogether. There's no pain like the kind you experience when being forced to walk past a sweet-smelling Italian restaurant on a daily basis, only to come home to your own soggy plate of spaghetti. Food never fails to taste better when prepared by someone else's hands. But even this quandary has a solution. And we don't mean running when the check comes around or feigning a lost wallet when out with friends. The old roach in the salad will only work once, and the fly in the soup is too clichéd to ever be effective. Anyway, we know you'd never even consider stooping that low. Dignified ways to scam a meal include splitting the statuesque portions with a friend or getting two meals out of one by taking half home to use for next day's lunch. Decrease your intake of restaurant food, and your waistline may finally be as lean as your dinner bill.

Cut-rate Glamour

Unless you're going for the overgrown frat look, no longer do the tried-and-true college colors cut it as a fashion statement. So, just as you've squandered your discretionary income on those trendy duds, there comes along yet another designer with a rad fad that's bound to make your days a living nightmare. As it turns out, you've spent your money on yesterday's paper. Now the tragic hipster in you won't get a wink of sleep until the what's "in" is what's in your closet. If your life is one such scenario after another, then, friend, it's high time you learned the art of dressing well on a college graduate's budget.

Without shelling out a cent on threads, a good dose of attitude will take you a long way into the world of chic. But since we can't all be Mickey Rourkes and Sandra Bernhards, we must express attitude through our clothes. Spending too much on clothes can make anyone's existence a mockery. Just think how absurd that calf-length leather coat will look when you're panhandling to pay it off. The optimum way to maintain that hip cat persona habit is to never, ever pay full price. Don't be ashamed to ask about unadvertised sales, because the horror stories are all true. Many is the time that some uninitiated schlemiel pays an arm and a leg for the coveted sports coat, only to find it discounted by 50 percent the next day. Another great entree into retail bargain paradise is a salesperson contact. If you butter up the help, in addition to being the first to know when the new line comes in, you might get your new pals to throw their employee discounts your way.

Thrift stores are a bargain hunter's dream. With "retro" being all the rage these days, the secondhand, thrift, and resale shops have been keeping penny-wise customers at fashion's hilt. Where else can you walk in with $10 and walk out with a stylish weather-beaten leather jacket, faded Levi's, and broken-in shoes? A word of caution: Wash and *then* wear.

Travel Steals

At some point you'll need a vacation. So you'll demand the week's worth due you, and then what? If your bargain travel sniffing is not up to snuff, you'll be home alone with nothing but soaps and bonbons to keep you entertained. However, flying the friendly skies need not involve stuffing yourself into an airhole-punched suitcase. There are plenty of inexpensive ways to get where you're going. Check the travel section of your weekly paper for cheap fares. When you notice a drastic drop in prices across the board, say hoorah for airline wars, and reserve yourself a seat on the pony express! Through our extensive searches, we have found round-trip flights to Paris for as low as $200, and to Germany for a negligible $149. Such prices should ensure that "the something special in the air" will be you.

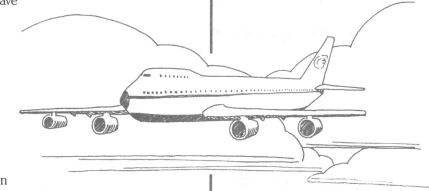

Make sure to volunteer as a "bump off," in case of overbooked flights. Talk about savings! Sure your flight plans may be postponed by an hour or a day, but it is worth it. When we volunteered to delay flying, we were handsomely compensated with $500 each in flight vouchers, free hotel accommodations for the night, and three hearty meals. Those vouchers alone pay for another trip to Europe, and we won't even go into the frequent flyer miles.

American Airlines has an appropriately entitled program called Savers Fares, and it has your name written all over it. One toll-free call (800-344-6702) is all it takes to get a rundown of the cheapest flights the week has to offer. Here's the hitch: The fares are advertised on Wednesday, and you'll be required to depart that Saturday.

On top of that, your return trip is only good for that Monday or Tuesday. Kind of short notice, but the prices can't be beat. If a weekend getaway in the continental United States is what you're after, look no further.

Flying Courier is also a trip. You are given very short notice and often required to transport a package. You are only allowed to pack one carry-on, but the prices are dirt cheap. Courier services are great for single travelers anxious to see the world. A small fee may be required to register with a courier agency, but who can resist the allure of flying to London for $50?

Fab Finds in Furniture

Forget reviving yesteryear's minimalist look only for a lack of furniture money. Sure you can roll your sofa and bed into one big, ugly futon, but we insist that you can do better. The archaic notion that furniture has to be expensive and brand new to look good went out with the all-white interiors. Think chic as you scour the local antique shops, rummage/garage sales, and even estate sales. Don't concentrate too much on the surface condition of the item; wood can be easily restored and cushions reupholstered. If it's all about being hip, then forget that ultramodern furniture fiasco. Bright colors and funky rugs are what you need to turn a bare space into a lively party place. Even your family is not without its share of oldies but goodies. Check out the attic for a pleasant surprise. Forget that original-owner snobbery, because as anyone who knows anything will tell you, Jethro's trash may well be Elli Mae's treasure.

Frugal Fitness

It's getting harder and harder to read the paper without being reminded that your abs need work. Okay, so what if the health club ads are right, and summer really is coming? Does that mean you have to spend hundreds of dollars to do what you could, in all honesty, do at home? While rollerblading, biking, swimming, and jogging make summer the choice time to save on fitness-related expenses, winter need not see you rushing off to the nearest health club. Exercising at home can save you time and money. No more pesky drives to the gym, and even peskier waits for the primo machinery.

You can change quickly and begin your workout the minute you set foot in your house.

If an endorphin boost is your remedy for the winter blahs, invest in an exercise video or a jump rope. If you need some muscular definition, invest in a set of barbells. They cost much less than a yearly membership to a health club, and you can lift in your underroos or while watching your favorite video. In all cases, exercising your right to sweat it off at home is a great way to say, "I'm not going to pay a lot for this body!"

Free Fun

Enjoying yourself should not be synonymous with spending money; but for some reason, that's exactly what has happened. Think about it. When you're ready for a night out and about, what's the first spot you hit? The most happening place in town, of course: the cash machine. A big evening could run into the hundreds, what with the cover charges, drink prices, and cabs. All this cash flow right out of your pocket, when in all likelihood you could have swung with a bevy of friends at someone's apartment. No shouting over loud music, no unsavory couples making out in corners, and no inflated prices to land you in the red.

No way, no how are you going to miss a happening evening clubbing? Okay, you too can save on the $10 to $20 covers by making friends with the staff. The bouncers, waiters, bartenders, and dj's all have reserved spots on guest lists, which they can extend to you. The owner has unlimited use of this V.I.P. list, so if you recognize the proprietor, strike up a conversation and don't beat too hasty a retreat. A spot on the guest list means no cover charge and no waiting in line in the cold with the rest of the little people.

Most importantly, fun is a state of mind. Have a great time wherever you go, and you won't feel compelled to shell out big bucks on substandard varieties of mirth.

NEST EGG START-UP

Climbing out from under the weight of a heavy debt is only one reason for cutting your costs. Another is saving money for your big

---

Budget-Friendly Entertainment

There's a world of fun and excitement to be had, even if you are on a tight budget. These ideas should get you off on the right foot:

- Gallery openings
- Museums
- Zoos
- Biking in the park
- Singing in the rain
- Window shopping
- Trying on clothes you can't afford
- Roof-top barbecues
- Driving with the top down
- Board or card games
- Matinees
- Beach volleyball/beach-blanket bingo
- Wild parties at home
- Test driving Italian sports cars
- Dressing up and walking the city's streets looking BAD.
- Attending talk-show tapings

future. It's never too early to start saving for concepts as remote as the white picket fence, 2.1 sets of little feet, and a front-porch rocking-chair retirement. Look at it this way: When you owe money, you lose a percentage in interest for the privilege; when you save or loan money, you're being paid interest. The choice is clear: debt is bad; saving is good.

Employer-Sponsored Savings

Everyone is on your side when it comes to cashing in on the American Dream. Companies often provide retirement-planning benefits to attract the best and brightest employees. Don't be so modest; you're no exception.

401(k)

If a company offers you this top-of-the-line investment option, don't be too quick to write it off as another corporate fraud scam. Keep in mind that not every deal is a gimmick to steal your money. This savings plan has great benefit potential, even though you won't be able to reap its rewards until the ripe old age of sixty-five. This may go against your "live for the moment" mentality, but if you plan on living into your sixties, it's a good idea to consider how you'll support your retirement when that time comes.

The 401(k) can ensure that your twilight years are not clouded with financial worry. A small percentage is deducted from your pay and placed in a managed investment account. Not only do you get a say in what type of program your money is kept in, but (and this is the kicker) your contribution is often matched dollar for dollar by the employer. In the long run, you end up with a big chunk of moolah that's just waiting for you to come of age.

Pension, Profit Sharing, and Money Purchase Plans

Profit sharing is a plan in which an account is set up in your name, and a crumb of company profits is invested in it each year. You must also contribute to this account, and it is not to be touched until retirement. Of course, if the company isn't making any profits, neither are you.

The Money Purchase Plan resembles profit sharing in that both employer and employee contribute a fixed sum every year. Even if the CEO is disgraced and there's a boycott on company products, you still get your annual allotment of dough.

The oldest type of company-operated retirement fund is the pension plan or defined-benefit plan. While it's not too common nowadays, you're one lucky employee if you stumble into a company that still employs it. If you stick your career out with such a company, they'll keep paying you once you retire. It wouldn't be as much as your original salary, but considering that these funds are provided entirely by your employer, it ain't half bad.

Self-styled Financial Planning

Many companies don't have the petty cash to take responsibility for your golden years. However, there are many ways you could take matters into your own hands. Since you're new to the capitalist game, we won't confuse you with the freestyle version and will just give you the basic scoop on the most popular—the Individual Retirement Account (IRA).

When a company does not subscribe to the 401(k) school of thought, it's time to look out for number one. Many lending institutions will let you deposit a percentage of your earnings into an IRA. Unfettered by taxes, this account is meant to grow and prosper. The funds can be managed by a mutual fund, a bank, or a broker. There is a steep penalty if you withdraw before retirement age, but at least you can shuffle the money from one investment to another. Keep track of how your account is doing, because as with any type of investment, you can end up a loser.

The Big "Bank" Theory

Before you go stashing your otherwise uninvested savings under the mattress, consider the convenience of a bank. Never mind the savings and loans scandals; now is not the time to sketch out a map and bury your treasure. First, in a bank, your money is insured by the Federal Deposit Insurance Corporation (FDIC). Then, there's the not-so-small matter of earning interest on your balance. And, most importantly, whenever you're in need of cash, it's there for the taking. Even after that cute teller has gone home for the night, you'll have access to the automatic teller dealing in cash twenty-four/seven.

Get the Facts Straight

Assume the informed consumer approach to picking a bank. Most people go by the proximity standard of choosing, but that would be like dating someone just because they sit next to you in homeroom. Some banks may offer a higher interest rate than others, have more convenient hours of operation, set up lower minimum balance requirements, and throw in that complimentary toaster you've heard so much about. Take all such factors into account before handing over your blood, sweat, and tear money. Make sure to investigate the many banks boasted by your area, and don't forget to run your own customer satisfaction survey. If your friends and family weren't satisfied with the services a particular bank had to offer, who's to say you will be any different?

Check Please!

Pay close attention to every institution's checking account policies. You'll be using this account frequently, and may end up paying steep fees if you're not up on the latest stipulations. Most checking accounts carry a minimum balance policy. If your funds dip below this line, the bank will bite some extra digits off your balance as a penalty. If a minimum balance sounds too rich for your blood, check out other banks for more reasonable offerings. The lower the required balance, the lower interest you can expect to collect. But even if you wind up with a zero interest return account, it still beats paying fines on a monthly basis.

The Savings Account

The easiest way to keep your money stowed away is to deposit it in a savings account. You can collect interest and take your money out at will. Keeping up both a checking and a savings account is the ideal banking situation. The checking account is for utilitarian purposes, and the savings is for that abstract time in the future when you need cash fast. When that happens, wouldn't you feel foolish going to your seventy-year-old parents for a loan? But that's nothing compared with the terror you'd feel upon hearing that their spring has run dry. You'd be lucky to undergo the humiliation of applying to younger siblings for help. Otherwise, you might have to move back home, live off of someone's couch, or hold down three jobs flipping burgers. So save now, or forever live in fear.

Money Market Accounts are a good alternative to standard savings accounts. The interest rates fluctuate with the market, but you'll usually obtain a higher yield than from a standard savings account.

Since every journey begins with just one step, your path toward financial security need only begin with one dollar. If you continue to deposit money toward your savings, they will grow. There's only one thing that can bust your saving strategy: the withdrawal. Make sure you limit this type of transaction to the checking account.

Final Tip

By far the most reliable method of pumping up your savings is to write out a check to yourself, and deposit it straight into your savings account. Most responsible parents will tell you the same thing: 10 percent of your monthly income should be stashed away in an interest-yielding account. Pretend you're a lending institution in the tradition of Jimmy the Knife, and never forget to write yourself a check. A savings account is your protection money. You never know when "Sunny Days Are Here Again" will segue into "The Sky Is Crying."

SHOPPING FOR WHEELS

Once the mechanic becomes that special someone in your life, you may be ready for your first major purchase—a new car. Now that you've washed your hands of the vagabond lifestyle, the car you park in the company lot should be presentable. A well-oiled machine will not only raise your life expectancy but also do wonders for your mature-adult image. With some careful financing, almost anyone can get the car of his/her dreams. Hopefully, you haven't been dreaming about Porsches and BMWs, because even a financing miracle won't get you into those leather bucket seats anytime soon. Cheer up! The market offers a wide variety of alternatives that are easy on the budget and won't embarrass their owners.

Shopping for a new car is not like any shopping you've ever done before. From all the bargaining that will be going on, you'll feel as if you just crossed into an Indian bazaar. You may just decide to enlist the aid of an auto-shopping pro, who will do all the negotiating and make sure that you don't get taken for a ride—maybe an older friend or a relative. But if you're forced to go hunting all by your lonesome, make sure you look and act the part of a seasoned car buyer.

Do Your Homework

There's more to a car than looks; so you'll have to do a little research to find the perfect match. Since you can't test drive every available model, consult the experts such as the transportation section of the city newspaper's Sunday edition and *Consumer Reports*. You'll also find a whole bundle of auto-buying manuals in the library or the automotive section of your friendly neighborhood bookstore.

Before you begin the in-depth research, reconcile yourself to one price range. Take our advice and don't torment yourself by drooling over the V-1000000 engines of cars you couldn't possibly afford.

Car-buying guides are also a good source of insider information. How are you going to pay a fair price for greased lightning if you don't know how much the dealer paid the manufacturer for it? You're not, and that's all there is to it. Once you're clued in to the car's wholesale price, otherwise known as the invoice, you'll also know how much lower you could force the sticker (a.k.a. retail) price. If the salesperson won't sell it to you for approximately 3 percent over the invoice, take your business elsewhere.

Rebates

Another good reason to keep your eyes peeled as you skim that transportation section of the paper is that you can often find rebates of up to one grand on new domestic models. Demo models are also a sweet deal, since you can get a couple of thousand knocked off because the car has been used for test drives. Those year-end rebates that the TV keeps yelling about could also be worth a look-see. There are so many special offers available that you should never pay the sticker price.

Rules of Negotiation

Unless you've got cash to burn, the "wrap it up and I'll take it" approach to car buying is not a good way to go. Cardinal rule number one: Never let them know how much you want the car. This nonchalance could be quite tricky if you've already picked out a pet name for the vehicle and are just dying to tuck your baby into the garage for the night. You have to stifle your glee long enough to convey that you are no stranger to the car-buying process. Save your poker face for the cards; now is the time to assume your most serious and critical look. Appraise the car with an air of reticence. Walk around it a couple of times as if you're just not sure. Your ability to convey a reluctant air may be all it takes to get a fair deal.

Check out as many dealerships as possible, haggling with each until you get a good quote. Once this preliminary step is taken, you're ready to do real business. Start pitting the dealers against each other by quoting the prices you were given elsewhere. Since no one wants to lose out to the competition, the dealer will probably try to outdo your lowest bid.

Because you don't want to pay more than 3 percent above the invoice price, start the bidding just below your target spending allowance. Move toward a price that both you and the dealer can live with at small increments, never raising more than $150 at a time. Car salespeople are notoriously slick; so watch your every bid and know when to draw the line.

Don't Pile on the Extras

If you accept every feature you're offered, your bill can get out of hand. Stick to the basics, like traction control and a radio. Power windows may add a nice touch, but do you really need them? And what about seat heat? Come on! Bypass such luxuries to avoid a nasty surprise when you see the grand total.

Used Cars

They say a new car depreciates something like 20 percent as soon as it's driven off the lot. That's quite a case for buying a secondhand car. Provided the mileage is not sky high and the condition is just fine, used cars are not the money pits they're thought to be. Check out the *National Dealer Association Official Used Car Guide* for estimates on the make and model you're looking to sink your money into. Before you lay any money down, have a reliable mechanic check the wagon out from top to bottom. Take it out for a spin, and listen carefully for any groans or cries for help. Check the acceleration, the steering, and the brakes. Many great-looking vehicles have failed the test run; so don't judge a car by its paint job.

FINAL THOUGHT

If you're really serious about making it on your own, you may have to do some pretty disagreeable things. While you won't have to peddle your wares on street corners, under the management of Leather Lou or Mama Rose, you will have to start thinking about matters as unrefined as money. You may have been Mr./Ms. Above-it-all Generous in your previous life, but in your present incarnation you'll have to understand the value of a dollar, and stop giving out those free lunches like they're going out of style. And who knows? You may even end up with a subscription to *Money* magazine.

COUCH POTATO

Chapter Nine

THE DAILY GRIND

LEAN 'N MEAN

Staying healthy, wealthy, *and* wise is quite a tall order! Even one out of three wouldn't be too shabby. While we can't all be rich or intelligent, we can all learn to take better care of ourselves. To live well, you have to feel well. And we're not talking about the short-lived Wite-Out-sniffing high you sneak in during office hours. Clean living means using each day to improve your well-being, or, in other words, eating well, exercising regularly, and learning to monitor stress. Anyone in Fingernail Biters Anonymous can tell you that behaviors are habit forming. Your college years probably did little to outfit you with a set of healthy lifestyle maintenance skills. But just because you screwed around in college—spent an average of four hours per night on sleeping and the remainder on drinking, cramming for tests, and watching MTV's Real World marathons—doesn't mean it's too late to clean up your act.

A wholesome approach to living should include a respect for yourself and your surroundings. Achieving a mind-body equilibrium becomes increasingly difficult when your environment is in disarray. There's a reason why mother kept telling you to clean your room! It was for your own good. Keeping your place clean, doing your laundry, and even decorating can give you a sense of control over your life. After all, why would you house the temple that is your body in a littered dive? There was a time when Mama made sure you ate and lived right; then it was Domino's turn, and now the baton has passed to you. It's time to acquire the skills to lead a healthy lifestyle and form good habits that will be with you for a lifetime.

DOING YOUR BODY GOOD

Twentysomethings are notorious for treating their bodies like dilapidated U-Hauls. We often disregard our physical wellness in favor of the momentary pleasures of eating high-fat foods, drinking alcohol, smoking cigarettes, and so forth. When we're told about the pernicious effects come long run, we scoff, "Long run! Yeah, that's a good one!" It's high time you reassess your situation. Sure, you're still young and vital and can afford to consume mass quantities of fries and Big Macs whenever an attack sets in, but how will these behaviors affect you as you age? Now is not a moment too soon to get on the healthy-diet-exercise-stress-reduction-awareness bandwagon. This is not another bunch of New Age balderdash; it is a clinically proven method to feel better immediately and in the years to come. Trust us when we say that an extra dose of energy will always come in handy.

Eating Right

Looking good is important, but it is only an aside to feeling good. You can cover both bases when you watch what you put in your mouth. Nutrition is a science all its own, but you don't have to be licensed to know what you should and should not eat. Proper nutrition involves getting the right balance of vitamins and avoiding high-fat foods. This balance is actually quite easy to achieve. You need only substitute your passé eating habits with ones that will have you riding a crescent wave to the future. A naturally high life is just waiting to be discovered!

The Basic Food Groups

Your daily total food allowance is divided into six categories. Forget what you heard about the four basics—that's strictly for the retro crew. You need to consume the proper amount of servings from each of the six food groups to become health wise. Variety is the key to achieving the proper nutritional content. To make the what and the how of a balanced diet easier on you, we've taken the time to outline the nutritional value of each grouping.

Bread, Cereal, Rice, and Pasta: 6-11 servings
1 serving = 1 slice bread; 1 ounce cereal; 1/2 cup cooked pasta
    This group of foods provides complex carbohydrates, B vita-
    mins, and fiber.

Fruits: 2-3 servings
1 serving = 1 medium apple, orange, or banana; 1/2 cup
    berries; 3/4 cup fruit juice
    Fruits are a good source of vitamins, especially Vitamin C.
    Fresh fruit is preferable to dried.

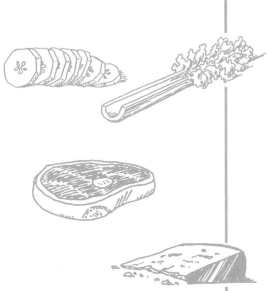

Vegetables: 3-5 servings
1 serving = 1 cup raw leafy greens; 1/2 cup chopped vegetables;
    3/4 cup vegetable juice
    Vegetables provide ample doses of Vitamin A, Vitamin C,
    and fiber.

Meat, Poultry, Fish, Dried Beans, Eggs, and Nuts: 2-3 servings
1 serving = 2-3 ounces cooked lean meat, poultry, or fish; 1 egg;
    2 tablespoons seeds and nuts; 1/2 cup cooked beans
    This food group provides protein, iron, zinc, and B vitamins.

Milk, Yogurt, and Cheese: 2-4 servings
1 serving = 1 cup milk or yogurt; 1-1/2 ounces cheese
    Milk products are a rich source of calcium and also provide
    Vitamin B-12.

Fats, Oils, and Sweets: 0-1 serving
1 serving = 1 tablespoon vegetable oil
    This food group provides Vitamin E.

Vitamins and Minerals

Instead of going into a lot of chemistry, let's just say that vitamins and minerals are essential to life. These nutrients have the power to ensure good vision, strong bones, and healthy teeth, as well as to reduce the risk of many cancers. To be frank, much of the hype is sheer old wives' hoopla. For example, overdosing on carrots won't necessarily give you a rabbit's keen eyesight, eating spinach won't have you dominating in the boxing ring, and drinking milk won't help you grow any taller. But a deficiency in any vital vitamin or mineral can stunt your growth, erode your muscle tissue, and keep you constipated for days on end. Ugh! Not a pretty picture!

For fear of ending up a carbon copy of a pre-op Phyllis Diller, you may turn to supplements to counteract your poor eating habits. Before you start putting away those Flintstones, you may want to consider that supplements must be combined with a healthy eating plan to contribute to your well-being. Looks like you're right back where you started from! That should teach you that there's no such

thing as an effective get-healthy-quick scheme. Only the regular combination of vitamin- and mineral-rich foods will keep you well nour-
ished—body and mind.

Vitamins

Vitamin A promotes good vision and helps to maintain healthy skin. It can be found in liver, eggs,
milk, fish, fruits, and vegetables.

Beta carotene reduces the risk of certain cancers. It can be
found in carrots, sweet potatoes, cantaloupe, leafy
greens, tomatoes, apricots, broccoli, and mangoes.

Vitamin C promotes healthy gums and teeth, may prevent
cataracts, and aids in iron absorption. It can be found in
citrus fruits and juices, potatoes, strawberries, cauliflower,
and cantaloupe.

Vitamin D promotes strong bones and teeth and may reduce
the risk of osteoporosis. It can be found in milk, fish oil,
and margarine.

Vitamin E aids in the formation of red blood cells and uti-
lization of Vitamin K. It can be found in nuts, vegetable
oils, margarine, wheat germ, leafy greens, almonds, and
olives.

Vitamin K promotes bacterial synthesis in the intestine.
It can be found in vegetables and cereals.

Minerals

Calcium promotes healthy bones and teeth. It can be found
in dairy products, leafy green vegetables, bread, and
sesame seeds.

Iodine plays a major role in thyroid gland activity and cell
metabolism. It can be found in seafood, seaweed food
products, and vegetables.

Iron is required for red blood cells. It can be found in leafy
green vegetables, whole-meal bread, eggs, and lentils.

Zinc is important to enzyme activity as well as the proper
functioning of the immune system. It can be found in
oysters, crabmeat, liver, eggs, poultry, milk, and beans.

The Big *C*'s: Cholesterol and Caffeine

In simple terms, cholesterol is artery fat. Even the skinniest minnies can have arteries clogged up with gobs of fat that do not allow the blood to pump freely to the heart. It's enough to make a person volunteer for a bypass. Fortunately, you need not take any such drastic measure. All it takes is a visit to the blood cholesterol testing center. Adults (that's you) should be tested at least once every five years to reduce the risk of heart disease. Even if you are given a clean bill of health, you can still gain from following a few simple guidelines to keep those cholesterol counts at sea level. Most importantly, you should keep away from saturated fat. The substitutions are easy once you start reading labels. For example, butter can be chucked in favor of olive oil, and protein can be ingested by way of white meat instead of red. Thus, the gourmand in you need not suffer one bit!

Unlike high-cholesterol levels, caffeine's bad rap is a lot of rubbish. Obviously, people with high blood pressure and irregular heartbeats shouldn't drink it. It doesn't take a neurosurgeon to figure out that a stimulant will only get the blood pumping faster, which is the last thing someone with high blood pressure wants. For the rest of us, caffeine has not been shown to present so much as one iota of an adverse effect. There's been no shortage of studies trying to link caffeine with everything from heart disease to breast cancer. The results have all come back negative. In fact, caffeine has been shown to boost energy levels during workouts, thereby indirectly improving the cardiovascular system and strengthening the muscles. And caffeine is not a gateway drug to the harder cacao/cola products. So if you're feeling run down, go ahead and indulge in a cup of java. Just do something productive with all that energy; and don't forget that too much of a good thing is never good. If you go over four cups per day, be prepared to suffer the consequences.

Up in Smoke!

Smoking can easily have you carting around an oxygen tank before your fortieth birthday. It's a serious business and should not be taken up or continued for the sake of looking cool or keeping your hands busy. Consider the rise in deaths due to lung cancer, the associated respiratory problems, and the many other health complaints being reported. The hacking cough you're sure to acquire is reason enough to brand smoking a gruesome habit and give it the final kick to the curb. Hypnosis, acupuncture, and nicotine gum have all been known to work. The patch has been heralded as the king of all habit breakers. And, if you're from the old school, go ahead and give your willpower a shot. Once you've got the monkey off your back, you can say you white knuckled it and succeeded without anybody's help. The accolades will be music to your ears and should keep you smoke free.

Miller Time

Alcohol ranks as the most commonly abused drug in the United States. For one, it is a whole lot cheaper than the designer variety; and it is socially and legally condoned. Being fresh out of college, you're probably used to handling your fair share of brews. But many people abuse alcohol and don't even know it. Binge drinking, otherwise known as a weekend of bar hopping, can take a serious toll on your health. High blood pressure, liver damage, and mental impairment are only a few of the problems associated with alcohol. Stress, depression, and a genetic predisposition are factors that are linked to alcoholism. So if your uncle is in AA, your significant other just broke your heart, and you're looking for some comfort, think twice about bending a bartender's ear. Call your friends; that is what they're there for. Or get some counseling if your problems are more serious.

Exercise

To those who don't partake in the natural endorphin rush, exercise is a thoroughly repulsive concept. What with all that sweating, jumping up and down like a mental patient, and running when there's no one chasing you, what's the point? Well, there is a method to all this madness. Some of the negative attitudes we hold toward exercise come from misleading claims that you have to feel the burn or do the deed on a daily basis to reap any

You May Have a Drinking Problem if . . . .

1. You get violent after a few drinks.
2. You drink alone.
3. You're spending more and more money on booze.
4. You think about drinking at work.
5. Your friends and family think you drink too much.
6. You start neglecting your responsibilities.
7. You don't feel comfortable in social settings until you've had several drinks.

Stay with the Program

It's all too easy to lag behind and lose sight of your fitness goals. Saying that you're too busy or you feel great as is are just excuses to keep you away from the treadmill or the Stairmaster. If you're losing your wind, you can still stay on top of your regimen by implementing a few safeguards into your program.

1. *Don't overdo it.* If you put too much stress on your bod, you'll be none too anxious to repeat the performance.
2. *Invite a friend.* The more the merrier or misery loves company. You decide.
3. *Chart your progress.* Your improvement will be marked if it's in black and white.
4. *Add some variety.* Boredom is the top reason for giving up on an exercise program.
5. *Inspire yourself with music.* Invest in a pair of headphones, and pop in your fave upbeat cassette. The rhythm will keep you moving.

results. But that is not so. Aerobic exercise, the type that gets you panting—running, cycling, or swimming—can be done as little as three times per week for half an hour each time. Supplement this program with anaerobic exercises, popularly referred to as strength training, on the off days. You'll soon see an improvement in health and physique, which will really give you something to smile about.

Aerobic activity enhances your cardiovascular endurance and helps you burn unwanted fat. Training your muscles can prevent the loss of muscle mass that comes with aging. A balanced program combines these two elements and will have you fit as a fiddle if you stick to it. Don't forget to stretch before and after your workouts. Inadequate stretching is the leading cause of sports-related injuries. No one's asking you to do the splits just yet. But who knows how far your body can take you?

Drab predictability doesn't have to define your daily workouts. Part of what keeps people excited about fitness is the variety of routines. You can ride a bike, play a game of tennis, rollerblade, or even go the squash route. There is no reason whatsoever why exercise should be boring. Keeping it lively and mixing it up is the best strategy for maintaining your lifelong fitness plan.

Battle of the Bulge

Are you tired of always feeling too big for your breeches, having to starve yourself for major social happenings, and hating your appearance? Well, you may just need a food attitude adjustment. This could entail a whole new way of living. Are you ready to say no to self-destruction and yes to self-preservation? You'll have to do some thinking before you can say it and really mean it. As a group, we are the fattest people in the world. You'd think with all those fat-free foods lining the grocery store shelves we'd be svelte and lean. Instead, one out of three Americans is obese.

Appearance is the least of the problems facing the heavy handed. Some people may even like living large. But the health risks include hypertension, coronary heart disease, diabetes, and cancer, and the list goes on and on. So if extra pounds have got you down, instead of reaching for the popular ice-cream panacea, try lightening up for a change. It's easy once you know how.

Weight-Loss Strategies

Losing weight takes time; so don't expect to become an overnight sensation. You have to make a serious commitment if shedding those unwanted pounds is truly a priority. Many people want to see quick results, and when the pounds are slow to move, they become despondent and go back to their unhealthy ways. Looking good is important, but it's more important to make changes that you can live with. And you should be happy with yourself no matter what you look like. People with positive self-images, regardless of what they look like, will be more successful in their attempts to lose weight than those who are constantly disparaging themselves.

1. *Fad diets don't work.* Every imaginable diet—the cabbage soup diet, the all-protein diet, the zone diet, the eat everything in sight but starve after 6 P.M. diet—has been circulated through every office across America throughout the years. Dare we say it? Stop the insanity! These approaches to weight loss are ineffectual because they promote behaviors that dissipate after a week or so. In order to lose weight permanently, you have to make changes that can last a lifetime.
2. *Never starve yourself.* Have you heard about Karen Carpenter? Anorexia is not a pretty business. Starving yourself lowers your metabolism, and you quickly regain the weight once you start to consume even a small amount of calories.
3. *Don't deprive yourself.* By all means, have an M&M if the urge strikes you; just don't swallow the whole bag. Depriving yourself of your favorite foods is the surest way to give up on losing weight. Food is not the enemy. Some successful dieters even promote eating large amounts of your favorite food to demystify its flavor.
4. *Cut out the fat.* You can eat hearty portions as long as you cut the fat out of your diet. There are plenty of low-calorie substitutes out there that will keep your meals tasting yummy without adding fat to your tummy.
5. *Eat slowly.* Stomachs need time to register that they are full. Develop a relationship with yours and listen carefully to its needs. On average, Americans consume much more food

than they need. The fast-paced lifestyle contributes to the national weight gain. If you rush through your meals, you'll be hard pressed to stop eating once you're full. So take time to smell the turkey. Savor your food; don't inhale it.

6. *Eat only half.* Many celebrities have sworn by this method. When you're given a portion of food, either at a restaurant or at home, eat only half and then save the other half for the following day. This is the easiest way to control your portions and get a grip on your appetite.

Guilt-Free Fare

Cooking light allows you to eat your favorite meals and not feel guilty about the calories being consumed. Salads and rice cakes are not the only low-fat food alternatives out there. Here are a few recipes that are both nutritious and full of flavor:

LASAGNA (6 SERVINGS)

1/4 pound lean ground beef
2 cups fresh tomatoes, chopped
14-ounce jar spaghetti sauce
7-ounce package lasagna noodles, uncooked
16-ounce container low-fat (1 percent) cottage cheese
2 tablespoons grated Parmesan cheese
1 cup shredded low-fat mozzarella cheese

Preheat oven to 375°. Using a nonstick frying pan, cook the beef over the heat until it is no longer pink. Remove the beef, drain the fat, and return the meat to the frying pan. Stir in the tomatoes and sauce and cook for another two minutes.

Spread a third of the meat sauce onto the bottom of a 7x11-inch baking dish. Place half of the noodles over the sauce. Spread half of the cottage cheese over the noodles and cover with another third of the meat sauce. Place the remaining noodles on top of the meat, and then add the remainder of the cottage cheese, followed by the mozzarella cheese. Cover with aluminum foil and then bake for 45 to 50 minutes. After baking, sprinkle with Parmesan cheese and you have a low-fat version of lasagna.

BISTRO STEAK SUBS (4 SERVINGS)

1 pound boneless beef sirloin steak, cut 1-inch thick
1 loaf French bread, split
1-ounce jar roasted red peppers
3/4 teaspoon garlic salt
8 ounces reduced-fat Monterey jack cheese
lettuce leaves

Place the steak on a grid over ash-colored medium coals; grill until cooked, turning once. Line the bottom of the bread with lettuce and top evenly with strips of pepper. Carve the steak into thin slices and season with garlic salt. Arrange the meat over peppers, and top with cheese.

CHICKEN CHILI VERDE (4 SERVINGS)

1 pound peeled and quartered tomatoes
8 skinned and boned chicken thighs
1 large chopped onion
2 cloves minced garlic
4-ounce can diced green chili
1 cup chicken broth
1 teaspoon ground cumin
1 tablespoon dry oregano
1/2 cup cilantro
2 tablespoons lime juice
1 tablespoon sugar

Place all the ingredients, except the cilantro, lime juice, and sugar into a large saucepan. Bring the mixture to a boil and gently simmer it for 40 minutes or until the chicken is tender. Add the cilantro 15 minutes before completion and add lime juice and sugar upon completion. Serve over rice or in burritos.

PEACH COBBLER (6 SERVINGS)

3 cups fresh peaches
1/2 cup water
1/4 teaspoon nutmeg
3/4 cup Bisquick-type baking mix
5 teaspoons sugar
1/4 cup skim milk
1 tablespoon margarine

Bring the peaches, water, and nutmeg to a boil. Pour half of the mixture into a 2-quart casserole. In another bowl, mix the baking mix with 2 teaspoons of the sugar and the milk until dough forms. Roll out the dough into a 1/8-inch thick rectangle and divide it into six strips. Place three strips over the peaches and add the remaining peaches. Cover with the rest of the dough strips. Brush the dough with margarine. Bake at 400° for 30 minutes until brown. Remove from the oven and serve.

STRESSED OUT

Stress can make your neurotransmitters go haywire when you least expect it. Life is riddled with minor nuisances—the freeway, the job, Thanksgiving dinner with the family, to name a few. The impulse to batter the ATM that has just dined on your cash card could be overwhelming if your car is at the towing service lot. But do you really need aggravated assault charges added to your list of woes? You always have a choice. Do you think before you leap or behave rashly and send yourself further down the spiral of shame? Studies show that those of us who work out constructive solutions instead of exploding whenever our plans are foiled end up healthier as a result.

Too much stress can do a number on more than just your easygoing image. Your blood pressure may rise; and after that happens, heart disease is just a stone's throw away. There are no two ways about it; stress should not be underestimated. It can, if left to its own devices, have a destructive impact on your psychological and physical well-being. Fortunately, everyone has access to stress-reduction tactics.

No Sweat!

The attitude with which you approach any obstacle can predetermine both the outcome and your stress rating. Every problem, be it great or small, can be viewed as a challenge or as an insurmountable obstacle. Those who choose the former are ultimately less anxious and more content than their stressed-out counterparts.

Stress often rears its ugly head when we're stuck in situations we cannot control. Gridlock, project deadlines, flashing lights in the rearview mirror, delayed flights, grocery checkout lines, screwed-up hotel reservations, lost luggage, and computer viruses are enough to drive a person to the brink of madness. You may not be able to control every aspect of your environment, but you can control your reactions. A cool head is a hot commodity in troubled waters. Angry people frothing at the mouth only makes for more chaos. React sensibly and watch out for yourself. If others want to fall victim to the adrenaline landslide, that's their business.

Work That Body

Exercise is by far the best method of tension redux. Built-up tension needs to be released. A good old-fashioned holler fest may seem like just the thing, but watch out. All that nasty stuff people say when they're angry will come back to plague them in the form of guilt and, there you have it, more stress. A bout of exercise will relieve that tension fast. Running has long been a popular form of exercise, and now boxing is quickly gaining followers. Whether you want to take long strides toward your goals or just pummel the opposition, either of these sports will make you feel like it's in the bag.

A Circle of Friends

Talking your friends' ears off about your problems is always an effective way to combat anxiety. Friends, if that's who they truly are, will affirm your actions and support you in times of crisis and doubt. Even scientific studies show that those of us with a network of close friends are much less likely to become stressed. The TV, a walk, or even a good snuggle session with your dog will not distract you from your troubles as well as a talk with your pals.

Just Relax!

Relaxation exercises can be lifesavers when you're caught unaware by stress. You'll never again be called uptight once you put these exercises into practice:

1. Maintain regular breathing.
2. Clench your fists for ten seconds, and then let go. Repeat the exercise.
3. Close your eyes and imagine swimming in the ocean.
4. Play a word game in your head: For example, *Bag* spelled backward is *gab*, *ABBA* is . . . and so on.
5. Imagine that the person stressing you out is wearing nothing but a pair of black socks.
6. Think of a fun activity you can do once you get home.
7. Call up a friend.

Get Your ZZZ's

If sleeping does not figure prominently on your list of priorities, you are doing yourself a great disservice. Sleep provides a valuable revitalizing function as well as one of the best times you can have without leaving the house. Maybe you take slumber for granted; after all, you did sleep whenever the mood struck in college. Envision it now: the nocturnal frolicking and the diurnal dozing followed by the midtermal failing. That was some life! Has it all come crashing down around you?

If peak performance is a must in your busy lifestyle, you'll have to figure out exactly how much snooze time you need to feel rested come sunup. Is forty winks enough or are you of the fifty to seventy demographic? Some of us are dead to the world without a tally of at least eight hours; others rise and shine on as little as five. Then there are the nappers. If you can come home from work and take an hour's siesta, you may not need to sleep as much at night. Sleep has no recommended daily allowance; you're the only one who knows for sure how much you really need.

Those who have experienced the horror firsthand know that little in life compares with the desperation of an insomniac. You're all alone in the conscious world, watching the clock's slow march, and short of a few false starts, nothing! A few such nights is all it takes to have you raiding your parents' stash of Halcion, at gunpoint if necessary. You must, we repeat, you *must* conquer this temptation and make an appointment with a physician. Insomnia is a medical disorder, and treating it yourself can land you in more serious trouble than you thought possible.

IS THERE A DOCTOR IN THE HOUSE?

Male or female, young or old, we all have a tendency to postpone the doctor's visit until the situation comes to a head. The "doctors are for pansies" ideology keeps most of us from taking up permanent residence at a clinic. Everyone should have a little faith in their body's own recuperative powers, but taking this belief to extremes can be dangerous. Finding a reliable physician to call your own cannot be stressed enough. You would be in good hands with a doctor who's known you through the years. (S)he would already know you inside and out, and (s)he would have all of your medical records on file. So look through your health plan and see if the practitioner of choice is a match. Then make that physician a permanent fixture in your life. You'll thank yourself down the road.

Which Doctor Is Right for Me?

Your pediatrician no longer takes your calls, the campus clinic has shut its doors to you forever, and you're at a loss as to where to go with your ear infection. You stumble into the nearest emergency room as if in a daze. "Help! Somebody help me," you plead at the top of your lungs. A stack of forms is all that comes to your rescue. "Fill these out, and then wait for the next available doctor." You get your shot in no less than three hours, and you're no less than $300 poorer for the experience. It's a darn shame! You could have just gone to a general practitioner, or maybe an internist could have helped. At least half of that money could have gone for new shoes. As for the wait, you could have been in and out in the time that it takes to read just two *People* articles instead of three full *New Yorkers*. There are plenty of doctors to choose from who will make it their business to look after you. All you have to do is pick the right one to begin a beautiful friendship.

Three Types of Primary-Care Physicians

Pediatricians are not for adults. We know. You're never planning on "growing up." News flash: Doctors don't care. If you're eighteen and above, your lollipop days are over. The following doctors specialize in the treatment of people who are old enough to vote.

1. *General Practitioners.* It used to be that one doctor was no different from the next. All were trained in the same medical procedures and were known as general practitioners. The twentieth century's medical advances made it impossible for each doctor to know everything that there is to know about every field, and so specialization was born. However, general practitioners are still around, and they make great primary-care physicians. They are usually associated with community hospitals and will refer you to specialists whenever they see fit.

A Good Night's Sleep

Sleep better and faster by adhering to the following plan. You'll never stay up nights staring at your alarm clock again.

1. Spend an hour or so relaxing before going to sleep; read, listen to music, or watch a documentary.
2. Never eat a big meal before going to bed.
3. Don't drink alcohol or smoke right before turning in.
4. Don't drink coffee after 5:00 P.M.
5. Try going to bed and waking up at a set hour.
6. Drink warm milk before going to bed.
7. Don't watch scary movies.
8. Take a bath two hours before retiring.
9. Do some stretching exercise before going to bed.
10. Don't watch your clock; turn it toward the wall.

Wouldn't you prefer to see a doctor who knows something or other about your ailment? The following docs are trained to treat and diagnose specific medical problems. They devote their whole lives to the study of one particular area, from skin disorders to heart disease. You'll feel better knowing you're in expert hands.

Anesthesiologists determine which type of anesthesia to use during surgery and monitor its effect during and after surgery.

Cardiologists diagnose and treat abnormalities of the heart and blood vessels.

Dermatologists diagnose and treat skin, hair, and nail disorders.

Gastroenterologists diagnose and treat digestive systems and liver disorders.

Hematologists diagnose and treat blood disorders.

2. *Family Practitioners.* Treating all age groups, these doctors are also equipped to handle most ailments. Family medicine is a specialty all of its own. If you sign up with one of these people, don't expect to get referred out to another specialist unless your problem is of a most complicated nature.

3. *Internists.* These doctors are qualified to treat a wide range of adult medical problems. They also have advanced training in the treatment and diagnosis of patients. Aside from a high level of expertise in such common medical complaints as heart disease, arthritis, and cancer, they may also have a subspecialty.

Choosing a Doctor

Before settling on anyone in particular, take the time to do some investigating. Call up physicians in the area, and probe into their educational background. Find out if they are affiliated with any professional associations or are board certified. Solicit the help of friends and family. It's a safe bet that if other patients are satisfied, you too will be a satisfied client. Don't forget to check out the doctor's availability before designating him/her your main source of medical assistance. How quickly does the doctor respond to emergencies? How many days in advance should you book appointments? Is (s)he available evenings and weekends? Finally, ask yourself whether you feel comfortable or uncomfortable with the physician. And, of course, if the doctor doesn't accept your health insurance, you may have to go elsewhere. Consider the insurance question prior to all others to save yourself some valuable time. Follow these guidelines when evaluating any medical professional, even a dentist, and you shouldn't have any problems.

Medical Records

Because of some serious lobbying on the part of consumers' groups, many states now guarantee you easy access to your medical records. If you are just curious, or have some reason for wishing to view your files, call the doctor or hospital where you were last treated, and they will brief you on the procedure for obtaining copies. You may have to pay a nominal fee for photocopies or postage. But if you simply will not rest until you get an eyeful, a couple of dollars is a small sum to pay.

THE HAPPY HOMEMAKER

Even though *Home Improvement* may be one of your favorite sit-coms, it has probably taught you little about the art of dwelling maintenance. You don't have to be Martha Stewart to run a tight ship, but you do need a grasp of the basics. For example, cleaning is not synonymous with strategic concealment, and pushing defrost on your microwave does not qualify as a culinary art. Even if you have been making your own peanut butter and jelly sandwiches since time began, it never hurts to brush up on your homemaking know-how.

Mr. Clean

Warning: A state of household disarray can lead to the scatter-brained dweller syndrome. While dust is the worst offender, it may be the least of your problems. Stains, an overflowing sink, a smelly fridge, and an unsavory myriad of other health code violations may qualify your initially spotless abode as pigpen of the year. It only takes one comprehensive cleaning session to experience the unfettered joy of coming home to a spic and span place on a hard day's night. Since Santa's elves won't be maintaining this state of decorum, you'll have to battle the grime monster on a daily basis. To keep up with your cleaning regimen, we recommend investing in a mop, a vacuum, some of those nifty dish scrub sponges, and a hand vacuum. This is the hardware. For software, we recommend a heavy-duty, all-purpose bleach, dishwashing liquid, glass and oven cleaner, and some air freshener. Stock your kitchen utility cabinet with such essentials, and in no time you'll be whistling as you work.

Each Room Is Special

Since every alcove in your home has its own unique purpose in life, you'll find that each one has a completely different style of messiness. Let's begin with the most unpopular room in the house to clean—the bathroom. This is where the bleach will come in most handy. Use it in your bathtub and on your floor to get rid of any unmentionable stains or enduring smells. Clean this room at least once every week, and be thorough. Consider buying one of those air-freshener toilet paper dispensers to clear the air with each use. An automatic toilet cleaner will also save you the trouble of scrubbing

---

The Specialist (continued)

Neurologists diagnose and treat brain, nervous system, and muscular disorders.

Neurosurgeons operate on disorders of the brain and blood vessels.

Obstetricians/gynecologists diagnose and treat reproductive system disorders in women.

Otorhinolaryngologists (ENTs) specialize in disorders of the ear, nose, and throat.

Pediatricians diagnose and treat children and adolescents.

Psychiatrists specialize in the treatment of behavioral disorders.

Radiologists specialize in administering imaging technology (i.e., Xrays and ultrasound).

Urologists diagnose and treat urinary-tract disorders.

the toilet bowl until your elbow grease runs dry. Change your towels regularly. Bacteria flock to moist areas, so launder that terry cloth bathrobe before it starts sprouting spores. This having been said, let's move on to less stomach-turning tasks.

Your living room and bedroom receive a major share of wear and tear. Excavate any dust and crumbs that may find their way into your carpeting by vacuuming every week. Crumbs are the progenitors of parasites. If your mind's eye views cable television and munching as intertwined, at least choose foods that don't have a high-crumb factor. Twizzlers, for example, are a great alternative to popcorn. Next, prepare to dust the premises. If you don't feel up to the French maid bit—feather duster and all—tear up an old t-shirt and go to it. Use the hand vacuum to get rid of dust on sofas and recliners, and then add a dash of that potpourri spray for a finishing touch. In your bedroom, don't neglect your bedding. Sheets should be changed at least once every two weeks—more frequently if sleeping alone is not your bag.

Now to the mother of all home disaster areas—the kitchen. Since this is a food-saturated zone, don't try to do too much all at once. Intensive kitchen detail does not have to be a part of your weekly or even monthly routine. Tasks such as cleaning the oven and the refrigerator can be done once every couple of months. The microwave, the dishes, and the floors, on the other hand, are completely separate cans of Campbell's. The naked eye will speedily alert you to the dirt piling up in these areas. If you've instituted home cooking as a common practice, dishes will need a daily scrubbing. Once your feet start sticking to unsightly stains on the linoleum, get a mop and wipe off the residue. If you get a queasy feeling in the pit of your stomach upon opening the microwave, go for the cleaning spray without our prodding.

The fridge and oven do present certain challenges. Keep a box of baking soda in the refrigerator to absorb odors. And every two months, you should empty the fridge of all its contents and give it a good rubdown. Make sure it looks as good as new, or the bacteria will soon be making your fridge their home. The oven also needs be cleaned every two months. Even self-cleaning ovens need a little help from yours truly. S.O.S. scouring pads and oven-cleaning mitts will come in real handy when you're giving the broiler a once-over.

Scrub the entire oven, top to bottom; just don't stick your head in without making sure it's been turned off.

Sorting Your Life

Cleaning is hard enough without first having to dig through all your worldly possessions just to find the floor. Once you've organized the space, your apartment's potential will be self-evident. Crates, boxes, and a storage cabinet for paperwork should all be acquired immediately, if you want to bring order to your messy abode. Discard junk mail upon arrival. Return clothes to shelves and hangers as soon as they're removed from your person. Also, keep those items that have nothing but sentimental value packed away in a remote closet corner. Tripping over your mountain bike or rollerblades is a sign that you should ask your landlord about basement storage space possibilities. Everything has its rightful place; the trick is to figure out just what goes where.

Fluff 'n Fold

Since laundry does not accrue in value, there's no reason to put off washing your skivvies. You may think nothing of wearing the same socks for days on end, but others may soon be raising their noses in disdain. Keep in mind that the longer a stain sits, the harder it is to lift. Hopefully, you had the foresight to check into a building with an on-site laundry facility; otherwise you'll have to haul those soiled knickers to a neighborhood washer/dryer emporium. Once you're ready to launder, separate your whites from your colors. The fragile items should go in with the gentle cycle, unless they clearly state "dry clean only," in which case you know what to do. Fight stains by putting the detergent directly on the culprit and rubbing it in. Only then should you throw the offensive garment in with the others. Carefully read and follow the washing instructions right on the machine. Then kick back and read a book, listen to a symphony, work on a crossword—whatever it is you do to pass the time.

Once you hear the buzzer or the machine shuts off, check the dashboard to make sure the cycle is complete. If it is not, open up the machine and have a look-see. It may just be that the clothes are improperly distributed. If you shift things around, you'll hear the machine's hum once again. When the washing is finally over, take out your laundry and stick it in the dryer. At this stage, don't forget to "delint the screen" for optimum drying. Remember: too long in the dryer and you'll be dressed in obscenely tight gear come morning; too short a time under the heat, and you're on liquids and bed rest from sporting damp duds. The final action is the pièce de résistance of proper drying; it's called adding the fabric softener. You'd better buy yourself a box quick, because people are loathe to spare one square of their own.

A Chef Is Born

If the thought of boiling water has you running for take-out, you may have some serious soul searching to do. Are you actually running from becoming your parents, and, like Oedipus, committing the fatal flaw of attempting to escape your fate? We'll give you a moment with that one. . . . Or have formative years spent watching *Dynasty* convinced you that cooking is hopelessly unrefined? Whatever your fears, fear no more. Look at mastering the culinary arts as simply another step on the road to becoming a complete person. Technology and social whims have done away with hunters, gatherers, and roasters. Now you can finally rediscover your primal nature. We're not talking New Age retreats. All you need is a quality nonstick pan, some baking dishes, a cutting board, a pair of oven mitts, a spice rack, and a set of Ginsu knives. You will be to the kitchen what Tom Cruise was to the bar. Knives will be spinning in the air as you catch them just in time to dice ten tomatoes with a single stroke. You'll have buns in the oven and teriyaki on the stove . . . well, maybe that won't happen, but you can certainly have some fun trying. The trick to cooking is not to take it too seriously. Be bold and create new dishes out of everyday foods. As necessity is the mother of all invention, you'll find that some of your best dishes are concocted on an empty stomach. If all else fails, buy yourself a cookbook. There's even one out there that tells how to make a zillion different meals with only three ingredients. You don't have to follow the directions exactly. When you're in the kitchen, you have the ultimate creative control. Once you figure out what your masterpieces are, you'll be able to whip them up at a moment's notice. So go ahead and give your parents something to really brag about.

You may think that when it comes to daily living, you know it all. However, you'll never know for certain until you quiz yourself. Here's a college-style popper. It doesn't count toward your final grade, but you may find it informative.

1. How many basic food groups are there? _____
2. What are they? _____
   _____
3. _____ promotes healthy bones and teeth.
4. True or False: Caffeine has adverse effects on the average Joe/Jill. _____
5. Name four effective weight loss strategies.
   _____
   _____
   _____
6. True or False: Eight hours of sleep is optimal. _____
7. What is a primary-care physician? Why would you want one?
   _____
   _____
8. What types of doctors make for good primary-care physicians?
   _____
   _____
9. What is a medical specialist?
   _____
   _____
10. What are the three essentials of proper laundry drying?
   _____
   _____

How Much Have You Learned?

Answers: 1. six; **2.** bread and grains, fruits, vegetables, meat, dairy, fats; **3.** calcium; **4.** false; **5.** eat slower, cut out fat, eat only half, exercise; **6.** false; **7.** a doctor who gives general physicals is cheaper than a specialist and an emergency room, has all your records on file so you don't have to fill out a truckload of forms and wait so long in the dreaded lobby, and can refer you to the proper specialists; **8.** general practitioners, family practitioners, internists; **9.** a doctor who has a very specific area of expertise; **10.** cleaning the lint off the screen, setting the proper drying time, and using fabric softener.

Scoring: Multiply the number of answers you had right by ten for the percentage of what you know about living well. If you're south of eighty, we suggest you not tell anyone that you really know how to live—you'd be all talk.

INDEX